Bike Lust

BIKE LUST

*Harleys, Women, and
American Society*

Barbara Joans

THE UNIVERSITY OF WISCONSIN PRESS

The University of Wisconsin Press
1930 Monroe Street
Madison, Wisconsin 53711

www.wisc.edu/wisconsinpress/

3 Henrietta Street
London WC2E 8LU, England

3   5   4   2

Printed in the United States of America

Library of Congress Cataloging-in-Publication Data
Joans, Barbara.
Bike lust : Harleys, women, and American society /
Barbara Joans.
pp.   cm.
Includes bibliographical references and index.
ISBN 0-299-17350-X (cloth : alk. paper)
ISBN 0-299-17354-2 (paper : alk. paper)
1. Motorcycling—Social aspects—United States.
2. Women motorcyclists—United States. 3. Harley-Davidson
motorcycle—History. 4. Joans, Barbara. I. Title.
GV1059.52 .J63   2001
306.4'81—dc21   2001000745

This book is dedicated to Ken Harmon, my husband. His love and patience got me into the wind.

This book is dedicated to Ed Gilbertson, my good friend. His biker editorial smarts and endurance got me through rough riding and rougher writing.

This book is dedicated to Rubin and Eleanor Levinsohn, my parents. In life, they would have hated motorcycles.

This book is dedicated to Howard and Deb, and David and Rosemary Schwartz, my children. They still hate motorcycles.

This book is dedicated to Ben, Laura, Mallory, and Jay, my grandchildren. They are their grandparents' grandkids. They love the wind.

Finally, this book is dedicated to the wonderful, amazing motorcycle communities that granted me entrance and acceptance and graciously allowed me to hang around with them.

Contents

Contents

Part 4. Polemics and Philosophy

Illustrations

Preface

Bikers talk straight. Since this book is about bikers, the preface is fittingly short and straight. *Bike Lust* can be read from either end. Or, you can rumble right into the middle.

For those who need order, start with the introduction, "The Love Run," and work your way through the book. Read all of part 1 first. Part 1 covers history and structure. The introduction and chapters 1 through 4 allow an easy entry into the community and provide both background and history.

For those who want cultural analysis right from the beginning, start with chapter 5, "Enter the Culture," and read all of part 2 first. Part 2 provides analysis of issues of gender, race, and class, as well as of traditional lifestyles and rites of passage.

For those who crave the armchair experience of jamming the wind (without bugs in your teeth), start with chapter 13, "An Intimate Account of the Redwood Run: Our First Year," and read all of part 3 first. Part 3 gives an up-close and very personal account of one of the most famous Harley runs in California.

For those of you who secretly desire polemics, try cruising through chapter 17, "Bikers' Dirty Little *Open* Secret: The Racism Rap," and join me in an exploration of racism, sexism, homophobia, and anti-Semitism within the motorcycle community. This chapter, which makes up part 4, explores biker myths as well as myths about bikers, in a summation of biker philosophy.

If you are reading this as an ethnographic account of a very American subculture, start with the glossary.

If you are reading this out of curiosity, to get a glimpse of a different world, start with the pictures and have fun.

PART 1

History and Structure

Introduction
The Love Run

"Hey asshole," shouts one of the 17,000 riders on the Love Run.
"Hey asshole," he shouts again, and everyone there turns around.
Us Harley riders, we know when our name is being called.

Six A.M. and the dense LA fog is thick enough to fondle. Six A.M. and I am already fortified with enough coffee and Bailey's to burst. Six A.M. and I am riding on the back of a bike, while the rider is tearing up the road at warp speed trying to catch up with our friends who left five minutes before we did. Six A.M. and I am already pissed enough at the rider to bitch.

Barreling down the highway at ninety miles an hour, trying to catch our friends, who themselves are all traveling at warp speed, is an almost impossible task. The fog muffles the world speeding by and casts an eerie silence around us. For once the roar of the motor is silenced by the thick, deep, early morning fog. The frigid wind bites right through our riding clothes, through our bodies, and into our bones. Freezing tears run down my face and burn into my neck, my fingers are numb to the point of pain, my body is pressed hard between the sissy bar and the rider's back as he races, in fog blindness, down the endless LA freeway.

Somewhere just ahead and out of reach, our friends are already pulling into the destination. We would have been riding with them instead of playing catch-up if the rider had gassed the bike the night before. He is now determined, deep in biker machismo, not to be left behind. We will catch up. We will ride with our group.

And ultimately we do, though we jam the wind on a shuddering bike, pass other riding groups with only inches to spare on this highway of fog, jump two curbs, and ride part of the way on city sidewalks to do it. Not a time to show how really pissed I feel. For this trip, I am a passenger, and I know that it is not a good idea to upset the rider.

"Hey asshole," shouts the anonymous rider, and I too turn around.

Seventeen thousand bikers have gathered in front of the LA–Glendale Harley-Davidson dealership to start the ritualized run up the Grapevine. The run raises money for research on muscular dystrophy. Bikers go to help and to party. We have traveled from Frisco, a fair distance, but there are bikers here from all over the country.

Exhaust fumes overwhelm the morning, mixing with the fog to make the air turn stiff. Frozen faces peer from beneath small, barely legal helmets while frigid fingers hold coffee mugs and light cigarettes. The moment of calm gathering is brief. The fog-muffled silence is broken by the sound of ear-splitting, soul-satisfying roars. Even the fog gives way as group after group revs their engines.

To the Harley rider, there are two kinds of bikes. There are Harleys, and there are all other kinds of motorcycles. The Harley world, as a separate American subculture, has been growing at a phenomenal rate. It started in a number of places, among very different kinds of people, and it is emerging as one of the more important social phenomena of the times. The Harley world. A new face on America.

Once, it seemed to be the private landscape of the One Percenters, members of the outlaw clubs so outrageously chronicled by Hunter Thompson (1967) and brilliantly documented by Daniel Wolf (1991). Once, it was the private preserve of the rebel, the social outcast, and the movie villain. From outlaw, working-class origins, the Harley world has grown to include people from a variety of classes and social statuses. Once, it was a male sanctuary; now it is shared by women. Men and women two-up, in partnership as passengers, or travel side by side as riding buddies. Women, who used to be excluded from any position except that of back-seat Betty or the bitch on the back, now ride the roads alone or travel in all-women riding clubs.

The old Harley world was a world in which membership meant belonging to the same race. Now there are numerous clubs that welcome racial diversity. The old world still exists, of course—indeed it is frequently fundamental in the organization of outlaw clubs—but it is no longer the only Harley world around. It is no longer the only game in town.

The new Harley world includes riding groups that are racially mixed. The new Harley world includes women who ride, as well as those who passenger. The new Harley world is filled with the affluent and the upwardly mobile, as well as the poor, the outlaw, and the working class. The socially successful snob rides carb to cam with the working-class stiff. The lady lawyer trades hand signals with the ma-

4

cho housepainter. The local plumber yells directions to the regional stockbroker as they share the road. The politically conservative, American flag–waving, small-town factory worker frequently parties at runs with the urban, rainbow flag–waving cynic whose politics veer to the left of liberalism.

This is the new Harley world in the process of being born. A world emerging from alternative culture and becoming mainstream. A Harley culture which, while denying it, is still rooted in the antique myth of the One Percenters, a legacy from which it draws its strength and from which it would like to disassociate. As middle America rides and parties with the urban middle class, neither discusses the skeleton in the closet. Neither draws attention to the fact that much of the Harley mystique, most of the unwritten rules of the road, and many of the values and ideals come from its unruly and bastard parent, the outlaw club.

The outlaw groups, quintessentially American, stand united, predictably, in their contempt for the new Harley culture. Within this mix of three cultural groups—the outlaw ancestors, the urban middle class, and the small-town working class—I ride with the only group that lane-splits between them all. I ride with women bikers.

Thus begins some really hot fieldwork. As a working anthropologist, as opposed to just an academic one, I am never without a people to study, a community to investigate, a subculture to join, or a counterculture to play in. The first rule is pretty simple: "when in Rome. . . ." If I don't like what Rome does, I don't study that culture. The methods are simple too: participant observation, fieldnote-taking, and analysis. And so are the ethical rules: love, respect, and appreciate the people you hang with. Identify with them *for the duration of the work* and never, never betray their confidences. If that requires keeping three sets of notebooks, keep them. If that means burning your notes, bring marshmallows. If you ever stop really liking and respecting the folk, leave.

Sometimes I get so close that I have difficulty telling where my skin stops and the cultural skin starts. When this happens, I write the work up fast because I know that soon I won't be able to write it up at all. Once identification is complete, analysis becomes impossible and even reportage feels like betrayal. Since I am on that verge with bikers, I am writing in furious haste.

This is about Harley culture. The one I have been riding with for the past seven years. I entered this world on the back of my husband's bike, moved to the front, and remained in the culture. I make no claims for any other groups. This work is about the Harley-riding men and women of California. Some are in HOG (Harley Owners' Groups) chapters, others belong to MCs (motorcycle clubs) of long standing.

Some Harley folk travel solo and ride only occasionally with others. But we all meet up at runs, rallies, swap meets, biker rodeos, and gathering places. We read the same biker rags and buy from the same dealers. We acknowledge each other on the road.

Whoever you are out there, I invite you to come along for the ride.

1

"Teach the Children Well . . ."

"Bikers are born, not made!"
"Everyone's got to learn how to ride, no one knows how at first!"
"Anyone can ride!"
"It takes a really special person to handle a bike!"

Ever since I started riding, academic friends have been making contradictory statements. And I have thought a lot about their words. Are bikers really born? Can only a special few learn to ride? Or is riding a skill that can be taught? And are there limits to that teaching? Must we all learn the same way? And what about the love of riding and the lure of the motorcycle? Must that too be learned?

In films, bikers are portrayed mostly as outlaws. But America has a taste for outlaws. Ole Jesse James once claimed that everyone loved an outlaw. He wasn't exactly sure why, but he knew it was so. Old horse thief that he was, Jesse never rode a bike, but then bikers don't usually ride horses, either. Horse riding now belongs to ranchers, rodeo performers, and the rich. Biking belongs to the working class and the modern-day outlaw. Until very recently, bikers mainly came from some part of the working class. Jesse would have felt right at home.

The connections between biker and outlaw tease our perceptions and cross our categories. A biker does not have to be an outlaw. Not all outlaws ride. But still the connections are made. In some places, the shoe still fits.

The outlaw's special place in the American heart is easy to explain and difficult to describe. Outlaws are not gangsters—although this group too has its followers. But gangsters present a different image. They inhabit a different landscape. Outlaws are mythologized. Outlaws are dangerous. They test and tear the social fabric of society. They thumb their noses at the social order.

Unlike gangsters, they may or may not be criminals. They may not have broken any laws. *What they have broken is the routine of the ordinary*

7

world. They refuse to fit into the normal world. They do not follow society's rules. They follow their own rules. They have their own ways of doing things. They reject common authority. They rebel against following orders even when that rebellion gets them into trouble. Their danger lies most often in their commitment to the unconventional, the unknown, and the untried.

Societies survive by imposing rules. The danger posed by outlaws is their indifference to these rules. Outlaws act alone as well as in groups. They are the loners, the drifters, and the rebels. Even the very successful, the rich and the famous, have been known to appropriate the term to justify both their private views and their public images.

When Waylon Jennings describes himself as an outlaw, he is not talking about robbing banks. He is talking about a state of mind. An outlaw is different from you and me even if he never breaks a law. The outlaw goes his own way and says "fuck off" to anyone who doesn't like it. He does what he wants *and* is willing to take the consequences for those actions.

Clint Eastwood in his old movie roles is an outlaw extraordinaire, most especially when he is playing a cop. One Percenters are outlaws because of their attitudes. They blow off authority. They fly the colors of independence up front even when they ride on the legal side of the law. Every isolated loner of a kid who longs to go his own way can identify with the outlaw.

Gangsters, on the other hand, while sharing attitudes with outlaws, make their living from breaking the law. They usually have a darker, more sinister image. Al Capone was a gangster, Willie Nelson is an outlaw.

Outlaw motorcycle clubs may traffic in illegal businesses or they may not. The defining aspects of the outlaw club are its attitude and its organization, not how it makes its money. Members may ride on the legal or the illegal side of the road. It's their business. Their comings and goings are private and you look too closely into their business at your own peril. Being uninvited into that territory, I leave descriptions of outlaw motorcycle clubs to Hunter Thompson and Daniel Wolf.

While I am unwilling to stick my nose into outlaw affairs, I have ridden with some of the outlaws' children. One of my most exciting riding moments came late one cold Frisco afternoon in autumn. I had ridden what seemed like nine hundred turns around Department of Motor Vehicles (DMV) circles in an endless effort to guide my Harley Sportster around the same damn testing circles I had earlier guided my Honda Rebel around. I had passed the motorcycle test on the light, small Honda and was trying to reproduce that effort on the larger Har-

8

ley. Since the Sportster is three times the size and twice the weight of the Rebel, it was a difficult task.

I had just finished the practice session when a small group of bikers from a local outlaw club rode by. While none of them were flying their colors, I recognized several of the men from runs we had all attended. They were traveling slowly up a San Francisco street. Each man had a young child riding on the back of his bike. Each child was being trained to ride. There were both girls and boys on the backs of the bikes and their ages varied from five to eight. There were no sissy bars and no large cushiony seats of the type that I need when I passenger. Each child had a leather strap to hold and was given specific instructions to never let go.

As I rode along with that small group, I became aware of the intensity of the training. As the riders eased in and out of traffic, switched lanes, speeded up and slowed down, the children never let go of those straps. No one wiggled around, moved in a dangerous manner, or bothered the rider. These kids were being trained for survival on the road. Since the fathers belonged to a serious riding motorcycle club, this was serious childhood training. On runs, children's lives depend on how well they learn their lessons.

I was impressed. I was pleased to ride with the group, and even though this was a children's riding lesson, I had trouble keeping up. I watched as the kids moved with the bikes, held on to the straps, and never, never let go, not even to wave to me as I smiled by. These kids with their careful training would later be so good at riding that everyone would assume they had been "born riders."

In one sense, because of their parents, they had been born to ride, but they still had to learn to do it. Each of them was special in their learning abilities, each a little different from the next, but they all learned. I followed this small group as far as I could through Golden Gate Park and a little beyond, then lost them as they headed down the great highway heading south.

I had often thought about the kids who rode. I had wondered how they were able to do so well on runs. At every Redwood Run, every Bridgeport Jamboree, every local toy run, I had seen these amazing children riding like pros on the backs of their dads' bikes. I never thought I would be able to find out how they did it. I never expected to run across an outlaw lesson in child rearing. Sometimes you just get lucky.

Outlaws aren't the only ones who train their kids to ride. I remember the first time we took our grandchildren on the bike. After calming down our son with endless promises of caution, we happily left the city streets for a slow putt through the Presidio. My daughter-in-law's only request was that we stay clear of traffic. Since the children were all old enough to reach the passenger pegs, they fit well on the bike. For their first trip, the kids were riding with my husband. As the experienced and confident rider, he was better suited to guide them on their initiation ride.

Mallory, our six-year-old granddaughter, went first. Since she is a wiggler, I worried that she could, if she tried hard enough, fall off. Harley Dressers are so cushioned, padded, and protected that a child could not fall off one even if she tried. We did not, however, own a Dresser.

We have a Low Rider, and the back seat is quite open and unprotected. The seat, big and sturdy, necessitated by my passengering days, has a lot of space on the sides. This did give me moments of great concern. Fortunately, my anxiety was groundless. Mallory was quite fearless; she was able to sit straight and still and hold on tight to the leather straps. She leaned against her grandfather and rode the wind. She laughed happily during the ride and wanted to stay longer when her turn was over.

Laura, another of our granddaughters, was older and better prepared to understand the dangers. At age eight, she knew enough to eye the bike with caution. She wanted to go for a longer ride because she was older. We explained about leaning with the bike, sitting still, and never letting go of the straps. Watching her climb on, avoiding the now-hot pipes, and arranging herself on the passenger's seat gave me a strange and scary feeling.

This riding experience was problematic. I felt the complexities and difficulties of being a riding grandparent, a parent of nonriding children, in the process of teaching my grandchildren to ride. This was risky business. The situation was full of psychological and emotional as well as physical dangers. Laura, however, was taking her first ride very seriously. Her trip was longer and more difficult than her sister's and she passengered with grace and ease. There was no fear in her. When it was finally her brother's turn, she gave up the passenger's seat with great reluctance.

Ben, being ten, wanted the longest ride of all. He had listened to all our instructions and could not wait to get going. Off they went, riding the hopped-up Low Rider, roaring into the wind. The bike is not called the Beast for nothing. It will detonate car alarms within a radius of three miles and looks and sounds like the Screaming Eagle carb and cam it sports. It is not a chromed and customized weekend show bike. This is a working Harley.

In our family, we each commute to our jobs. We live midway between our work worlds and go in opposite directions. We own one car and two bikes. Since I drive to work, my husband commutes on his bike. In the worst and the best of weather, he rides. I have absolute confidence in his riding. But that was my ten-year-old grandson on the back, and they were jamming the wind.

The gentler ride my husband had prepared for the younger children was not the ride he gave to Ben. They rode as partners. Later he claimed that it was Ben's age and not his gender that caused him to change his style. I have my doubts. But Ben still talks about his ride, and all three children want to get bikes when they get older.

Riding parents and grandparents have serious safety issues to face. The risks they assume for their children are life threatening and sometimes life ending. Taking a child on the road opens up the possibilities of dangers unknown to nonriding parents. No one takes this responsibility lightly. All riding parents and riding grandparents understand this. One moment in time, one wrong instant, and you can lose your whole family. Every time Ken and I think of our own grandchildren, the concerns emerge. If anything ever happened to them, it would destroy the entire family. We would never forgive ourselves. Our grandchildren's parents, our own children, would never forgive us (nor should they), and it would shatter the family unit.

So why ride with kids? Why risk harming the people you love most, your grandchildren?

We know the risks and they scare us. But we also know the pleasures. We know the extraordinary pleasures of the road. We want to share with our grandchildren some of the very best pleasures available. If biking is part of our lives, the kids may want it to be part of theirs as well. There is a grandeur in riding that comes from nowhere else. The skills one needs to gain mastery over a bike are skills that come in handy throughout life. That sense of adventure, bravado, accomplishment, and courage is indispensable. It keeps you alive and vital all of your days. Our grandkids want to be part of this heritage and we want them to have it as well.

"So tell me, Bernie," I asked one of my passengering friends, "did your kids ride a lot with Dick when they were younger?"

"Only Cynthia liked to ride with him."

"Were you ever really nervous? Did she have any problems learning?"

"Not really. My daughter didn't ride until she was a teenager so I didn't have to worry like if she were young, and Dick's a good rider. I wasn't nervous at all. If she had wanted to ride as a child, it would have been different."

It was different with Robin. She was barely five and Linda was terrified. Robin couldn't reach the foot pegs, so her father adjusted them higher and turned them into princess pegs. Linda finally allowed Robin to ride because she felt she couldn't fight both daughter and husband anymore. Don, riding a Softail, sat far back in the seat and wedged his daughter between himself and the backrest while she sat in the passenger's seat. She stayed put. For all her fears, Linda saw that Robin rode well. She stayed still, never wiggled, held on tight to the leather strap, and loved the ride. The backrest came up almost to the top of her daughter's head, so there wasn't much chance of her falling backward.

"Robin really wanted to go," Linda explained to me. "Don sat back and Robin was squished between him and the backrest. She rode on long trips. She rode most of the way to Bridgeport and that's a hard ride, but she never got dragged out. She never got tired of riding. She was always excited and always happy to ride. After a while, I just stopped being scared with her riding. They knew what they were doing."

I remember that Bridgeport trip. We camped right next to Linda, Robin, and Don. They showed us how to make camp beside that frigid mountain lake. They loaned us one of their air mattresses and taught us how to position our tent in all that wetness. It rained ceaselessly that first Bridgeport year, and a number of our friends went down while riding over the High Sierra passes. But no matter the weather or the danger, Robin wanted to ride.

"So were you nervous when Miles started riding?" I asked Marjory when we visited over coffee. "He's still a pretty young kid!"

"I wasn't nervous at all. I was fine with it. It was no big deal. He was riding with Tim so it was okay. I mean, once we decided that he should be able to ride, it was easy."

"Yeah, but didn't you have to teach him how to ride?"

"No, he wanted to ride, and Tim's got a big Dresser. That seat is so safe, it's like sitting in a recliner. He couldn't fall off if he wanted to. And just to add a bit of extra safety, we bungeed him to the back seat. We tied him in with a bungee cord."

As I listened, I reflected upon the differences between riding parents and riding grandparents. I wished that I had come to riding earlier. I wished that I had taught my kids to ride. As in any culture, parents socialize their children into it from an early age. I remembered my friend Debby riding around with her two-year-old grandson crammed between herself and her twenty-two-year-old daughter. She was a riding mother and a riding grandmother. Biking is a way of life, and within Harley culture, kids learn early.

2

Harley Culture
An Emerging Community

"Sure as shit, there's a Harley culture, and it's what we're doing now. We're riding."

Something is going on in America. A unique culture is rumbling into life. Beneath a sea of suits, stockings, sweaters, and skirts, a culture cloaked in leather is roaring its way to birth. The office cubicles, trading floors, reception areas, and conference rooms have been forgotten. There is wildness left in America.

The lure of chrome and steel challenges tired workers and transforms them into bikers out to jam the wind. They are riding. As the shirts, ties, and pumps give way to leathers, chaps, and shades they start their search. Office-exhausted and weary of spirit, they are out on the road looking for something not found in law or business or teaching, something more. They are looking for something with soul.

While bikers have long existed as a fringe element, invasion into the American mainstream is new. Motorcycle riding as a way of life has been around since the first motorcycles appeared. Riding a Harley meant having a free, devil-may-care attitude toward life. In the twenties and thirties, it was also good transportation. Both men and women rode. Both took pride in their skills. World War II changed all that. Returning vets, in the forties, made it very clear that they wanted their Harleys and they wanted them *now*. Like all vets both before and after them, they came home restless and expectant. They had trouble inside themselves and something had to calm it. Some quieted that restlessness in family and work, but others roamed the roads, refused to settle down, and maintained their hold on the edges of danger by riding.

By the end of the forties and into the fifties, outlaws claimed Harleys as their own. Through the very lean and hungry Harley years of the sixties and seventies, only the few, the faithful, the fearless, and

13

the fanatical, continued to ride Harleys. The Harley-Davidson Motor Company was close to broke. The bikes demanded constant maintenance and every rider needed to know how to tear down his bike and rebuild it. A biker had to be able to wrench.

In those years, being a biker meant being a member of an alternative and very fringe society. You could join only if you had the experience and guts to survive the road. If you couldn't wrench a bike, you didn't own one. If you weren't tough enough to defend your turf, you didn't have one. The Motor Company had its troubles. The riders had their troubles. And while motorcycling became respectable in some quarters, bikers remained outcasts, living in a world of their own.

In the mid-eighties, the biker world began to change. A new pattern, a new rider, a new Harley order was rising phoenix-like from the stubble and rubble of the fringe. New Harley riders come from all kinds of classes, races, regions, and backgrounds. And despite the lack of a common territory or community, a biker culture is emerging. And it is shared. There is a strong and vital bond. Harley riders share some impressive traits in common. They share attitudes, values, dress, and language. Linking it all together is the profound love for the bike.

Harley culture is out in the open. It's no longer fringe. It's roaring toward mainstream. It's proud, loud, and pushy.

American society is so large and so amorphous that most people identify with just the big stuff. We share cultural icons. But sometimes it's hard to find the America in Americans. Most identify with only the things we know. We know the flag, the eagle, Uncle Sam, baseball, McDonald's, Norman Rockwell, and apple pie. Harleys are becoming part of the shared stuff. They are cultural icons.

Harleys are not amorphous. They are not ephemeral. Like the other icons, they are very concrete, very real, and very identifiable. Harleys may have started as hard-assed bikes, good rides for fringe folk, but they have transformed. They have become cultural symbols, and as such they have the power to unite separate groups.

Harleys have always been the vehicle of choice for a large group of hard-working, politically underrepresented, risk-taking, frequently ignored middle Americans. They are the vehicle of pleasure for a large number of office-working, career-training, overpaid, overworking professional Americans. They are uniting in spirit many groups across great lifestyle divides.

Middle Americans look at Harleys and smile. Here is something grand, something American-made, something powerful, something uniquely ours. In the heartland and in small towns on both coasts, Harleys play a role in reaffirming pride in America.

Daniel R. Wolf wrote that "becoming a biker constitutes a search for identity" (1991, 30). Daniel rode with the Rebels, an outlaw motorcycle club in Edmonton, Alberta. His portrayal of outlaw bikers rings true. It wasn't until I read his work that I realized just how many behaviors all riders share with outlaw clubs. Outlaw biking is part of Harley history. Most of the outlaw rules and values make good road sense. They started as road smarts, survival tactics, and remain so to this day.

Hunter Thompson, the infamous author of *Hell's Angels*, wrote: "The California climate is perfect for bikes as well as surfboards, convertibles, swimming pools and abulia. Most cyclists are harmless weekend types, no more dangerous than skiers or skin-divers. But ever since the end of World War II the West Coast has been plagued by gangs of young, wild men on motorcycles, roaming the highways in groups of ten to thirty and stopping whenever they get thirsty or road-cramped to suck up some beer and make noise." (1967, 59). He continues,

> The whole thing was born, they say, in the late 1940s when most ex-GI's wanted to get back to an orderly pattern: college, marriage, a job, children—all the peaceful extras that come with a sense of security. But not everyone felt that way. Like the drifters who rode west after Appomattox, there were thousands of veterans in 1945 who flatly rejected the idea of going back to a prewar pattern. They didn't want order, but privacy and time to figure things out. It was a nervous, downhill feeling, a mean kind of angst that always comes out of wars, . . . a compressed sense of time on the outer limits of fatalism. They wanted more action, and one of the ways to look for it was on a big motorcycle. By 1947 the state was alive with bikes, nearly all of them powerful American-made irons from Harley-Davidson and Indian [now defunct].

The label "outlaw motorcycle club" originally meant any club not registered with the American Motorcycle Association (AMA). A registered club receives a charter and rules of membership, which allow the members to participate in regularly sponsored motorcycle events and the all-important motorcycle racing circuit. Nonregistered clubs are labeled "outlaw" and called the "one percent fringe." It's this one percent that most folk think of when they see a biker.

"The root definition remains the same . . . a dangerous hoodlum on a big, fast motorcycle. And California has been breeding them for years" (Thompson 1967, 59). And Wolf adds, "today, many outlaw club members wear one percenter badges as a supplement to their club colors; or as Sonny Barger, President of the Hell's Angel's, first did in the sixties, they make a very personal and uncompromising statement on where they stand on the issue of being an outlaw by having the one percent logo tattooed on their shoulders" (1991, 5).

Ed Youngblood, president of the AMA, says that the exact origin of the famous one percent statement is lost in the past. It was well after the Hollister riot of 1947 that some AMA official in some national forum made the statement, which has since passed into folklore.*

It goes something like this: "Most motorcyclists are law-abiding citizens. It's only one percent of the motorcyclists who are outlaws." The outlaw groups heard this statement, adopted the one percent logo as their symbol, and have kept it ever since.

Regardless of one's preference in lifestyles, regardless of which side of the law one rides on, the problems on the road do not change. Whether one is an outlaw, a member of a Harley Owners' Group (HOG), American Bikers Aimed Towards Education (ABATE), or the Modified Motorcycle Association (MMA), a new rider, an old rider, or part of a Christian MC, the difficulties of jamming the wind remain the same. Whether one is a RUB (Rich Urban Biker), a rural blue-collar worker, a middle-class suburbanite, a working-class urban rider, or a townie, there are common difficulties. How bikers relate to the police, the nonriding population, and the world in general may vary depending on whether they belong to outlaw or AMA-approved groups, but the road never varies.

There are common problems. There are common solutions. All groups share the problems of maintaining their bikes, maintaining road-worthy clothes, and maneuvering through rough weather, rough terrain, and rough times. All groups get hassled by the cops. All groups have to deal with downed comrades, highway accidents, and hospital calls at 2 A.M. All groups maintain Harleys which growl and smoke and at times leave us at the side of the road.

Riding paraphernalia is shared. Riding clothes all look alike. Most of the men, to outsiders, look alike. All but the RUBS and new bikers share some version of long hair, beards, or tattoos.

It is not, however, the differences in appearance or bikes that separate the outlaws from the rest of the Harley world. It's attitude. It's commitment. Daniel Wolf's view that becoming a biker constitutes a search for identity holds true for all groups. But it holds true differently. Identity is earned by each rider within each group, but it means different things to each group and it is earned differently. According to Wolf:

*For those who want a Hollywood dramatization of the Hollister riot of 1947 check out the movie *The Wild One*.

16

The outlaw biker is a product of urban industrial society. A survey of the socio-economic background of bikers furthermore indicates that becoming a biker is a class-specific response to the general problems of self-actualization. Whether outlaw bikers are loners or club patch holders, they tend to come from the lower working class. None of the Rebels or any of the bikers with whom I associated during my ten years as an active biker originated in the upper-middle or upper class, and few held professional, managerial or administrative positions.

He continues,

Why does the lower working class produce candidates for a biker sub-culture? The answer lies in the culture of the streets and in the work-place. It is a modern-day urban setting that lacks symbols and activi-ties around which to build a personal identity, and is largely devoid of meaningful collective endeavors around which to build a sense of community. While he receives a pay-cheque, he finds himself short-changed in meaning. Whether you call it "alienation" or label it "anomie," he is deprived of adequate psychological payoff in the way of life-expanding experiences and identity confirming ritual. Isolation from meaningful social participation and the subsequent psychological experience of inadequate identity fulfillment may result in a personal search for self authenticity. If the laborer is a young man in search of himself, he will find nothing in his self-image at work that will excite him; he had best look elsewhere. Men who are chained to these circum-stances share a compelling desire to escape. (1991, 31)

Thompson, three decades earlier than Wolf, observed, "In a world increasingly geared to specialists, technicians and fantastically compli-cated machinery, the outlaws are obvious losers and it bugs them. But instead of submitting quietly to their collective fate, they have made it the basis of a full-time social vendetta. They don't expect to win any-thing, but on the other hand, they have nothing to lose" (1967, 54).

Wolf writes, "A man who enters this sub-culture in search of an identity looks to the outlaw-biker tradition to provide him with long-standing values, behaviors, and symbols. What he will find are heroes and role models, a personal legacy that is consistent with what he dis-covered on the streets about the complete man. He will adopt attitudes and learn behaviors that gravitate around lower-class focal concerns with independence, freedom, self-reliance, toughness, impulsiveness and masculinity, all of which will be embodied in a highly romanti-cized image of the anti-hero" (1991, 33).

The attitudes and backgrounds of outlaw bikers, as described by Wolf, are not so different from those of many bikers I ride with. Yet I rarely ever ride with outlaws. Most of my first companions came from blue-collar working-class backgrounds and my later ones from the middle class. Sometimes both groups rode together in the same club. They came from both small towns and large urban areas. Some had ridden all their lives, some were riding their first bikes. In my experience, it is not class, but age, commitment, and attitude that separates the outlaws from the other Harley riders. That, and the willingness to openly ride on the wrong side of the law.

The Harley world is vast. It is also being transformed. Its strength and durability lies in both its diversity and its continuity. A tradition that began in 1903 in a shed in Milwaukee continues today as an American institution. It is a tradition that exists in chrome and steel and also in the heart.

3

The Early Years

"There's almost a hundred years of history here. Someone's got to tell it."

My husband's been riding motorcycles almost all his life. But after he returned from Vietnam, it became a serious, if quiet, passion. Through a long, busy, messy, and moving life filled with kids and work, his love of bikes endured. During Harley's lean and terrible years, he rode Hondas. In his youth, like so many other American men, he had fallen in love with Harleys but never quite got the money to buy one. After the war, with some bucks in his belt, he went to the shops to compare bikes. As an adult, he had not fallen sufficiently under Harley's sway to buy one. He didn't want to endure the long roadside breakdowns, the constant wrenching, and the endless oil leaks. Ken loved Harleys, but he kept on buying Hondas.

In the winter of 1990, all this changed. We had been visiting in Santa Cruz where our friend Bill Shaw had just bought a Mazda Miata.

"Great car, Bill!" I yelled as Bill grinned at us from the front seat of his little sports coupe.

"Great car, Bill!" echoed Ken as he examined the new Miata.

Bill just kept grinning.

"Great car?" I asked his wife, Carolyn Martin Shaw.

"No comment," was her reply, "but Bill's really happy with it."

Ken looked interested but not impressed.

"Want one?" I asked in a light, but *I really don't think so,* voice.

Ken's response was a surprise. "No, I don't want a sports car, I want a bike! A big bike!"

Next day he went down to the Honda shop and rode away on a Shadow. Ken had ridden a lot of Hondas. But this time, when he rode the Shadow home, he carried an issue of the Harley magazine *American Iron* under his arm.

19

Ken bought a Honda but for the next four months he read about Harleys. He read the magazines and the papers and the trade reports. He rode a Shadow but lusted after a Harley. At that time, I could see no difference between a Honda and a Harley. But Ken could.

The yearnings of youth returned and he started hanging out at Harley shops. He wore a deep path between our home and the Dudley Perkins Company, our local Harley dealership.

But there were no new bikes available. To his shock, everyone else also wanted a Harley. "You'll have to wait a year for delivery" was the dealer's response. Being new to the Harley world, I could not believe that Ken would not be able to get his bike.

I called every Harley shop within one hundred miles of San Francisco. They all said the same thing. "Want a Harley? Wait a year."

He couldn't wait. He had been waiting all his life. He wanted his Harley, and he wanted it *now*! So I stretched my anthropological skills, learned some bike vocabulary, and started making phone calls. I called all over the state of California and far into Arizona and Nevada. There were two, just two, new Harleys to be had. Both were Low Riders and both were available in California. Two lone bikes not yet spoken for! And at the same dealership! Within minutes, both these bikes had Ken's name on them. The shop was in Rosemead, in Southern California, and the owner was willing to take Ken's Shadow in trade. Ken could buy either Low Rider. His choice.

A good business deal. Good for the dealer, good for us. Ken would ride down on his Shadow, open his wallet, and ride home on the Harley of his choice. It was the Fourth of July when Ken rode the four hundred miles to Rosemead. Fourth of July and everyone was celebrating, not traveling. With concern, I called Bob Laidlaw, the Rosemead Harley-Davidson dealer. I asked about motels along the way. Bob wouldn't hear of it. And that's when Ken and I both learned that things really are different on a Harley.

Bob insisted that Ken stay at his home and share Fourth of July dinner with his family. The next day, they would go together to the shop. I was impressed. Bob Laidlaw was inviting a stranger to his home. On trust, he was offering Ken his house, hearth, and hospitality. Eight hundred miles and two days later, Ken rode his FXRS-SP Low Rider home and life has never been the same since.

Ken's story is not unusual. Over the phone (I never did meet him in person), Bob told me other stories of Harley hospitality. And it was not limited to Harleys. "In the old days," Bob recalled, "anyone riding an Indian motorcycle would also have been welcome."*

*Harleys and Indian have always been linked as *the major* American motorcycles.

Ken Harmon (Courtesy of Noel Paraninfo)

The Harley world is filled with stories of friendship and camarade-rie. It's part of the mystique that reinforces the legends. Out-of-town strangers are welcomed at local dealerships. If you are stranded on the road, bikers will stop to help you out. Harley camaraderie touches something deep in the American psyche, and the modern explosive increase in the sale of Harley motorcycles and goods and in club mem-bership is a living testament to that need. In a country rich in diversity, Harleys act as a symbol of unity. In a country that is divided into sub-cultures and regions, Harley culture cuts across the divisions and pro-vides some very important common ground. The blue-collar construc-tion worker in Utah and the white-collar social worker in New York swap stories and addresses at national rallies. Harleys provides a com-mon language and common identity in a land often scored with conflict.

"As a boy it didn't take long to realize that I was related to a very special company. Born the son of H[arley] D[avidson] President Wil-liam H. Davidson and a grandson of Founder William A. Davidson, I recall seeing my father attired in a conservative business suit as he

21

pulled away from the door each morning on a motorcycle. Not just any motorcycle but—as it has turned out—the only American motorcycle that remains in production today" (Wright 1993, 34).

It started in a shed in Milwaukee in 1903. The three Davidson brothers, Arthur, William, and Walter, and their friend Bill Harley created their first motorcycle. At the time it was rumored they made only one. By 1907, however, the distinctive V-Twin engine was born, and the rest has become part of American history.

From 1910 through 1920, the bikes were ridden over dirt roads, over impassable, impossible mountain lanes, down steep ravines and cow paths. They were ridden from coast to coast. They were the great escape. Bikes were the call to adventure. Racing circuits formed and Harley riders made names for themselves. Harleys were fun, but they were also working bikes. The motorcycle, complete with sidecar and sometimes top covering, had its practical side. It delivered goods, hauled materials, and transported people. Harleys were useful machines. In 1916, Harleys went to war. Before there were tanks, there were Harleys.

In 1916 an army division of machine-gun-wielding men on Harley-Davidsons rode into Mexico chasing Pancho Villa. In 1917, during World War I, the motorcycles were shipped to Europe. Thousands were used in France. They were also used at home. Women from the Women's Army Messenger Corps rode Harleys. They were the police vehicles of choice in over 2,500 cities and counties around the country. Gray military bikes were working machines.

During the twenties, production dropped. In spite of their functional uses, Harleys stalled in sales. They had become old news. There was something new on the horizon. Henry Ford built an automobile, and Americans loved it. A car, like a bike, gave Americans mobility. A car, unlike a bike, gave Americans privacy. In a world where many young people lived at home, a car promised dating privacy. Bikes were nice, but cars offered seclusion. The car was dubbed "the rolling bedroom." Bikes were left in the dust.

By the end of the thirties the Motor Company was again gearing up for war. Between the police purchases, the war effort, and the racing industry, Harley-Davidson kept going. Its fortunes rode the American economic wave. It jammed the wind in the good years and bottomed out in the bad ones.

The year 1933 was a very bad one for Harley-Davidson. Like most other companies, it suffered in the Great Depression. Struggling through crisis after crisis, it picked up in the war years only to crash and burn in peacetime. After World War II, most Americans wanted cars. By the middle of the forties, only the returning vets remembered motorcycles. The Indian, the only other American-made motorcycle, gave up the ghost in 1953. This left Harley-Davidson riding alone. America's last motorcycle.

When Brando, in *The Wild One*, led his outlaw club through Hollister, he led them on a British-made Triumph. The film is remembered for many things: Brando's portrayal of the alienated, urban antihero, town fear in the face of rampaging bikers, and a romanticized view of the outlaw image. Here was American youth, misguided and lusting after adventure. Here were bikers looking for freedom and excitement. Every alienated teenager in America could identify. Every parent in America could fear the bike as a symbol of rebellion.

The bike could transport its rider right out of middle-class boredom and into exotic adventures. The bike offered unpredictability. The bike beckoned. The road, the unknown and the mysterious, lay just beyond the next hill. It was irresistible. It still is.

In *The Wild One*, the character playing the real sleaze was Lee Marvin on his chopped hog. Brando may have been the "wild one," but Marvin was authentic.

As if Harley didn't have enough competition already, with automobiles offering both transportation and smooching space, overseas motorcycle companies started building better bikes. The opening shot in what has been called the motorcycle wars was fired in 1959 when the first Japanese Honda motorcycle rolled ashore.

By the end of the sixties, Hondas were everywhere. Harley was hard pressed to survive. Harleys had always appealed to the blue-collar working-class guy. The Harley had both rural and urban appeal and drew its strength from its American roots. But it had acquired, along with its reputation for strength, the unsavory tinge of the outlaw. It was linked with the One Percenters. They were clear about their love of the Harley. It was the only bike they would consider riding. Ironically, it was also the only bike most police officers would consider riding. Both groups insisted on power and the "made in America" label. While only a small percentage of Harley riders were outlaws, the image persisted. For forty years, the AMA has been fighting the outlaw image, as Thompson explains:

> The AMA includes all kinds of motorcyclists—from those on 50-cubic-centimeter Hondas to devotees of full-dress Harley '74s—but it centers on competition riders, either professional or amateur, who take their bikes very seriously, spend a lot of money on them and ride all year round.
>
> Unlike the outlaws, they frequently take long trips either alone or

in groups of two or three, and often into areas where anybody on a motorcycle is automatically treated like an—outlaw,—a raping brute unfit to eat or drink among civilized people.

Unlike the general public, many competition riders have had painful experience with the outlaws, for they move in the same small world. Their paths cross at bike-repair shops, races or late-night hamburger stands. According to respectable cyclists, the outlaws are responsible for the motorcycle's sinister image. They blame the outlaw for many of the unpleasant realities of being a bike-owner—from police harassment to public opprobrium to high insurance rates. (1967, 166)

Honda took the offensive. It created a different image. Honda wanted its riders to look respectable. It began running ads that read: "You meet the nicest people on a Honda" (billboards in Southern California, circa 1968).

Honda went after the middle-class rider. It went after the family man, the man whose wife would support his riding. It showed ads of smiling women cheerfully waving their husbands on as they rode down suburban lanes looking for an afternoon of innocent merriment.

Honda's advertising presented the image of riding as good clean fun as opposed to the rough and tumble, down and dirty image of Harley riding. If Honda was striving for respectability, Harley kept appealing to the fringe. The movie *Easy Rider,* Peter Fonda and Dennis Hopper's ode to disaffected youth in 1967, typified the Harley image in America's collective consciousness and reflected a deep yearning on the part of counterculture young. To quote Fonda's famous lines: "We want to be free. We want to be free to do whatever we want to do. We want to ride. We want to be free to ride our machines without being hassled by the man. And we want to get loaded."

Honda sent a different message.

In the seventies, Japanese bikes started taking a larger bite out of the high-end motorcycle market. They were increasing in size and speed and were well constructed. People joked that constant oil leaks were just the Harley's way of marking its territory, but Harley was waging a losing battle: "Compared with the state-of-the-art, smooth-running, oil-tight engines on Japanese bikes, Harley engines were primitive. It was commonly said that you could always tell where a Harley had been parked by the puddle of oil it left behind. Vibrations made long trips distinctly uncomfortable" (Reid 1990, 61).

Harley still maintained the dominance it had held in the big-bike niche for over twenty-five years. Then catastrophe struck. Honda came out with the Gold Wing. It was big, well made, absolutely reliable, and considerably cheaper than a Harley. By the mid-seventies, Japan had managed to outbuild, outclass, and outsell the last remaining American motorcycle.

Reid offers the interesting theory that some Harley dealers, in a last-ditch effort to cater to their core clientele, tried to perpetuate a type of bad-guy, tough-guy atmosphere in their shops. They rented storefronts in run-down neighborhoods and deliberately presented sleazy images to the world. To make matters worse, in terms of its image, Harley was no longer owned by the Harley-Davidson Motor Company. It merged with AMF (American Machine and Foundry) in 1969 and remained a division of AMF until 1982, when it was bought back by Harley corporate officers. Without the merger, it is unlikely that the company would have survived.

To the hard core, however, this merger meant defection. Harley desperately needed the capital AMF offered, but AMF had little interest in motorcycles. The Harley businesspeople knew it. The riders knew it. The company floundered. All during AMF's reign, the bikes sported the dreaded AMF logo alongside the Harley one.

In an attempt to outrun the competition, the Motor Company, under the auspices of AMF, filed charges with the government against the Japanese imports. Harley claimed, on the basis of considerable evidence, that the Japanese were selling their bikes far below market value. They also claimed that the Japanese were changing the calendar dates on specific models so that more bikes could enter the country. The Motor Company requested that a tariff be placed upon Japanese imports. At first, the tariff was denied.

Then the Japanese started building Harley clones and shipping them to America. To the untutored eye, Yamaha's Virago, Honda's Shadow, Kawasaki's Intruder, and Suzuki's Vulcan all look remarkably like Harley Big Twins. About the Virago, Reid remarked: "This Harley clone had it all: the buckhorn handlebars, the stepped seat, and most important of all, the big V-Twin engine that had been so distinctively Harley for more than 70 years. Moreover, this brash impostor ran better than the real thing and cost 25 to 75 percent less. Here was a bike of higher quality and lower price. The Harley mystique wavered. Hard times for Harley! Hard times for the men who made them, for the American workers who ran the factories, worked the machines, and sold the bikes." Reid continues, "The Company now was depending on die-hard fans who wore T-shirts emblazoned with sayings like 'I'd rather see my sister in a whorehouse than my brother on a Honda'" (1990, 61).

In the early eighties, Harley was hurting. By 1981 there were more Japanese bikes than Harleys sold in the big-bike market. There were so many problems that Harley dealers offered inducements: "Buy a Sportster! Trade up!" The Sportster was sold with the understanding that the owner could ride it, return it, and trade it in—for its original purchase price—for a Big Twin. Still it was not enough. Harley kept hurting. The Milwaukee company offered more incentives, including rebates. But the blue-collar, working-class men who traditionally rode Harleys were out of jobs. The general economy grew worse. With their core customers unemployed and interest rates high, Harley-Davidson almost went under.

In 1983 the Motor Company finally convinced Washington that it was in the economy's best interest to charge a tariff on all Japanese bikes in the Harley big-bike range (over 700cc's). Honda had fun with this one. For several years, a large number of Japanese bikes rolled to American shores at 699cc's. Eventually, however, Harley got what it wanted (and needed) and Honda paid the tariff. Once more, with the tariff in place, they owned the big-bike niche.

In the eighties there were three basic Harley models. Once there had been only two. There had been Dresser touring bikes (FLs) and smaller Sportster bikes (XLs). The original touring bike, big and heavy, arrived from the factory padded and loaded. A fully dressed, factory-ready Harley, complete with saddlebags, fairing, sissy bar, crash bar, and extra gadgets, was what most touring riders wanted.

The hard-core rider, however, would have none of it. The original FLs were stripped, chopped, and streamlined before they became good enough for One Percenters. The cams, carburetor, and pipes were changed. A bored-out engine, extended forks, and lowered seat usually completed the process. The finished bike was loud, fast, and customized. It expressed the rider's tastes and needs. And it was still big.

The other original Harley, the Sportster, was lighter, faster, quicker handling, and sparser. It lacked the gadgets and geegaws of the FL. It was designed as a street bike. It was the complement to the long-distance-traveling FL. In a romanticized view of the two motorcycles, David Wright noted, "If FLs were the kings of the highway, the XLs were the studs of the street and strip" (1993, 72).

In 1972 Harley-Davidson engineered another type of bike. It combined the size of the FL with the sports features of the XL. It was big and powerful like a Dresser but fast and lean like the Sportster. The company called it a Low Rider, and it was a hit. Born in the seventies, the FX came of age in the eighties and became one of Harley's best-sellers. (While the factory used the term Low Rider to specify only particular FX models, many used the term for most FX types of bikes.)

In 1983, when things were starting to get better for the company, a new and different line of bikes was added. Called Softails, they were a stylistic coup and a runaway success. One kind of Softail had the leaner front end of the FX while another had the more traditional front end of the FL. Both looked as if they had been ridden right out of the 1950s. Instant nostalgia! For the burgeoning middle-aged market, that look was irresistible. So what if they were not rubber mounted and had no rear shock to speak of. So what if the rest of the FX and FL lines were better rides. So what if the Low Rider cornered cleaner and the Dresser rode with greater comfort. This bike, this Softail, had the look of youth. Their youth.

The Softail spoke to a generation of men who longed for their youth and mourned the changes in America. America had become a different land from the one they had grown up in. The old U.S.A. was barely recognizable to the working-class guys who grew up on Harleys. They, like other Americans, were confused. There were new rules. For men there were new jobs as the market shifted from industry to service. For women there were new relationships and few guidelines. No one was sure quite how to behave. America had participated in, without winning, two wars, in Korea and Vietnam. The Vietnam War and the civil unrest it caused at home still burns in the heartland of America.

Scores of skilled and semiskilled jobs were lost to automation. The country's need for skilled craftsmen hit an all-time low. Electronics started taking the place of mechanical knowledge, and the skills learned in high school no longer guaranteed a job. Hard work no longer guaranteed a job. Computers defined a new literacy. American factories were being built abroad. Labor unions lost ground and people stopped buying American. The eagle still flew, but the wings were hurting. Civil rights, affirmative action, gay rights, feminism, and extensive government programs were new ideologies. The old ways didn't hold. Bikers were suspicious. Workers had made a deal with America, but America was reneging. Unemployment kept rising. Men could no longer make enough money to support their families. Pensions and retirements could no longer be taken for granted. Loyalty to a particular company no longer promised security. A land they had fought for, a land they thought they understood had changed the rules. And worse, no one had told them about it.

The Softail looked like the America of the fifties. The Softail looked like the bike men wanted before their world changed. The Softail represented the era of American prosperity. In that era, America won its wars, and had jobs for working-class men and safe neighborhoods for their children. That America was a land where women knew their place, gay liberation was in the closet, and racial conflict was confined to urban ghettos.

Ride a Softail and the world becomes a simpler place. Ride a Softail

27

and feel young again. Ride a Softail and remember a time of male superiority and American ascendancy. Softails became instant best-sellers. Harley pitched nostalgia. American working men remembered their past. And the bikes flew out of the shops as quickly as they rolled in.

But we know America cannot go home again! That fifties world is as dead as a Shovel's battery. And for lots of us, that's a good thing, too. Because America's promise belongs not only to blue-collar, white-skinned, hard-working family men, but to all of us. It belongs to the poor, brown, gay, female, and ghettoized as well.

Change happens. Lots of us have it better now than we did in the fifties. Some of us have it worse. But for the hard-core Harley rider, change came hardest of all. In the early eighties, the American working man could no longer routinely expect to own his own home, raise his family, keep two cars in his attached garage, or send his kids to safe schools. He could no longer do what his father before him had done. And it hurt.

He didn't know or care that those who were poor or female or ghettoized couldn't do that either. He only knew that something very important had been taken away from him. His belief in himself had been taken away. And he wanted it back. America used to promise success to the hard-working man. The Softail gave him the illusion of its return.

Through hard work, his father had become one of the *haves.* In the early eighties, the white working-class man was in danger of slipping into the ranks of the *have nots.* Working-class men felt that they were being pushed aside by minorities. They did not care that the minorities had no choice in their scramble for upward mobility. They had to encroach. America had made a promise to them, too. America had made a promise to all the people. The promise to minorities was never fulfilled. So they let their anger boil up out of the ghettos and the kitchens and the closets. By the time the Softail came out, America was in chaos and workers wanted to forget about their downward slide. The Softail came out and working-class men grabbed it. They have held on ever since. It is like holding on to a piece of old America.

Change keeps happening. Things got better. The economy took an upswing. People started buying American again. New industries emerged. There were new jobs. Many women got the work they needed and there were still jobs to go around. Against incredible odds, against formidable foreign competition, Harley staged a comeback. The fiercely loyal customers who had stuck by Harley despite all their problems were vindicated.

The success of the Softail was due in part to the reorganization that had taken place in the company. In 1983, thirteen Harley-Davidson executives bought the company back from AMF. They ushered in a new era for motorcycling. Harleys rolled off the assembly line reborn and roaring. Major improvements were made. Everything on the bikes was revamped. There were changes in engine design, in style, in performance, and in attitude. With new management, the entire organization was restructured.

All who stayed agreed to have their salaries frozen or cut. The product was to come first. There were massive layoffs, but management promised to rehire when production improved. The promise was kept. Harley representatives went to the Japanese companies and studied their production methods. They studied their managerial methods. In Milwaukee, there was hope for the first time in several decades. The workers bought into the dream. For the first time they were included in the production, evaluation, and decision-making processes.

Harley developed radical and innovative techniques. Customers— honest-to-God bikers—were consulted about design. They were asked what they wanted in their ride. In 1984 a new engine was retooled. The Evolution engine, or Blockhead, replaced the Shovelhead. Since 1966, the Shovelhead design had ruled the Harley world.

With the Blockhead came rubber mounting on Low Riders and Dressers. The ride became smoother. The bike stopped shaking and dripping (mostly). The company used top-of-the-line, up-to-date technology. The bike did not leak or vibrate loose its parts (mostly). It did, however, keep the original Harley look. It kept the Harley sound. It combined the best of both worlds. It combined modern technology with nostalgic looks. While the bike still leaves you at the side of the road, it leaves you there less often. The Evolution engine vastly improved the overall ride and outperformed the earlier models. But it managed to maintain the raw Harley look and sound.

Aesthetically, everything still hung out. No nuts or bolts were concealed. No engine parts were covered up. The powerful-looking V- twin engine remained remarkably visible. The V-twin was seen as an integral part of the bike's beauty. Harley riders, unlike the rest of the motorcycle world, want to *see* their machinery. They want the satisfaction of hearing the sound of shifting gears. They want to hear that distinctive *clunk*. They want to experience the rumble and pulsation of the engine. Those sounds and sights and feelings are part of the Harley experience. Harley riders don't want the smooth comfortable silence of a Honda Gold Wing or Yamaha Voyager. They want to hear, feel, and see all the parts of their bike. That is a big part of Harley's success. That is part of the mystique.

The Motor Company added one final ingredient in its makeover. It added HOG. HOG (Harley Owners' Group) is a factory-sponsored motorcycle group. (The company intentionally avoided using the word "club.") Anyone buying a new Harley is automatically registered in HOG, a national association with regional affiliations. Every Harley dealer is encouraged to have a local HOG chapter associated with the shop. The local chapters organize rides, parties, and charity events. The dealers, in their efforts to remain close to their customers, coordinate their own events with their chapters. At the time of this writing, HOG has over 300,000 members. For the dealership, selling the bike is just the first step in a long-term relationship. The dealer hopes to maintain a lifelong partnership. The creation of HOG—pure brilliance.

The national HOG puts on regional gatherings around the country and sponsors riding events. At regional rallies, demo-rides take on special importance. In many areas this is the only way riders can have access to new or retooled bike models. With the formation of HOG, Harley is now selling more than bikes; they are selling the Harley-Davidson experience. HOG, the only official Harley-Davidson group backed by the corporation, provides social and riding activities all over the country. HOG has turned motorcycling into a respectable way of life.

Buying a Harley has become more than buying a product. Customers are now offered a ready-made community to join. The community is laced with patriotism. The nationwide network gives riders the feeling that they are joining with other American riders in supporting the country. They are buying an American product and keeping the economy strong. The connection between buying a Harley and supporting American business is frequently made. Harley sales are strong!

Harleys have now become the "in" bike to buy. Not since the early years have Harleys been so respectable or so chic. Milwaukee is merchandising the image. The Harley-Davidson trademark is appearing on a great variety of products: "Fashion magazines feature models sporting Harley T-shirts or draped over a vintage Harley bike wearing what *Mademoiselle* magazine calls 'truly cool again' motorcycle jackets" (Reid 1990, 32).

Museums exhibit motorcycles as works of art. The Motor Company now places ads in many nonmotorcycle publications. The implication is clear. You don't need to ride a bike (or even own a bike) to join the Harley family. The dealerships sell an impressive line of new Harley products—from functional and protective road gear to household goods. Go to the shops and check out the baby clothes, sleeping attire, wine, watches, pocketknives, Tiffany-style lamp shades, and shaving mugs. From blankets to bibs, the Harley-Davidson logo is likely to show up everywhere. It even appears on jukeboxes and cigarettes. The marketing has been so successful that sales records keep soaring and bikes remain on back order.

In the 1980s, customers were offered rebates and trade incentives; now Harley puts their customers on waiting lists. It is not uncommon to wait a year or more for the model of your choice. The Harley message—buy a Harley and join the American family—has become so successful that Honda has started marketing their own bikes with a similar promise. They offer clubs to join and activities to enter. They stress that Honda motorcycles are also made in America. While Hondas used to be manufactured exclusively in Japan, today there are Honda factories in many parts of the United States.

Since its inception in 1983, the national HOG has grown in size and in numbers of services provided. It has a Fly and Ride Program that permits members to rent Harleys when traveling. It initiated an LOH (Ladies of Harley) program to assist women within the Harley community. Since only a small proportion of Harley business comes from women (five to eleven percent), at first blush this emphasis on women seems like an odd business strategy. It appears less odd, however, when viewed against the backdrop of family buying patterns.

Men may buy bikes, but women often handle the family finances. If the wives have a piece of the action, their own place within the organization, they may be more cooperative about the purchase. Bikes cost a lot of money. Milwaukee wants wifely approval. If a woman does not ride, if her only contact with the bike is from the back seat, she may not feel comfortable on the road or at rallies. LOH was created to make her feel at home. It was created to give the passengering wife a sense of belonging. As more women ride their own bikes, however, this organization is coming under criticism.

Many women appreciate the program. Others resent its presence. Some see it as reinforcing a secondary-status position for women. Others see it as helping women take that first big step toward riding. HOG's ladies' auxiliary program may yet turn out to be Milwaukee's own affirmative action plan. Some women need a leg up. Some women don't. Women who come in as riders may resent the double standard. They do not see themselves as *ladies* of anything. They see themselves as bikers. They neither need nor want the program. Nonriding women, however, often find this group the first place they feel at home, the first place they feel accepted. Often this is the only place passengering women get to meet with riding women. Sometimes, this is the only group that encourages passengers to try riding.

Dealerships now sell "the whole Harley experience." At 7:00 P.M., far from home, when the bike has broken down and both rider and wife are sore and hungry, it helps to know that the closest dealership will offer assistance. Charisma and mystique sell bikes, but services and assistance keep them running.

The dealership network did not spring up by accident, or overnight. It is part of Milwaukee's marketing strategy. Belonging to the Harley family is one of Harley's strongest selling points. Once in the family, if you break down, there is someone to help you in every town across the country. The rider, especially the long-distance rider, is no longer riding alone. Dealerships offer services that reinforce customer loyalty. Milwaukee has hit upon marketing magic. It is somewhat ironic that the image of the independent biker riding alone down the lonely country lane is, in reality, backed by a national network of dealerships. Independence may look and feel good, but every Harley rider knows that breakdowns on isolated roads are no fun.

In 1987 the Harley-Davidson Motor Company informed the U.S. government that it would no longer need the protective tariff. It did this several years before the tariff was scheduled to expire. This was a political first. And it cleared a path for another first. The path to putting the Harley-Davidson Motor Company on the stock market.

When Harley went public, Wall Street got a parade. When companies go on the New York Stock Exchange, the event is usually celebrated by a quiet luncheon. When Harley-Davidson was listed on the New York Stock Exchange (in the summer of 1987), a Heritage Softail was suspended from the ceiling above the floor of the exchange. The Harley flag was flown outside. A large motorcycle parade led by Harley executives rumbled down Wall Street. From 59th Street to Wall Street, with an escort of Harley-riding New York City police officers, Harley-Davidson roared its entrance into the market. The parade was joined by independent Harley riders along the way. Several hundred bystanders watched as the riders reached the exchange, revved, then shut off their engines. This was the first time that the welcoming ceremony was conducted on the sidewalk.

From a Milwaukee shed in 1903 to the New York Stock Exchange in 1987, the Harley-Davidson Motor Company has come a long way. Bikes are selling, service is up, aftermarket merchandising is booming, peripheral products are flying out of the stores, and economic indications are strong. Harleys are a success story in marketing.

But what about the Harley riders? What about the men who stayed with the Motor Company during all the lean years? What about the wives who put up with oil puddles in their garages, bike parts in their living rooms, endless waits by the sides of roads, and Harley paraphernalia strewn throughout the house? What about the blue-collar, hardworking men who supported it all? Will the company continue to sup-

32

port them? What about the outlaws? Will they continue to ride Harleys now that so many professional, respectable folk choose them? Harleys now represent both respectability and scuzz. But the "wild one" image has changed. The gut-loyal guy who stayed with Harleys throughout all the bad times walks into an upscale dealership and doesn't recognize the place. He sees T-shirts and mugs and gimmicks. He wonders, Where are all the bikes?

Change happens. The Harley-Davidson Motor Company is still in the process of transforming itself. Much has happened since William Harley and the Davidson brothers, good friends and fishing buddies, created a motorized bike and changed America.

4

Movers and Shakers
Some Key Players

"In the Harley world, you can't tell the players without a score card."

I'm a Northern California Harley rider. My references are all territory specific. In my small corner of the Harley world, I am fortunate to have interviewed a few of the important folk who make things happen. I was privileged to speak with Dudley Perkins Jr. and Tom Perkins, owners of the Dudley Perkins Company, the San Francisco Harley-Davidson dealership. (Dudley Perkins died a few years after I interviewed him.) Also connected to the Dudley Perkins Company was Steve Zarwell, who sold Harleys for Dudley and Tom for over five years. I interviewed Reg Kittrelle, founder, editor, and publisher of *Thunder Press*, the premier monthly West Coast Harley-Davidson newspaper. I interviewed Mike Molinari, who was at the time CEO of Performance Productions, Inc. PPI puts on motorcycle events, including the very famous Bridgeport Jamboree. I spoke to Mike Felder, an insurance broker specializing in Harleys. Finally, I interviewed Brian Halton, founder and owner of *CityBike,* the oldest and one of the most successful San Francisco Bay Area biking newspapers.

My first interview was with Dudley Perkins Jr., whose business card reads:

DUDLEY PERKINS CO. Est. 1914
World's Oldest Harley-Davidson Dealership
A family tradition for three generations
66 Page Street, San Francisco, CA 94102

Dudley Perkins Jr. inherited the business from his father and had just formally passed it on to his son Tom when I spoke with him. While Tom had that busy, distracted look of someone trying to run a highly complex business (all from a tiny office), Dudley was calm and serene.

Dudley, who was referred to affectionately by customers and admirers alike as "the old man," was an imposing figure. Still strikingly vigorous after recovering from surgery, he wore his seventy-plus years with great dignity. In his shirt and tie and dressed-for-business clothes, he had the relaxed look of someone who had seen it all. In many ways, Harley history is also Perkins's history. His family and Harley-Davidsons have been intertwined for three generations.

We visited in a small office adjacent to and no bigger than his son's office. We talked about his early experiences in the family business, about the pitfalls and pleasures of spending a lifetime with Harley-Davidsons. We discussed the spiffy and unique Dudley Perkins Company dress code and the changes in bike quality over the years.

"In my father's time, he knew all the principals in Milwaukee. He went there regularly. He was in Daytona every year. The races couldn't start without him."

Dudley Perkins Sr., founder of the dealership, was a hill climber, flat-track racer, and all-around Harley rider. He was one of the famous old-timers who regularly appeared in the racing journals. He ran a shop staffed by racers and motorcycle enthusiasts.

"I used to go every Sunday with my father to watch the races and hill-climbing events. He rode with his customers. My father, the employees, and the customers were all very close. They were like a fraternity. My father was busy racing all the time. He constantly pulled money out of the business and put it into racing. We had a full-time mechanic on call just for the events. A lot of the business supplies were spent supporting racing. But the racers used the shop's resources and then kept all the prize money. The shop supported them. In the early days not enough money was put back into the business.

"My father was very close to his customers. To be a successful dealer, you must be close to your customers. But not so close as to be intimate friends. It's a fine line. You get close, you see the same people over and over, but you are in business, and that has to be respected. You do get to know the needs of your customers. If you are fortunate, they stay with you a long, long time."

When I asked if he too was interested in racing, Dudley Perkins Jr. answered in the classic way of all sons who work in family businesses.

"I raced a little but not professionally. I grew up in the business, so after school I came to work. I didn't have much time for racing. I was encouraged to go to school and get an education, but then I was expected to work. My father grew up racing. I grew up in the family business."

One of the remarkable things about a Harley shop is the mix of people who enter it. I remember that on my first visit to the Dudley Perkins Company I was surprised at the number of employees who were formally dressed. This is a motorcycle shop. I expected something more casual. I was wrong.

"All my life, I remember my father always wore a tie. He ran parts and service and sales, and it didn't matter, he always wore that tie. It made our dealership unique. We had a dress code. While other motorcycle businesses were run with people in dungarees [Dudley and I were probably the only two people in the shop who remembered that term], all the people at my father's shop wore jackets or suits and ties. Tom has kept up that tradition."

I wondered if Perkins had kept up the family tradition of wrenching. Did he do his own bike maintenance?

"I was never really interested in being a mechanic. I was always more interested in the selling end. I can fix a flat but that's all I'd care to do. Father always had qualified mechanics. Curiously, I was in the Third Motor Transport Battalion of the Third Marine Division during World War II. But they were all four-wheeled vehicles. I remember I got to Guam on August 15th, the day the war ended. It was very fortunate. I never really needed mechanical skills. If a bike broke, I called a mechanic. My son Tom is following in my family tradition."

"Are you still riding?"

"I can still ride, but if the bike fell over, I wouldn't be able to pick it up. I never got all my strength back after surgery. I rode a lot just before I got sick in '93. I went on the '92 New Year's Day Run (another Perkins family tradition), and I rode to Milwaukee in 1990 for a special celebration. Even though I rode a full Dresser with everything on it, my back was sore for weeks. That was my last real ride. The last long one."

"And the changes? What kinds of changes in the bikes have you seen over the years?"

"In the early days, when I worked for my father, the arrival of the bikes was a serious event. We had no forklifts. The bikes would come in on a flatbed truck and it took five or six mechanics to get them unloaded. It was hard work. The bikes would come skidding off the off ramp. A lot of the bikes arrived in bad condition. This made for poor factory-dealership relationships. Now the packaging has greatly improved. Also back then, the quality of the bikes wasn't as good as it is now. Even after AMF bought the company, the quality didn't get much better. After the buyback, however, quality improved. But even with better bikes coming from the factory, the factory-dealer relationship was not good. That relationship is, at best, adversarial. Sometimes what's good for Milwaukee is not what's good for the dealers. The factory wants the dealers to do whatever Milwaukee dictates, and the dealers want to stand up for their rights and the rights of their customers. Tom is continuing in that tradition too. You always stand up for your customers."

Dudley Perkins Jr. died in April 1997. On that day the world of motorcycling lost one of its leading players, one of its formidable champions. He was not only a San Francisco personality; he belonged to the entire world of motorcycling. It did not matter if you lived in Novato, Nebraska, or New York—the Perkins name was synonymous with bikes. He wore his age with dignity, just as he did his perennial shirt and tie and dressed-for-business clothes. It is always sad when a well-loved person dies, but Dudley Perkins Jr.'s death created a sadness in the whole biking community. He was more than a motorcycle dealer. He carried within him the history, legends, lore, and love of motorcycling. He was the living link between the beginnings of motorcycling and the contemporary scene. He provided stability and continuity in a changing industry.

Tom Perkins sat in an office that was small but wonderfully filled with biking memorabilia and motorcycle books. Having redesigned the shop three times in four years, he was a busy man. Running a large Harley dealership with a long family tradition had taken its toll on Tom. He was not only a busy man, but a harried one. He could not find time for lunch while juggling his multiple responsibilities. He threads his way through a Harley world where he must find a way to relate to *all* bikers. He must stay on good terms with everyone, including Milwaukee. His dealership, his reputation, and his ethics demand that as the third-generation Perkins to run the family business he must carry on family tradition. Yet like all young businessmen, Tom, still in his mid-thirties, wants to put his own stamp on the dealership. He had no time to give a leisurely interview. He jumped right into the middle of the issues.

"Harley culture is a world unto its own. Until you own a Harley, you can only view it from the outside. Even if you buy a Harley, it takes awhile to get fully initiated."

"Then what makes up the culture?"

"All the varieties of people and organizations who are involved in Harley business. From Hells Angels to the Christian motorcycle organizations. And every other 'believer.' For all of us, riding is very important. If I couldn't ride a bike, I would go crazy.

"I credit HOG with being very important in getting people back on bikes. Harley riders started riding with other Harley-oriented folk. There are other organizations, of course; there is AMA and ABATE and to a lesser extent the MMA, but all point to the same thing. Harley riders like to ride together. When we have a dealership-sponsored ride, we get over a hundred people showing up every time."

"What groups do you belong to?"

"AMA, HOG, SFMC [San Francisco Motorcycle Club], and the Ugly MC."

"Do you want to comment on that last one?"

"No, not really. It's just a bunch of guys getting together and riding. It is for males only. I see nothing wrong with having separate leisure-time activities. Women usually stake out the house as their domain and men have the garage.

"Up until very recent times, Harley riding was one of the last bastions of male-only activities. And yes, it was mainly white males. All through the fifties and sixties, it was a white male–dominated sport. It was also a strong bastion for the 'tough guy attitude.'"

"Tom, when did that attitude start?"

"Well, you must remember, riding Harleys was seen as very masculine *from the very beginning.* It began in Milwaukee. German immigrants started it. That was pretty much a male-dominated culture. And it remained male dominated, in both riding and in the work force, until the early eighties. It was all those tough old guys, those one percenters and ten percenters, who kept Harley alive in the lean years."

"Do you have a name for them?"

"Yes, to me, they are Motorheads. They are the mechanical types, the tinkerers, the garage Harley builders. They are guys in love with engines. They just keep on tinkering. For some guys, it is a way to get out of the house without the wife being mad at them. Many guys have a solo seat, which means that they don't have to take their wives on rides. They could ride alone. Many of the old runs were not family oriented. They were places for men to get away from their wives and children and relax. I still think that the Redwood Run is not a family run. It is not for everyone."

"Tom, if all this motorcycling took the men away from their wives, didn't the women object?"

"Some did. But those men kept a double seat hanging in their garage for when their wives rode with them. They would change their solo seat to the double. As a couple, they would go out with a few other riding friends, have a good dinner, and then take a moonlight ride under the stars. It could be very romantic.

"Much has changed in the past few years. There has been a major

38

transformation. Women are less leery of attending HOG events and other events too. Women's liberation has opened the doors. We have many women riding now. They make up a good strong percentage of our business."

"Do you think that this culture, this Harley phenomenon, is going to last?"

"Well, I hope that it does, but I also think that it will. It now covers a wide range of people in all walks of life. It also opens the doors to adventure. You get to explore your world. You don't get this in cars. And then there is the camaraderie. People in cars do not wave at one another. There is a general bond among all motorcyclists. Sometimes Harley riders will only wave at other Harley riders, but I think that is shortsighted. All of us are on the road.

"Riding can also be seen as an extension of the frontier. It's an iron horse. And Harleys are as American as mom and apple pie. Harleys carry on a tradition. There is that streak of independence in all of us. And a little bit of recklessness too. Kind of like, if the world gets too close, you can say, 'Screw it, I'm getting on my bike. Goodbye.'"

"Can you wrench? Do you service your own bike? Can you repair and build and do the mechanical things your grandfather Dudley Perkins Sr. did?"

"No, not at all. I never saw Dad wrenching in the garage. Dudley Jr. never repaired his own bikes. I don't wrench either."

"Tom, there used to be a joke around the shop. When asked what kind of bike Tom rides, the answer was always, 'Any one he wants.' What bike do you ride?"

"Over the years, I've ridden almost every kind of bike. The one I ride now is a customized Road King."

"What about the kids? Do your kids ride? Do you take them on the back of your bike?"

"I do take both my children on the back. But neither my son Chris nor my daughter Nicole are motorheads. They don't, yet, share a passion for riding. Also, they see me with one foot missing from my bike accident and they think, Do I want to do this? It's a tough call. It is a high-risk life. My wife and I are very aware of this."

"How does your wife feel about your riding the kids?"

"She puts it very plainly. She says that if anything ever happens to the kids while I am riding them, it better happen to me too. 'Cause if the road doesn't kill me, she will."

Some parents shield their children from the bike as long as possible. Some say it will be their kids' choice when the children are old enough to make a choice. I sympathize with Tom and all other parents and grandparents caught in this dilemma. Parents who take their children to ski or sail or surf are all caught up in this issue. Tom and his wife have voiced it well. He rides. She doesn't. She intones, "if the kids are harmed, don't come home." He hears the message and fully understands. Part of him agrees. Part of him says, "I cannot deny my kids this experience." All of us who ride hear that message too.

When I interviewed him, Steve Zarwell had been selling bikes at Dudley Perkins Company for over five years (he has since found employment closer to home). He got into Harleys in 1971. His first bike was an XL1000 Sportster. This model, he made sure to tell me, had both an electric and a kick start.

"In those years, most people were buying Yamahas, Hondas, and Kawasakis. I wanted to buy something different. And I didn't like the idea of buying something that was not made in the U.S.A."

Steve Zarwell, with his long-sleeved shirts, bright ties, and carefully pressed pants, looked like he could be a salesman for any high-priced, big-ticket item.

"Harleys have never been cheap. I remember in '71, I bought my new car, my Plymouth Duster, for less money than I paid for my Harley. When Tom hired me, I had to think about it. I had always been able to sell things. Even as a little kid, I was good at selling. Yet, I had never sold bikes before. I had, however, been a customer."

Since taking the job, Steve had been commuting from San Jose. This was a serious commute. But he was very serious about the Dudley Perkins Company. He was also aware that they were riding the crest of Harley popularity and the good times were rolling.

"We *never* take a customer for granted. The Motor Company must understand that this is merchandise that *nobody actually needs*. A motorcycle, for most, is a leisure-time vehicle. Being a salesperson means that I will never take for granted what people buy. And I appreciate whatever they buy from me. The factory must realize that no household ever really needs a Harley. It's not like a refrigerator or a stove. The factory almost went out of business once. It could happen again. What I like about working here is that it is a family-owned shop. It's my kind of Harley-Davidson store."

Steve and I talked about Harley culture. He would sit right up in the front of the store and could see everyone who came in. He got the wide-angle perspective. To him, all Harley riders are people who don't want to be part of the mainstream "normal" world. All these riders are individualists. When I suggested that his life would be easier if there were more bikes on the sales floor he disagreed. The Harley waiting list can be as long as a year, depending upon the model and color desired. I thought it would be great to see lots of bikes available for purchase. When you walk into any other bike shop, any non-Harley shop, the bikes are lined up four or five to a model. When you walk into a Harley shop, you see the display bikes and the used bikes, and you take a number and get in line for a new one.

"If you made too many Harleys," Steve explained, "you would eventually have more bikes than there would be people to buy them. If people stopped waiting for these bikes it would be all over."

Soon Steve was commenting upon little-known Harley tales. He talked about the bikes that people bought but never picked up. I didn't understand. He said that for some people, owning a Harley was like owning a fine piece of jewelry or art. Some people would buy a Harley, change bike parts continually, but never take the bike out of the shop. The bike was always a work in progress. It was never completed. I asked, "How come they kept it around?" Steve looked puzzled and then realized my mistake. The bike stayed at the shop because the owner constantly had work being done on the bike. The owner kept paying the bills on the makeover. But the bike was never ridden outside. Strange though this sounds, it is more common than one would think. One month, he explained, there would be a complete paint job. The next month the pipes would be changed, and so forth. The bike would always remain a dream just beyond the horizon. Either that, or the owner just didn't want to ride.

Steve told me other stories.

"There are people who buy motorcycles and want no one to know they ride. Not their parents or their wives or friends. They are closet bikers. They create separate facilities just to house their motorcycle and their motorcycle gear. No one from their home will ever know about their biking activity."

We spoke of how much the community of riders had changed during the past ten years.

"It's now socially acceptable to own a Harley-Davidson. The Evolution engine changed a lot of things. People who didn't know how to maintain their own bikes could now ride. And as the demographics changed, Harleys became news. All of a sudden, there were many celebrity riders. This has changed the Harley image.

"I do not miss the way it used to be. A long time ago, when I would come home with my old Sportster to my nice upper-middle-class neighborhood, I was seen as a threat. I was treated badly. My parents were OK. They knew that I maintained the bike and always had it insured. My parents were basically accepting of the motorcycle. But, in general, most places treated you badly. No, I'm not sorry at all that the attitude's changed. As more people ride, opinions about bikers change. Since I do not have a bad attitude, I've been treated well for the past few years. I have never been denied a motel room or a seat in a restaurant. If you cop an attitude instead of going with the flow, you *will* have problems. Years ago there were many bikers with attitude problems. You could see why they had difficulties."

Steve had worked for the Dudley Perkins Company for over five years, but he had been coming to the store for twenty.

"This place is the center of the universe. You can sit here on a Saturday from nine to five and every kind of person will come in. From judge to outlaw, they are all here. You see the cop over there, talking to the guy with all the tattoos? He knows that one day he may have to arrest him. But for now, they are talking. They are talking bikes. This is neutral territory. Everyone who comes in knows that this is their store. Everyone can feel comfortable when they are here. You can be black or white, male or female, lesbian or gay or straight, cops or robbers and still feel that it is your motorcycle store. This is Harley culture, right here, in the middle of San Francisco. And it's as diversified as it gets. The San Francisco biking community comes in all shades and types. When I sit here, it is just where I want to be. This job fulfills my dreams *and I get paid for it.*"

When I asked Steve if there was anything he wished to add he responded: "Motorcycles are definitely dangerous. There is no doubt about that. But I am against all the protective legislation. I am against the helmet law. I do not like anybody telling me what to do. This should be a choice, not a law. I would not be wearing a helmet if there were no law about it. It's a violation of all our rights. It's a denial of our right to choose."

Steve ritualized the event of selling a bike. After he had finished the paperwork, retrieved the bike from the garage, and was ready to turn the keys over to the new owner, he went through a ceremony. He would hand the new owner the key and welcome him or her into the Harley world with a little speech. Whether this was the person's first or fifth bike, he performed the ritual handshake. It was joyous and sobering all at the same time. The year when I received my FXD Low Rider from Steve, I got more than the traditional handshake. I also got a hug.

Thunder Press started in January of 1992 as a small Northern California newspaper and grew to cover Southern California as well as several bordering states. It has recently gained national distribution and is also exported overseas.* It started small. It is small no longer.

Reg Kittrelle, looking competent and full of energy, sat at his clut-

*I now contribute a monthly column called "BikeRest with BJ."

tered desk in a cubbyhole in Scotts Valley, California. This was his *big* space. *Thunder Press* had just moved up the hill from smaller quarters. Like the proverbial California freeway, he was out of space before the new move was completed. Having loved *Thunder Press* from the day it hit the streets, I asked Reg about its creation.

"I was always frustrated," he responded, "when I viewed the so-called objective press within the Harley world. It was either filled with T and A or rhetoric of only the most positive kind. It was hard to get real coverage of Harley products or events. The reporting was usually biased one way or another. I was also fascinated with newspapers, *as an art form*. Combining one's avocation and vocation is totally seductive. Starting the paper was right for me."

He added that his goals had altered since he started the newspaper. He had become more realistic about publishing and had lost his illusions.

"The general mystique doesn't exist for me anymore. It's been replaced by reality. It's no longer a mystery. I know why people ride. It's been demystified. The allure is still there and the mainstream press still capitalizes on the mystique but we can spell it out."

And he did!

"Harley's growth happened at just the right time. The timing was perfect. There was brilliant marketing from Milwaukee and there was a lack of domestic competition. Harleys are the only American motorcycles. There was a backlash against Japan and Japanese products. The Harley-Davidson Motor Company officers bought back the company from AMF. There was a resurgence of patriotism, and a push to buy American was in the air. Riders supported the company not only by logic but by legacy. Their dads had ridden Harleys. These were guys who were just waiting for Milwaukee to do something right, and it did. The new bikes are good bikes. Now there was a solid reason to buy a Harley. There are no other bikes like them.

"And this is an important plus: there has been an ever-increasing disfranchising of the population. Individuals feel pretty distant from their government and they were looking for things to identify with. Everyone wants an identity. It's pretty much lost in most people's workplaces. None of us feel that we have much voice in government. The vote doesn't count. So people look around and say, 'What am I? How do I count as an individual?'

"Riding a Harley provides an outlet. Now the rider is in control of his own destiny. Gone is the remoteness of modern life. If the rider makes a mistake on the bike, he's going to pay for it. There is the satisfaction of knowing that the rider has made some decisions concerning what he does with his time and his life.

43

Reg Kittrelle (Courtesy of Noel Paraninfo)

"And again, don't forget the brilliant marketing. Milwaukee doesn't focus on other motorcycles. It ignores all other bikes. Harley riders are ignorant of other motorcycles *by choice*. They don't want to know!

"When a whole bunch of people are riding on Harleys together, riding the actual bike is secondary. What is primary is that it gives the rider an identity and a group of friends to ride with. These are people he might otherwise not have befriended.

"This was a revelation to me. When I switched to Harley-Davidsons, I found that everyone was my friend. The friendships started with the first meeting. It's up to you to fuck it up. If you don't fuck it up, everyone remains your friend. This is the opposite from the rest of the world. In the rest of society, you start out neutral, and then over time, build up friendships. In the Harley world, the bike unites you. You have to really fuck up to lose that connection. The amount of initial trust is astounding. Everyone is a bro unless you screw it up. A man can go to a HOG meeting and leave with fifty friends he never knew he had. I remember the first one I ever went to, here were all these men hugging me. It broke me down. It opened me up. These men had no compunction about throwing their arms around other men and accepting them (if they were on a Harley). It's part of the Harley culture."

"Reg," I interjected, "you know that the words 'Harley culture' strike close and dear to my heart. What is it?"

"Like any other culture, it's many things to different people. It straddles different groups and ages. It covers fifty-year-olds who have ridden for forty years on Shovels and Pans and are disdainful of any-one on an Evo. It covers fifty-year-olds who have never ridden before but because of Harley exposure in *Forbes* or *Time* magazine, they sud-denly become interested. These riders drive up to the dealership in their trucks and trailer their bikes away. Then there's the twenty-five-year-old kid who has been convinced by the media that it's cool to ride a Harley. And for some it's only an image. For others it's a political statement about the way things are going in the country. The need to ride gets equated with the need to feel some freedom in their lives.

"And let's not forget, it's an incredibly enjoyable experience. Per-formance and mechanics are good. I can take my Harley and hustle. I can ride through Mt. Herman Road damn fast. To a lot of new Harley riders, it never occurs to them to push the bike. I ride an FXR and it's a pure visceral sport. Then when I have to make long trips down I-5, I ride my FLHS. Different bikes for different needs. I've had thirty-seven motorcycles in my life. I've had all kinds of Japanese bikes, British, German, and Italian ones. My latest bike, is, of course, a Harley.

"The Harley allows me to make a statement. It says, 'Take me or leave me.' For better or for worse, this is who I am. It also represents for me my love of my country. I'm putting my country up there and supporting it. I can't get satisfaction out of the government, but I can still support and love my country. It also allows you to choose your own statement. It sets you apart."

"Reg, I wanted to interview you because I see *Thunder Press* as the center of the Harley communications network in California. It's like the newspaper itself is an integrative mechanism. It helps define and hold the community together. No single other force does that."

"If we are a force in this community, it's because we *do not speak for the Harley community, we listen to it*. Newspapers that claim to speak for a community violate the tenets of good reporting. They should listen. Think about the important organizations. There's HOG chapters and AMA and ABATE. All these groups represent unique places in the Harley world. The outlaws and the Christian bikers all have their places within the community. It's not my job to judge peoples' activities that are not relevant to the motorcycle world. There are Harley magazines that pander to the outlaw clubs and ones that seek out the newer, richer riders. I report on all the relevant Harley activities."

"Reg, if you had one thing to add what would it be?"

"I care about individual rights. That's my passion. If the general public would become more aware of what goes on in regard to minority groups and the loss of people's rights, it would help us all. As a minority, our rights have been trampled on by the passing of the helmet law. People who don't ride don't realize what a violation that law is. The government is making rules about something it doesn't understand and trampling on our personal freedoms and our minority rights. We had no voice in that decision. Remember the old bumper sticker 'Question Authority'? That was a good one. I wish I had come up with it."

Reg Kittrelle, with the production of *Thunder Press*, has a secure place within the Harley world. If something is happening out there, Reg is covering it. Mike Molinari, who was CEO of Performance Productions, Inc. (PPI) when I interviewed him (he has since left that position), had a different place and a different perspective on the same community. Mike's voice adds both weight and contrast to the other voices.

I interviewed Mike Molinari at his home in Daly City. The back part of his house doubled as an office and, like Reg, he had a desk piled high with motorcycle information. Also like Reg, Mike knew where everything was and could pull material out in an instant. If *Thunder Press* is the circulatory system of the Harley communications network,

PPI is the heart. Mike Molinari, then head of PPI, put on motorcycle events. PPI, he informed me, had its roots in HOG. It grew out of the very first Bridgeport Jamboree run. The jamboree started as a regional HOG event in 1990. Bob Hansen, then a HOG regional director, was put in charge of finding a place for this next event. He and his biker buddy Ken Hennings wandered the Sierra hills until they rode into Bridgeport. It was love at first ride. This small town, with the traditional main street running through it, was willing to play host to a large group of bikers. Being a biker-friendly town can have great compensations. Riders have been contributing to Bridgeport community institutions from the very beginning.

The first Bridgeport HOG event was so successful that riders pushed to hold the rally there every year. By the third year, HOG events had moved elsewhere, away from Bridgeport, so PPI formed to keep the Bridgeport run alive.

Right from the start, the jamboree kept to HOG philosophy. It was, and remains, a family-oriented event. Much of the wild abandon typical of outlaw and mixed (outlaw and family) events does not occur at HOG events. The type of naked drunken dancing, sans T-shirt contests, and other festivities like those experienced at Redwood Runs, do not occur at HOG rallies. Drag races and tattoo and arm-wrestling events do take place and beer flows like water, but the wildness and intensity are absent. Bridgeport is the quintessential HOG event even if HOG no longer sponsors it.

"We keep the HOG family philosophy," Mike informed me. "If Bridgeport turns into a drunken orgy and wet T-shirt contest, we'll shut it down. Bridgeport is a family event. We want to keep it that way.

"Performance Productions, Inc., does put on more events than the Bridgeport Jamboree. And we put on all-bike events as well as Harley-only affairs. We aim our events at motorcyclists. We look for serious riders, but not just Harley riders. As president and CEO, I feel I should make it clear that I love all motorcycles. There are many kinds of bikes and they are all valuable. If you limit yourself only to Harleys, you miss a lot. It's like only having sex in the missionary position. It's nice. Sex is always nice, but it becomes routine if you try no other positions. Why limit yourself? Sex in many positions is good. Lots of motorcycles are good too. All bikes are fun to ride.

"PPI's aim is to put on classic motorcycle events. I want riders to feel impatient to return each year to our events. I want them to be proud that they participate and I want them to tell their friends about it. It's a time to ride with friends, relax and have fun. It's a great way to go on vacation and a great way to party."

At various times, PPI has sponsored not only the Bridgeport

Mike Molinari and D. C. Dick (Courtesy of Noel Paraninfo)

Jamboree, but the Yerington Classic and the New Carson City Run. The Yerington Classic featured a wide variety of spectacular events, including boxing matches and trike races. The New Carson City Run featured name bands and bike events such as slow races and the weenie bite. The weenie bite, an ultraclassic bike competition, is the comic relief of the games. A hot dog is suspended from a pole just out of reach. A biker with a passenger on the back, just about always a woman, rides slowly toward the hot dog. The passenger raises herself on the seat and using her mouth alone attempts to bite into the hot dog. If she fails, she is usually given another try. The one who bites the biggest bite of hot dog wins. Skill in riding slowly is important, balance is important, and, most important, it helps to have a sense of humor. The weenie is hung with or without mustard.

Mike, a native of the Bay Area, has explored the back roads and superhighways from San Francisco to Idaho. He spent three years as director of a local HOG chapter learning the needs and wishes of bikers. His expansion plans included rallies in Santa Maria and San Diego as well as Arizona and Oregon.

"To be honest with you, it's a great position. I create events that make people happy. What biker wouldn't want to wake up to the sound of motorcycles! PPI is made up of people who love to ride and share that passion with their friends. We put on quality events, each with their own unique flavor. Creating motorcycle events is a great way to make a living.

"Harley-Davidson has come a long way. They are responsible for making cruising popular again. In the seventies Honda got people back on bikes. What Honda did for general riding, Harley did for cruising. All riders are important to PPI, and I meant it when I said that I have an appreciation for all kinds of bikes."

Since Mike organized events and came in contact with thousands of bikers, he was in a perfect position to reflect upon Harley culture.

"Yes, there is a Harley culture but it's all over the map. All different kinds of folks have Harleys and very little communication goes on between them. There is very little common ground. The one percenters, and most of the ten percenters, tend to look at the rest of the riders with disdain. The rest of the riders have no idea that this is so. They haven't a clue. To a hard-core one or ten percenter, they truly live and die by their bikes. They don't live by anyone's rules but their own. And they only ride Harleys.

"Now the new bikers, they'll be ready to make a bike move if they want to. They don't have that built-in loyalty to the brand name. They check out BMWs, Ducatis, Hondas. If I were rich, I'd own every kind of bike. I'd have my Harley, of course, but I might ride that least of all. It would depend upon the kind of riding I was doing."

"Well Mike, if that's so, why did you buy your Softail?"

"The reason I bought this last Harley was because D.C. Dick and Bob Hansen told me how much fun they were having with this new thing called HOG. How different it was from the old days. The social aspect had been added to it. The trips to Sturgis and other rallies were great. You got to ride with a large group. HOG brought me back to riding Harleys. It was the bike and it was the recommendation of D.C. Dick. To me, D.C. was the Fonz."

When I asked Mike to describe himself he said: "I'm a husband, a father, a grandfather, and a biker."

Interviewing Mike Molinari was an eye-opener for me. I had not realized that PPI had such an avid appreciation for so many different kinds of bikes. The next two men I interviewed also make their livings from dealing with all kinds of bikes and all kinds of bikers.

Mike Felder sells motorcycle insurance. In California it is illegal to operate a motorized vehicle without insurance. Mike runs a big business. He sells insurance and he rides. From the mid-seventies through the mid-eighties, Mike sold bikes. He sold Hondas in Pasadena, BMWs in Hollywood, and Kawasakis in LA. Now he just sells bike insurance. He also writes a column on insurance for *Thunder Press* and has had biker articles published in many magazines.

I asked him about his early years in the motorcycle business.

"These were bad years for Harley. They were dying on the vine. Hondas were making out like crazy and Milwaukee was hurting. In those days Honda had over fifty percent of the market share. Harleys then were badly made, badly managed, and badly marketed.

"All that started to change in the late eighties. Harley picked up the over 800cc market. Even with Honda Gold Wings and Yamaha touring bikes out there, Harley owns the big-bike market now."

"What do you see, Mike, as the reasons for that dramatic change?"

"A number of things happened all at once. There was the tariff, of course. But also, the bikes just started getting better. There was the buyout from AMF too. But most of all there was this incredible marketing strategy. You cannot underestimate the importance of HOG. All of a sudden, a guy could buy a bike and become an automatic member of a motorcycle association. The first year's membership in HOG is free to all new Harley buyers. Remember, this is the Harley Owners' Group, not the Harley riders' group. Lots of times you will see forty or fifty people at a meeting, but only three or four coming out on the weekends for a ride. Of course, it's all right with me, I sell insurance to all of them.

"You can't realize how important the HOG chapters are in terms of business. They provide an introduction to motorcycling. And all you need for entrance is the price of a bike. Dealers now are pretty much happy to sponsor a chapter. That way you get built-in customer loyalty. The guy who comes to your shop every month for a meeting also returns every week for accessories and repairs.

"It wasn't always like that. When the chapters first started, Milwaukee had to give inducements to get dealerships to sign up. There used to be contests between the dealerships, and the winners got sent on a Caribbean vacation. The dealers got points for sponsoring HOG chapters. This gave the dealerships their initial motivation to start. Good business and common sense gave them the reasons to continue.

"There's an irony here. You take all these riders. Some of them are new riders but many of them are experienced riders, and you put them all into a HOG chapter. Here you have some of the most independent-minded people in the world and Milwaukee starts putting rules on them. The HOG chapters are given corporate rulebooks. It's kind of funny when you think of it."

Mike's been riding since he was fifteen but it's only since he got his Harley that his involvement has intensified.

"It surprised me that I fell so hard. I had sold Hondas and other bikes but to me they were only hunks of steel. Then I got my first Harley. I fell over the edge. It surprised the hell out of me. Now I need the shirt and the chaps and the saddlebags. I recently sold my '85 Low Rider because I wanted an FLHS Electra Glide Sport. I wanted a rubber mount. I'm in my forties and I want to be comfortable.

"Yes, it did surprise me. It still surprises me. I always wanted a Harley. But I never considered that I would go over that edge. In fact, I'm turning into one of those people I used to hate.

"When I see the bumper sticker that says, 'My wife says if I don't sell my bike she's gonna leave me—well I'm sure going to miss her,' I now understand. When my wife was pregnant with my son (nine months pregnant), I called her from the bike shop. I had just taken a trade for a bike. I asked my wife to drive the truck to Dudley Perkins so that I could pick up the bike. My wife complained. She said that she was so big that she couldn't fit into the seat. I told her to pull the seat back. 'What happens it I get dizzy?' she asked me. 'Just open the window, but get down here.' Here I was, turning into a person I barely recognized. But I wanted that bike."

"Do you ride a lot, Mike?"

"I ride to cover as many bike events as possible. It's not just because I love the riding, which I do, but it's also good for business. People see me on my bike, get to recognize my face, and they know that I share the same problems of the road that they do. Then they become my customers. It helps. It also keeps me in contact with the different Harley groups.

"In a funny way, you could summarize the differences within the Harley culture by specific road examples. Everyone has to make pit stops. The youngsters, the speed kids, wouldn't be packing women so they wouldn't be making many stops. But the other groups would have to. They would all have to. When the passenger says she has to go to the bathroom, a one percenter might answer, 'Hold it.' A working-class rider might answer, 'Yes, dear.' And the rich urban biker might suggest they find an acceptably *nice and clean* bathroom."

"Tell me Mike, do you want your daughter riding?"

"If she wanted to ride, I would want to teach her how to do it. Right now she doesn't show much interest. I get scared that when she's fourteen or so, some young man will take her for a ride on the back and they will go too fast. You have to realize, in my profession I see and hear all the horror stories."

As we neared the end of the interview, Mike Felder stopped me from writing and told me a story. It exemplified his feelings about the drama and mystique of riding; the way the mind gives weight to commonplace events.

"I remember a bike," Mike said; "it was cutting the silence of the night. It had straight pipes and could be heard miles away. It was a pitch-black night and it was during my first Redwood Run. The bike stopped right in front of where I was sitting. I could hear the man's boots thumping as he walked toward me. The man was wearing a B.C. patch. He was tall and thin and wore a western duster. Time stood still as he walked toward me. He was a figure straight out of the mythic past. He looked like pure theater: spiderweb tattoos, western hat! When he finally reached my side, he looked me in the eye and said, 'Mate—what's the prospects of lodging in the vicinity?' In a split second, this mythic character became just another rider looking for a room. But in that second before he spoke, he could have been anyone. He could have been a Wild West hero. That's part of riding. We make and remake ourselves. We fashion who we are when we get on the bike. It's a great way to live."

Interviewing Mike Felder in a local coffee shop was fine. Having him pick up the breakfast tab was even better. He revels in his Harley experience. It is business, but it is also his life. Riding a Harley is the way he wants to live. Riding is part of his definition of self.

Brian Halton (Courtesy of Brian Halton)

Unlike all the other people in this chapter, Brian Halton is not a Harley aficionado. He is, however, a serious motorcycle rider and publisher of one of the most important local biking newspapers. Brian Halton produces *CityBike*, San Francisco's local motorcycling newspaper. It's a monthly newspaper distributed free around the city. It's paid for by its advertisers. According to Reg Kittrelle, "Brian set the standard for free motorcycle publications. He proved it could be a business. For eleven years he's been putting out that paper. He identified a small niche and he developed it. He proved that there was a market. A free motorcycle publication could work. It made me think that there was room for a free Harley publication. I copied the idea from Brian."

Tucked away at 323 Tenth Street in San Francisco is the office of Brian Halton's *CityBike*. According to some, this is the most important motorcycle newspaper in California. It was certainly the first. Publishing out of a small storefront in SOMA with only two rooms, Brian runs a neat operation. Compared with the clutter of *Thunder Press* and PPI, *CityBike* is a model of neatness.

53

Everything in the first small room, from books to T-shirts to tapes to papers, is arranged for optimal show. The second room, the inner space, is designed for work. It is divided into work areas with bulletin boards, shelves, desks, and all the materials of publishing. Brian has made good use of a small inner-city space.

Waiting for Brian gave me an opportunity to cruise his book display. Reading enthusiasts' publications about Harleys is always productive. Situated prominently among the biking books was Harry Sucher's *Harley-Davidson: The Milwaukee Marvel* (1990). Flipping through this Haynes publication history reminded me of how much Harley interest has grown over the past several years. But it wasn't until I picked up *Cruisin 'n' Posin: All Part of the Harley-Davidson Experience* by Malcolm Birkitt that I realized how much Harleys have become part of the American scene. Birkitt sets just the right tone when he says: "Anyone who buys a Harley for its top-end performance or as a way of getting from A to B as fast as possible is completely missing the point. We all know that it's the rumble and the roar and the feeling we get from riding a Harley" (1992, 90).

This quote set me in just the right mood to interview Brian Halton, motorcycle publisher extraordinaire, and no fan of Harley-Davidsons. Brian got right to the point.

"Old Harley culture was blue collar and brand faithful. The culture changed with the Evolution engine. When Harley made the Evo, more people started to buy into the Harley experience. The Evo did it.

"Harley dealers can be tough to deal with. They used to be jealous of the success of the dealers who sold Japanese bikes. When the Evo engine first came out, I remember going in and looking at the bikes at Dudley Perkins and thinking, 'Who would want one of these?' They are big, slow, heavy, and not very good looking.

"But then I thought, most customers going in and out of Harley shops were raised on Harleys since Word War II. These were the blue collar and the brand faithful that I talked about. They had absolute brand loyalty. It was almost like a religion. Actually, it was beyond religion. It was like they were raised to be Harley riders. Once a Harley rider, always a Harley rider. But for the rest of us, I thought, why buy one of these big, slow, ugly machines?

"Then the bikes got better. Evolution engines were definitely an improvement. Sonny Barger said he got one of Harley's best engines, so he kept riding them. Management changed. Not only did the bike get better but they came up with some very shrewd marketing strategies. Finally, they got Willie G. With his flair for style and his outgoing personality, he has helped in both bike design and marketing. Willie

G. Davidson, grandson of one of the original Davidson brothers, is one of several heirs of the Harley-Davidson legacy. He is responsible for major contemporary stylistic changes, including factory built custom bikes.

"This has made a big change in Harley's success. I remember in early '87 going down to Bob Dron's Harley dealership in Oakland and spending hours with him shooting the shit. There were no customers. He stayed alive by working on Oakland police bikes. Now he's always busy. The store is filled with people. It's like a boutique.

"Then, of course, Harley came out with the Buell. This at least looks like a good bike. This looks like a sports bike. I remember one day I was trying to park in front of Dudley Perkins. They were having some kind of bike street fair. Someone, upon seeing me ride up, shouted, 'Get that asshole out of here.' Since the Buell didn't look like any traditional Harley, people thought it was some kind of Japanese bike. They thought it should not be parked at that street fair. Just try to park another kind of bike in front of DP and you will see the reception you get. I felt out of place. I wasn't *one of them*. Everyone was also very aware of the way I was dressed as well as the motorcycle I was riding. I kept thinking, 'What's wrong with these people?' I felt alienated."

Brian looked up, as if trying to decide whether he should continue along this line. He needed to say more about his perception of Harley riders.

"One of the primary sources of controversy among non-Harley riders is the feeling that most Harley riders are unskilled. They have just enough ability to ride from bar to bar or do an afternoon of showboating. Their skill level is highly questionable. Fortunately for them, it doesn't have to be all that high. You can't do much with a Harley except ride it in a straight line. A lot of BMW riders and other professional riders find the sight of Harley-Davidson riders paddling around parking lots pretty comical. They ride with their girlfriends on the back, dressed in all their fancy clothes and those cheap $10 helmets. It all looks pretty funny. And another thing. They seem to feel inferior if they are not in large numbers. They like to travel in large packs."

Brian has spent a lot of time figuring out the Harley culture. By the time we talked, he had a pretty firm idea what it was all about.

"They are not bad people. The guys are usually in their forties with their kids all grown. Business is good. The couples are still married and now they are looking for things to do. The guy was always into cars, now he's into bikes. They like hanging out with friends. They like to drink beer, ride with a group, and visit. This is not a highly sophisticated crowd. These folks form the major part of Harley culture.

The old culture consisted of young, reckless, blue-collar, brand-loyal bikers. Now they have grown older, settled down, married, have grown kids and gotten some respectability."

"The really new Harley culture is different. They have moved up the scale. They have gone from blue collar to white collar and celebrity status. They want Harleys for the status, the look and the sound. These new shiny bikes have attracted very trendy, celebrity-type personalities. You wind up in the Church of the True Believer of True Motorcycles. For these true-believer types, they ride their Harley-Davidson three miles to a café in LA and that's it. For someone who really rides a motorcycle, this is sacrilege.

"Part of this new Harley culture revolves around the American male. He is buying his way into manhood. He perceives the bike as virile and macho. He senses that there are some things lacking in his professional life. There is a vacuum. But if he can get his wife on the back, pay a lot of money for the bike, he can buy his way into manhood. He buys into the whole package. Harley markets its bikes by saying, 'You are not just getting a motorcycle, you are getting a life.'

"Another reason for all this success is that these buyers are the same guys who were seeing movies about bikers in the forties and fifties. They were kids then but they are middle-aged now. Again, it's just this manhood thing. They want to knock back a couple of cans of beers, take the wife out for a Sunday ride, and shoot the breeze with their buddies.

"Some of the criticism leveled at the new Harley riders by other motorcyclists is that their skill level does not equal their financial level. Their skill level is lacking. This is also what is scary for the dealers. When these guys get a little older, they are going to stop riding. Their next purchase will be a mobile home. They will sell their bike and head for the Sierras. The dealers should be trying to protect themselves. They are all heading into an elephant's graveyard. Gray, balding bikers will soon be buying retirement homes. Remember, the bald eagle is the Harley-Davidson symbol."

There have to be more reasons for the phenomenal Harley success. Brian had some interesting theories about it.

"One of the real reasons that so many middle-aged guys buy Harleys is that it matches their perception of what a motorcycle is all about. It's what they have seen, not only in the movies, but on TV as well. Most of the guys are afraid of the looks of a sports bike. To them they look like bullets. They are sleek and smooth and none of the working parts show. This frightens them. Then they see movie guys paddling around on Harleys with their low seats and wide wheels and they think, 'It's just like an old tractor. I can see all of its parts. I understand it.' That bike is really just like an agricultural vehicle. These guys want a toy to ride around on. They want a two-wheeled toy. Harleys are perfect."

Brian kept coming back to skill and performance levels, his major themes about those who ride Harleys.

"Northern California has some of the most committed and articulate motorcyclists in the world. But, mainly, they are not Harley-Davidson riders. Even though Harley has attracted some of the rich and famous, the riders do not have a great deal of knowledge about bikes and bike safety. For example, I hear this kind of conversation around Harley riders all the time: 'What kind of motorcycle is that, honey?' 'Oh, I don't know,' answers the husband, 'Forget it, it's not a Harley.' The knowledge just isn't there. Another example. We all buy really expensive gear, but that's where the similarities end. My gear is safety oriented. Their gear is great looking."

"Brian, is it true that Harley riders don't tend to wave to people on other kinds of bikes?"

"Unfortunately, yes. You have all these upwardly mobile jamokes with their low skill levels riding around trying to prove their manhood, and you wave at them and they ignore you. It's very annoying. Now the old Harley guys, they won't wave either, but at least they know how to ride motorcycles. Their skill levels are high. They are guys who have ridden their motorcycles all their lives and I relate best to them. I too have ridden a lot. I don't even own a car. I have four bikes and a truck and I am constantly honing my skills.

"One thing that has always amazed me about Harley riders is that they engage in this outrageous riding behavior. Especially in traffic. They are willing to drink and ride, and that's unconscionable and really stupid. Fortunately, most Harleys go too slow to get their riders into real trouble. Plus they like to ride in packs and that slows them down even more."

Brian, deservedly, is very proud of *CityBike*, which he sees as reflecting the heart and mind of the motorcycling community. He was one of the first to put women riders on his cover. He suspects that seven or eight percent of his readership consists of women. While most of the women readers are passengers, many of them are riders. Some are both. His paper covers many diverse groups of people and bikes. He reports on the performance of motorcycle products and bikes. His columnists raise controversial issues and help create a lively and informative paper. Brian reflects upon the aspects of biking that the entire community holds in common:

"Everyone reads *CityBike*. The old Harley guys read it, the dirt-bike riders read it, the young sports-bike riders read it too. We have a real common readership. There's a real hard core of riders who couldn't give a fuck for you unless you tell them something they don't know. They want real bike news and real bike views. A lot of motorcyclists are independent. These are the guys who own guns, are politically conservative, and total individualists. They take no bullshit from anyone. These riders who read *CityBike* have all that in common. They are very direct."

"OK Brian, why do you really not like Harleys?"

"As bikes, they don't work for me. I like to go fast, especially around turns. I don't care for the laid-back style of a Harley. I want a bike that gives good value for my money, is very functional for the type of riding I like to do, has saddlebags that snap on and off and can go in the dirt too. Mainly I ride my BMW. The guys I ride with have their own kinds of problems, but these bikers ride the way I like to ride. And yes, the BMW crowd will wave back at you. It's a tradition as old as motorcycling itself.

"But remember, as much as I wouldn't want to ride a Harley, I'm really glad they are out there. If they weren't selling so well, we'd all be in trouble. They have kept motorcycle enthusiasm high while the entire economy has been really low. For that, I am grateful."

I was enormously pleased that Brian Halton consented to this interview. Never a Harley aficionado, he was willing to share his reasons and his views. Brian wants a machine that rides like the wind, corners like a pro, and turns on a dime. Most Harley riders would rather cruise the highways than rocket through them. Harley riders and BMW riders are looking for different things in a bike. Brian has found what he wants. His newspaper is a tribute to all riders of all bikes.

PART 2

Cultural Analysis

5

Enter the Culture

"OK! That's the history and the structure, but where's the culture?
"Relax, relax, it's here now."

Mr. Harley and the Davidson brothers made a motorcycle. They had the idea, ran with it, created a bike, and started an industry. They were businessmen with a very American dream. Build a product and make a fortune.

Harley-Davidson went on to become a success story. Although the company had its ups and downs, it endured. But for generations of riders, Harleys were more than a product. They became a way of life. "Live to Ride, Ride to Live" was a slogan, a mantra, and a creed to live by. The original Harley builders were all born in the nineteenth century. The culture grew up with the kids.

The kids, the ones born between 1910 and 1925, started it all. They were the first generation to grow up knowing about motorcycles. Harleys weren't the only bikes around, but they were the important ones. These kids, now all in their seventies and eighties, represent the living history of the biker legend. They didn't know they were making history. They didn't know they were starting a culture. They just loved their bikes and rode them. They rode them for transportation, they rode them for sport, and they rode them for fun. The mystique came later. But it started here. It started in garages and cow pastures. It started on dates and on milk runs.

Americans have always loved the open road. The road does not get more open than on a bike. Long before Kerouac, bikers were having an affair with the highway. Here in Northern California, land of great open spaces, curvy mountain roads, and stunning ocean highways, motorcycle life took hold.

Those early bikers, those on Flatheads and Knuckleheads, formed a small core of dedicated riders. They were into something that grabbed their imaginations and fired their lives. My friend Easy Ed would say it grabbed their animal. They were mostly, but not exclusively, men. They rode with friends and formed loose communities of riding buddies. They rode on dirt trails, straight up mountain paths, and across the country. They created a racing circuit and dedicated their lives to it. They rode solo or they short-coupled. The guy sat on the tank while the girl sat in the saddle.

"Wasn't it painful to ride a long distance sitting on the tank?" I asked Dick McKay one afternoon.

"Nah, you're young. You can ride forever. It doesn't bother you. You could go for miles."

Dick, in his seventies, remembered the old days of riding. A veteran rider of the late 1930s who rode a '37 80-cubic-inch Harley and '39 and '40 Knuckleheads, he reminisced about the Harleys he had owned.

"The best bikes ever built," he recalled, "were built in the forties. They could go anywhere. They could follow a cow trail. They could go right up the side of a mountain. They were low and well balanced and you could trick ride. Great bikes."

Besides his '37, '39, and '40 Harleys, he also owned a '74 Sportster, an '80 Shovel, and an '85 Evo. He rode a right-shifting Triumph in the dirt but reserved his best riding for the Harleys. After he claimed that the best Harleys ever made were Knuckleheads, I asked why he wouldn't just get a restored Knucklehead instead of an Evolution engine?

"Not practical. You can love a Knuckle, but when you spend $15,000 you want it to be a new bike."

Before World War II the motorcycle community belonged to anyone who threw a leg over. They were all bikers. They varied by region, sometimes by class and bike choice, but they shared a common set of road rules, the most important of which survives today. It is still the number one rule of the road. Protect your own. You see a biker in trouble, you help. You see a biker at the side of the road, you offer assistance. Rule one is the common denominator among all who ride. Sometimes it takes awhile for new riders to learn it. Sometimes there are riders who just don't give a damn and ride by anyway. But, in general, it is a thread that runs through the biking world.

Who rides in the Harley world? The simple answer: anyone with enough dough to buy a Harley. The complex answer: the people who ride together in the clubs, the people who create their identities around their bikes, and the ones who behave in predictable ways when they ride.

To someone like Dick, the Harley world has changed so profoundly it has become unrecognizable. In the twenties, thirties, and early forties, the Harley world consisted of individuals and sometimes groups of men who fell in love with bikes and rode. Mostly they didn't formalize their groups into clubs. They just rode.

Today's Harley world is vast. It covers a lot a territory. It consists of seven major but overlapping groups of men: Old Timers, One Percenters (outlaws), Ten Percenters, Old Bikers, New Bikers, Rich Urban Bikers, and Occasional Bikers. The last three groups have come into existence since the easy-starting, better-engineered Evo engine came out. The first four have ridden forever. These categories help explain some of the divisions within the contemporary Harley world.* They can best be described in the following categories. Old Timer, in his seventies and still riding Harleys. One Percenter, outlaw, club member and patch holder. Ten Percenter, always rode a Harley, not a joiner. Old Biker, rode whatever was available, wrenches his own. New Biker, rode intermittently, just started riding Harleys. Rich Urban Biker, new rider and passionate about it. Occasional BIker, new rider and not so sure of his passion.

True to form, however, all Harley riders are unique, and no individual fits one hundred percent into a category. Still, there is something recognizable about each of the groups. There is also a common link that ties them all together. They love Harleys.

The earlier riders are dwindling now, though many still ride with great vigor. They are the first-generation builders of the Harley world. The bike was part of their youth and helped shape their personalities and character. While it may not have formed their entire identity, it helped form part of it. The bike shaped them as they shaped the culture. It helped them to belong to something larger than themselves and their neighborhood. It gave them a wider reference point and a community that extended beyond local borders. The bike was something to be built or bought, ridden, and cared for. Owning it created competence and self-confidence.

If you rode a Harley, you knew how to fix it. If you rode, you could wrench. It made a man feel confident about his machine and his own abilities. It made a woman confident too. Women also rode in the early days. The bike was a wonderful machine to be used and enjoyed. It was not, however, used as a rite of passage into manhood. It was not a male thing.

Other aspects of their world defined masculinity and femininity. Job, money, home, kids—these were the markers of gender and adulthood. Success was measured against survival in the real world. Men and women measured their self-worth against the real-life problems

*These divisions reflect male riders. Female riders are discussed in the following chapter.

Cultural Analysis

of supporting and raising a family. Bikes made them feel special, but were not the foundation upon which they built their lives, or their total identities. They shaped a culture out of common need but came to this culture as girls and boys, men and women.

With World War II, the reference points changed and the definitions of both adulthood and gender came into question. With so many men overseas, American women staffed the factories, worked the farms, and ran their own lives. For the first time, many women got a chance to be boss. It felt good. It made women feel competent. They talked differently. They walked differently. They swaggered. Running things at home liberated the forties woman in unique ways.

She wasn't just Rosie the Riveter. She was Cathy the Carpenter and Patty the Plumber. She was her own person. Then her man came home. He was not pleased. Gone was the smiling, unsure, high school sweetheart. The woman who had taken her place was strong, confident, and a bit sophisticated. She knew what she was capable of achieving and what she wanted. She wanted her man, but she wanted her job too. She liked making money. She liked making her own decisions. Her man took one look and freaked.

After having fought in a successful war, he wanted no lip from anyone, most especially his woman. He had paid his dues. He had watched his friends die and his brothers mutilated. He had seen too much. Some men wanted peace. Some wanted excitement. None of them wanted competent women competing with them and demanding equality. His father's world had died in Okinawa. His world was waiting to be born.

But first, women had to be pushed aside. They had to make room for him, for his employment, his decision making, and his ego. Some were pushed back into the home. Some were just pushed. Those women with well-paying union jobs were switched into clerical slots. Being clerical meant having lower status and lower pay. Men took the union vacancies. Women returned to the kitchens and became full-time housewives again.

Registered Harley clubs, solo riders, and outlaw bikers formed a great part of the forties and fifties landscape. Then Harley went into its decline. Only loyal, enduring customers kept Harley alive in those years. The Harley mystique had been born in the thirties, but it came alive after World War II. Harley was the bike of choice in middle America. It was the bike of choice on the desert flats and in country lanes. It was the essential American bike. The Indian had its defenders, but Harley remained the mythic bike of the small-town kid who wanted to grow up and ride a cycle. Throughout the lean years, Harley

64

kept its biker base. The One Percenter, the Ten Percenter, the Old Timer, and the Old Biker remained faithful.

The Old Timers rode for fun. The returning vets rode to live. A lifetime of meaning separated these two types of riders. In the thirties and forties, women rode alongside men. Anyone with an adventuresome spirit and steely courage was welcome. By the end of the forties, a new kind of biker had emerged. He liked women all right, but he liked them on the back of the bike. Women riders were looked upon with suspicion. Women riders were not accepted into the new clubs or sought after by Harley-Davidson.

All through the twenties, thirties, and forties, the Harley-Davidson Company had encouraged women. It sponsored an organization called the Motor Maids. Many of the early advertisements showed men and women riding their bikes together. Women were more often seen riding than passengering. They were depicted as smiling, competent, resourceful, *and* in love with their bikes. The organization helped women over the rough spots. It provided a supportive atmosphere.

Women responded. They rode. In the Women's Army Corps (WAC), women rode spectacularly well. The Motor Company highlighted all these women in its promotional campaigns. Then came the Change. By 1948 all the Harley ads showed women in the rear. The Harley campaigns featured big, unsmiling, tough-looking men on their bikes. They rode solo or with their women perched upon small, high, ass-viewing seats on the rear bumper, the princess seat. Gone were the smiling faces of the thirties everyman. Gone were the smiling faces of riding women. The new Harley rider was a biker and he was tough.

"Biker" is a funny term. Some people love it. Others don't. It runs the definitional gamut from asshole to zealot. Most agree that a biker is usually a man—tough, paid his dues, ready to fight, hard drinker, doper, and shitkicker. He can mellow as he ages, but not by much. He's got to teach his sons to be bikers. This is done by modeling the role. He's usually working class, often poor, sometimes rich, and he made it the hard way. He is proud of this. His identity is tied into biking. He reads the biker rags, studies the specs of the new bikes, schemes to own them, and spends much of his life involved in bike business. He wrenches. Every biker worthy of the name can tear his bike down and rebuild it. A lot of time is spent in the garage. It's pretty much a male club, as is made clear in a response by D. C. Dick, a Ten Percenter, to a letter written by an enthusiastic women rider to *FogHog News:*

> Ladies, Believe me when I say I would not say or do anything to dampen your enthusiasm or take away from your ability to ride a

motorcycle. The fact is, I understand some of you ladies ride really well. I guess this is OK, but only OK. I'm an old dinosaur and a Chauvinist (and you thought DC stood for Daly City) S.O.B. I still believe a woman belongs on the back of a bike with her hands on the hand warmer. Yea, yea, I know; this is the '90s and you'll pardon me if I tell you that some parts of it suck. I bought my first Harley when I was 15 years old and I've been building and maintaining my own bikes for the last 39 years, so maybe you can understand why I get pissed off when someone who can't change their own spark plugs or change their own oil calls themselves "Bikers." Believe me, you are NOT bikers, you are not even close. If you try hard, and if in a few years you are able to take a few boxes of Harley parts and build a strong running motorcycle, get your ass kicked a few times, end up in jails and hospitals any number of times, develop an asshole attitude, then maybe, just maybe, we can discuss it. Earn the name biker and don't insult yourself by just using it. Most will never make it. Some do not want to and that's fine too. It all depends on you. Thank you for allowing me the space to express myself. If I have, in fact, offended anyone, it's just too damn bad, we're even. (*FogHog News,* Dec. 1992)

D. C. expressed a view that's common among a lot of bikers. It is, however, only one view. The riding world is changing, and even D. C. Dick's clear voice is no longer the only voice in town.

What remains a point of agreement about the term is that a biker must be able to maintain the bike and take riding seriously. It is a fundamental part of his identity. To a biker, riding is an essential part of life. It is not just a hobby. It is *essential.*

Harley culture is growing, but it has its roots in the past. The Old Timers, those who grew up in the thirties and forties, were the first generation to know there was a Harley in their future. The Old Timers remain endlessly interesting. They have literally seen it all. They were around before HOG, before the AMA, and before the One Percenters. Born sometime between 1910 and 1925, they were the second generation to ride and the first to grow up with Harleys. They are the living part of the legend. And they share their memories. The only earlier riders were the builders of the bike.

Dick McKay belongs to this group. He will ride as long as he can throw a leg over. He and Bernie, married forty-two years, keep the earlier traditions alive. They two-up; she rides the passenger seat with pride and—mostly—fearless pleasure. They intend to keep it that way. Unlike the later generation of men, however, Dick would have had no problem with Bernie riding her own. It is Bernie who wants no part of the front seat.

Dick McKay started as a kid of seventeen on a '37 Harley-Davidson. Harley history was only one generation old. He rode with friends and

Bernie and Dick McKay (Courtesy of Bernie and Dick McKay)

he rode with two clubs. He joined the San Francisco Motorcycle Club (SFMC) and the Bay City Motorcycle Club.

"In those days," says Dick, "in them years, I lived on my bike. I bought it from a kid. Bought it right away. We had no insurance. Nothing was enforced, like today. You had a group of friends and you rode with them. One week it was SFMC and the next, Bay City MC. Both of them are still around today."

"Were they all Harley clubs in those days?"

"In those days there was only Harleys . . . well, there were a few Indians around and maybe a few English bikes, but mostly there were Harleys. Bikes were part of your life. You got up and rode."

"Did you ride with a lot of other bikers? Racers? People we would remember today?"

"Hell yes! I rode with Hap Jones. He owned the Indian dealership over on Valencia. Old man Perkins, he owned the Harley shop on Ellis. I bought three bikes from Perkins. I remember Hap and Rose—we would stop at North Beach for dinner. For a buck you got a big meal."

"Did you ride with other groups too?"

"I rode with the Hells Angels in the early forties, but they were a mom and pop club then. They didn't become radical until after the war."

"Dick, what's a mom and pop club?" I asked, thinking that his definition might be different from mine.

"You know, like the FogHogs today. Husbands riding with their wives, guys riding with their girlfriends. A lot of the girls, they rode too."

"They didn't just passenger? They rode?"

"Lots of girls rode and I mean lots of girls. And they was good riders too. They could really ride."

As an Old Timer, Dick has more than his memories—he has his Harley. He rides his '85 Electra Wide Glide with his wife Bernie on the back. He keeps his solo seat hanging on the garage wall for the times when he wants to take off alone.

Harley culture is still tied in inextricable ways to the image of the One Percenter. Outlaw clubs flourished in the late forties with the returning veterans. Those were rootless men who refused to settle into sedentary ways *and* felt that the American dream could not be dreamt by them. The outlaw club became home to groups of men who chose to live on both sides of the law. They became police targets by their choices and paid some heavy prices for those choices. The outlaw identity, with its emphasis on a kind of kick-ass masculinity, defined a whole group of bikers. They may have had their start in the forties and fifties, but they are still going strong today. Like the Old Timers, they came from the past and continue to be represented in current culture. No other rider comes closer to the biker image than the One Percenter.

Harley culture would not have survived this long if it were not for other Harley faithfuls. These guys approached their bikes with the same dedication and spirit as the outlaws. But they didn't join. They were loners. They were too independent to accept the rules even of an outlaw club.

A century earlier, they would have been called drifters. They would have ridden into town on a horse. Throughout the fifties and sixties, they rode Harleys. When everyone else gave up, they still rode Harleys. Along with the One Percenters and the Old Timers, they form the hard center of Harley culture. These dedicated riders, the Ten Percenters, are Harley riders to their core. If they couldn't get a Harley, they would not ride. They're not outlaws, they're not Old Timers, but they never ride anything but Harleys.

I'll never forget the look my husband got in 1974 when he went searching for a bike. He hit all the shops from San Jose to San Leandro. At a shop in San Jose, I was talking to two guys who were looking over the bikes.

"What kind are you going to get?" I remember asking.

The look I received was pure scorn. What kind of bike indeed! There was only one kind of bike, and anyone who didn't know that was an idiot! True Ten Percenters.

These are men in their forties and fifties who still remember what it felt like to start riding at age twelve. Men born and reared in small midwestern towns who bought their first Harleys in high school. Easy Ed Gilbertson, Ten Percenter, columnist for a number of Harley rags, formidable and easy going all at the same time, remembers it like this:

"I was born in a small town called Devils Lake, North Dakota, and I've always been in love with Harleys. Some of the older guys, particularly returning vets, got into them and I started saving at a young age for one. I started riding motorbikes and scooters in 1948 at age eleven. In 1953, while still a junior in high school, I got my first Harley, a 1947 Knucklehead. My bikes are my best friends and I keep them. Had my Knucklehead twenty years before I got my Shovelhead."

"Is that the Bumble Bee?" I asked.

Having ridden to some of the same events as Ed over the years, I was familiar with the incredible roar of his pipes and sleek style of his bike. It was the black and yellow Bumble Bee then. But Ed has made additional changes and the paint is now roadhouse blue. The bike is called the Blue Max. He has had this Shovel for over twenty years and plans to keep it. But that does not prevent him from getting a new one.

"Tom Perkins called and asked if I wanted the last FXR. The shop had gotten notification from the factory that there would be no more. As Tom put it, 'If you want it, it's yours; if you don't it's already sold.' Since I consider the FXR one of the best Harleys ever built, I was interested. Besides, the Shovel was getting up there in years and it seemed like the time to buy a new bike. Every twenty years isn't bad. My Shovel was one of the first of the FX series, and my Low Rider is the last. They're both great bikes; after you completely modify the suspension and beef up the engine, of course. Those early bikes needed a lot of wrenching. You had to wrench continuously. But the Evos are easy. You just punch the button and ride."

Ed rides constantly. It's a big part of his life. Ed's first wife wouldn't ride and they soon parted. He fell madly in love with his second wife but waited to see if she would fit into the lifestyle. She did. They married twenty-five years ago and have been riding together ever since.

"For years she would go on every single run, sleeping in the dirt and listening to all us wasted bikers telling the same old war stories over and over again. She doesn't drink or toke but even now she misses only a few of the hard-core runs. She has tried riding on her own but prefers to be a passenger."

Easy Ed Gilbertson (Courtesy of Noel Paraninfo)

Ed started with Harleys, stayed with Harleys, and has never wavered in his appreciation. He recalled the kick starts with fondness.

"You had to kick a Harley to life. I used to believe that if you didn't kick start a Harley you didn't deserve to have one. My Shovel came standard with an electric starter and I converted it to kick start. In those days, if you used an electric start, you were in danger of being called a pussy. On the bikes, in the old days, everything had to be just

70

right. The goal was a *one-kick Harley*. You'd go out on a run, put in the key, and immediately crank up. Bikes had to be in good running shape to do that. If the bike wasn't set up right, you'd kick and kick and maybe twenty kicks later it would start. It was always a challenge. Nothing was more embarrassing than having all the guys looking at you, ready to go, and you're still kicking the hell out of your reluctant mount."

"Ed," I asked, "didn't the kick start serve a really good function? Didn't it insure that everything was working right on the bike? Like if you were wrenching properly, the bike would start. So it forced you to always pay attention to the machinery."

Ed thought about it, agreed, and then added that the electric start has sure made things easier.

"So I use the electric start on both bikes now. The Evo changed a lot of things. Before the Evo you had to have basic mechanical skills. You had to be able to take the bike apart and put it back together again. It's different now. The Evo is helping a lot of women get into riding because they don't have to do any wrenching."

Harley culture to Ed is clearly defined.

"Every true biker is a libertarian. You don't want Big Brother telling you what to do. Being a biker is live and let live. Grab yourself some space and do your thing. A biker is an independent character who wants to be left alone and will grant others the same privilege. Like my straight pipes, for example. I always run open pipes. I try to cool it through town but when I'm out in the countryside I like to crank it on. Good sounds are important. There isn't anything that sounds better than a strong-running Harley. Despite the high taxes and goofy politics in California, the scenery and the weather make up for a lot. By offering some of the best riding on the planet, California is biker country. It's the main reason I live here."

"Do you expect to ride all your life?"

I looked at Ed, and, although he looked young, big, and strong, I knew he was in his mid-fifties. He expects to ride Harleys for as long as he can, and he figures that would be until his mid-eighties.

"As the years wear on," he said, "I look at the oldest people on Harleys. I never see anyone on a Harley beyond their middle eighties. There are just a few riding into their seventies. The hard-core Harley rider may make it a few years beyond that. Those who stopped riding I asked why! They all say the same thing. 'My legs gave out. The desire and the spirit were there but the legs just gave up.' Well," continued Ed, "I'm in good shape and I expect to ride into my eighties but probably not into my nineties. When I go, I plan to be buried at Sturgis. They have a national military cemetery outside Sturgis and as a vet,

I'm eligible to be planted there. It's right on the main road to Sturgis, so when the bikes roll by every year, they'll be rolling right over me. I first rode to Sturgis in 1956 and still make the run every year. The spirit of Sturgis, the Black Hills, and great memories of our many rides there will live on."

Ed's a Ten Percenter but no outlaw.

"That's a full-time commitment," he states. "You have to give it your all. For me there's more to the world, more things I want to do. Besides, I'm too independent to live by the rules of the average outlaw club. I hang out with a dozen brothers. We have been riding and partying together for several years. You might say we have a club without the visibility and hassles associated with running colors."

Harley culture is growing and still creating its own legends. There's a whole generation of Old Bikers out there who are not Old Timers. They're younger but they never joined the outlaws or became Ten Per-centers. They share some of the sensibilities of both groups and they're fiercely independent. They could be Ten Percenters 'cause they ride hard, wrench their own, take no shit, and have been riding all their lives. But unlike the Ten Percenters, they ride whatever is available. They prefer Harleys but will ride anything that comes their way.

These men, these Old Bikers, also in their forties and fifties, grew up riding. As it is to those in the other groups, riding is important to these men. They may have wanted Harleys, but unlike the others, they did not always ride them. Sometimes they lacked the money. Some-times they lacked the time to wrench. Sometimes they just gave in to the lure of the easy start and easier maintenance. Some bought crotch rockets. Harleys were good, but riding anything was better than not riding. If you couldn't get a Harley, you rode whatever you could get. A lot of them were drawn to British bikes and to this day still have garages full of old BSAs, Triumphs, and Nortons.

Pablo Lopez is an Old Biker. Although still in his early forties he has the look of someone who's been riding a long time. He started riding at twelve, got his first Harley, a Sportster, at seventeen, and now has half a dozen bikes in the garage. Road wise and impatient with idiots, he's says emphatically:

"Riding is a very serious endeavor. Unless you pay attention, *you will* get hurt. You have to ride very, very defensively. Look out for the idiots who don't see you."

He's been to Sturgis three times, and when I asked if he was going back this summer he responded: "Been there, done that."

There are too many other places he wants to travel. He toured Rus-sia on his bike with his daughter riding the rear. His wife Jayne rode

Jayne Kelly de Lopez and Pablo Lopez (Courtesy of Myrna Horta)

beside him on her own bike, with her son riding on the back. The trip lasted three weeks.

"Even if I have to rent a bike, the joy of riding's the same. But when you have your own motorcycle there, it's the best. It's comfortable. You know what to expect."

73

Pablo's first bikes were not Harleys.

"Too expensive. I had a chopped Honda because I didn't have the money for a Harley. As a kid, I wanted to be a badass. You had to have a bike if you wanted to be a badass. You'd get all the girls."

When I asked about joining a group he responded: "I never joined a club even though a part of me wanted to be a Hells Angel. But I was too independent to go by the rules. Anyone's rules! Even outlaw rules. I ride by my own rules. I've paid my dues. I've started far too many runs in the rain and ended them in the rain. I've torn down bikes and rebuilt them. You're out on a run, the bike breaks, you fix it any way you can. You got guys waiting for you, you get moving. Do what you must. Get that bike going. Then at the end of the day, you can tear the bike down at your leisure. But when you are on a run, you move."

Pablo has gone on many runs over the past thirty years. Sometimes he takes a passenger but he prefers to ride solo. His ole lady, his wife Jayne, rides her own. With a sidecar they were able to take the family for rides.

"A run is a minimum of a weekend. A month's trip is a run. The one-day poker run came about as a way of assembling riders. But it's just a putt. To me a run is a run to somewhere. You've got to put some miles on. You go a minimum of a couple of hundred miles. You've got to realize, a four-hour trip [in a car] can take ten hours on a bike. You can be at the side of the road. You can sit out bad weather. You can party along the way. Five hundred miles is a lot of hard riding on a bike. You can break down. Today, on an Evo, to do your own wrenching requires a great expense of tools.

"I've now become a fair-weather rider. I'm not a diehard anymore. I wait for a nice day. I don't have to prove anything to anybody. With two Pans, one Shovel, two Evos, one Flathead, and a Knucklehead on the bench in the garage, and a brand-new Indian in the oven, I ride when I want to."

"Would you call yourself a biker?"

Pablo looked up, thought about it for a moment.

"Yeah, some people have. That's not what I would say. That would limit my view of myself. I'm many things and one of them is a biker. If I had to find one word to describe me I'd say 'lover.' I love everything: life, antique cars, new and old bikes, and beautiful women."

When Harley-Davidson built a better bike in the mid-eighties, another whole group of guys started riding Harleys. These were men who had started on Hondas. They still wanted dependable mounts. When Harley came out with Evos, they started switching. The men who didn't like wrenching started switching. Finally, Harley had made a bike they could ride with a turn of the key. These were men who had wanted Harleys, but the wrenching, the undependability, and the price kept them from owning one. Now they could.

They switched in droves. Like the One Percenters, the Ten Percenters, and the Old Bikers, these are guys in their forties and fifties. They are not rich. Still fundamentally working class, they have jobs and could save their bucks for a bike. Their love of the machine is primal. They are road wise. They had been riding a long time. Biking, however, was never a fundamental part of their lives. They rode Japanese bikes for transportation and the love of riding. These men are not racers. They are not into the sport of motorcycling. They just like bikes and want Harleys. They liked the mystique but never joined it. They had ridden as young men, but it was never a defining part of their lives. Now in their forties, they finally own their Harleys.

These New Bikers are probably the largest group of Harley riders and the most diverse. They are old riders, but New Bikers. They have, at last, fallen under the Harley mystique. Having put off owning a Harley most of their lives, they have finally come under its sway. They come from all regions and cross color and class lines. Some of these guys join motorcycle clubs, but mostly they ride alone. Like the Ten Percenters and the Old Bikers they are not club people. They are loners. And they ride. They go on runs, campouts, and poker runs, and go the distance. As individuals, they are not, at first, respected by the other groups. They have to prove themselves. They are not hard core. They have ridden too many Japanese bikes. But they ride. Some of them have learned to wrench, but most of them have not. Some may eventually even cross the line to outlaw, but most remain in a group all their own. These new riders are a new force in the Harley world.

Bradley "Rooster" Brown grew up in a middle-class California neighborhood. All kinds of folk lived there. It was racially and culturally mixed. Both his parents worked, and he and his two sisters and two brothers grew up pretty tight. When I asked him how he would describe himself during those growing years, he looked thoughtful and answered, "mellow." Then things got changed around a bit. He went to Nam. He did drugs on that very first day. He had not done them before. "If I'm going to die," he said, "I'm going to die high."

After that he got a lot more aggressive or, as he put it, "Don't call me nigger—whitey!"

He became part of the Black Power group. In the military he was considered a troublemaker. Everyone labeled him "black man from Watts." Didn't matter that he had not grown up in Watts. Didn't matter that he had never even been to Watts. The stereotype stuck.

"I'm a three-part mixture: African American (black—the word doesn't matter), white, and Native American. But I identity most with

Bradley "Rooster" Brown (Courtesy of Noel Paraninfo)

the Native American side. I'm part Native American on both sides of my family. I'm the all-American boy. After Vietnam I went on a spiritual quest 'cause nothing made any sense anymore."

Bradley is six foot two, tall, slender, with hair to his waist and a Tai Chi symbol tattooed on his shoulder. He's into martial arts, Harleys, and his wife Susan. She two-ups, and while she intends—one day—to ride her own, she has yet to do so. His identification with being Native American is also where he taps into his spiritual side. It's the part that brings him peace.

Rooster's need for transportation in 1977 led him to buy a used Kawasaki KZ 300. He loved that bike and rode it continually till it got stolen. He upgraded to a new 4- cylinder Kawasaki KZ 1000. This bike was bigger, lightning fast, and pretty reliable. Four years later, on the job at the Oakland bus service, a coworker showed up on a '78 Harley Low Rider and offered to let him take it around the yard.

"Sure in hell sounded good. I was hooked."

His friend said that when he rode it for the first time it was like "riding with God!" There were some serious feelings behind those words. Three months later Bradley bought his first Harley. He bought a Low Rider.

"And I knew, right then, just what he was talking about."

"But Bradley, why a Harley? You were already riding. Why did you have to buy a Harley?"

After a moment's thought he replied, "Relaxation. It's the Milwaukee vibrator. It relaxes you like nothing else can. After I got my Harley I didn't care about any other bike."

"How do you feel when you ride?" I finally asked.

"Unlike so many other Harley riders, I never used to feel tough. I used to associate Harleys with the tough guys, the Hells Angels. Having it all hang out, being exposed to nature, to the elements, to the cars, toughens you up. I started riding my Harley and it was like living on the edge. And I loved it. It started happening to me too. I began to toughen up. Plus I was being treated differently. Motorcycle people are always being treated differently. *It's the only civilized way to be uncivilized.*"

At this comment his wife Susan leaned over and added: "You guys need to play out those primal instincts. You don't hunt anymore. You need a space where you can feel independent and free. You need a place to be wild."

"It's not solely a man's world, Susie," Bradley remarked. "Women were into Harleys way back. They rode them as part of the WACs in World War II. Harleys were used stateside."

"What happened to your Low Rider, Bradley?" I asked.

"It broke, so I sold it."

"You know why it broke? I'll tell you why it broke!" Susan leaned over. "It broke because he dinked and dinked and futzed and putzed around with it. It broke because he put so much stuff on it, it wouldn't run."

Bradley shook his head. "No, I got tired of kicking the sun of a gun over."

Susan looked bemused. "And why was that?" she added. "It was originally an electric start and he *put a kick start in it.*"

They kidded each other with affection born of long-time association. You could tell they had been married eleven years. Bradley, hooked on Harleys, went out and bought an '89 Dresser. A black FLHS. Susan warned that since they had only one car, he would have to ride it in the rain. She took her car to work. He didn't care. After saving up their money, they got the new bike.

And life was different.

"The very first day I came home from work Susie noticed a difference. I was really changed. The bike helped me relax. Aside from martial arts it's the only thing I do all day that really feels good. I drive through heavy traffic in the worst commute of the day and it takes twenty minutes. I just glide around the cars. It feels great."

Bradley made it clear that he was not part of the Ten Percenters. He was not an Old Biker. He had no intention of ever becoming an outlaw.

"There is a Harley culture and it's the people who eat, sleep, and breathe Harley-Davidsons. They've been at it all their lives. Outlaw or not, they live to ride. I'm not a trendy rider either. I ride to work every day. I'm a rider. Hells Angels are bikers, I'm a rider. Outlaws are bikers."

"I don't tend to join clubs. I'm a lone wolf. If I had to make a self-description, I'd say I'm a hippie riding Harley man. If I could get away with it I'd have on tie-dyed T-shirts, stick a pot bowl on my hat, and have my hair flying in the wind."

Upon hearing that description, Susan said: "That's Bradley. That's the man I love."

Bradley represents the New Biker much in the way Pablo represents the Old Biker, Easy Ed the Ten Percenter, and Dick McKay the Old Timer. These are not hard and fast categories. They overlap. Bradley can wrench but he does not have the intense dedication of Pablo, and neither fashions their world around motorcycles the way Easy Ed does. Dick McKay alone remembers the early Harleys and the pre–World War II world.

These four groups plus the One Percenters represent part of the contemporary Harley world. Up until the late eighties, they would have represented that whole world. These five groups would have described Harley culture. Since then, two new categories have emerged: the Rich Urban Bikers (RUB) and the Occasional Bikers (OB). They are much talked about. They are infamous. RUBs are most frequently new riders. Harleys are usually their first bikes and they dress them to perfection. While the term Rich Urban Biker describes a group of folk, not all are rich, not all are urban, and most other groups would not consider them bikers. Their backgrounds and professions tend to put them at odds with other bikers. They do not wrench and most have no intention of learning. They are, however, serious riders.

Karl Svensson, in his early thirties, is blond, Swedish, and smart. He owns and runs a San Francisco computer consulting firm. He's very comfortable talking about his bikes. He says that as a kid he was always assembling bicycles. Putting all these assembled parts together has a particular name in Sweden: Hopplockade Delar (HD). As a kid he screwed around putting ape hangers on bicycles, removing chain guards and fenders. He made his bicycles look like choppers.

"We played that it was a motorcycle. The motorcycle we all had in mind was always a Harley-Davidson. When I came to the States and got a bike, it was a used Kawasaki 'cause it was cheap and I knew I would only have it for a short time. I wanted a Harley. As soon as I started riding and discovered that I really liked it, I wanted to get *the real thing*. The real thing when you are growing up in Sweden is a Harley. And I'm glad."

Karl bought a Sportster two years ago and tricked it out to perfection with paint and chrome. He hopped it up to increase its power and handling and rides it everywhere. Just this year he bought another Harley, a Road King. This stripped and modified Dresser on an FL frame is Milwaukee's bid for engineering and style compatibility.

"I bought the Road King for convenience reasons. It's more convenient for passengers. It makes camping easier. When I travel I have to tie everything on and the Sportster's a bit too small for that. All the current publicity about Harleys had nothing to do with my getting a Harley. It had nothing to do with my getting the Road King."

"Hey Karl, you gonna sell your Sportster now that you have a Big Twin?"

"Never. I like it too much."

We talked for a while about Harley culture and how Karl sees himself within it: "Bike culture has several different levels and all kinds of people. There are some people who *live for it*! They are similar to some football fans who spend all their money going to the Super Bowl. They

79

are fanatics. People who love motorcycles spend all their money, all their savings on bikes. If you are that dedicated you take care of the bike. You go to swap meets and patch a bike together.

"Another group just goes riding. They thoroughly enjoy riding. They get a bike and really, really like riding it. They take the time to do it. Then others have a bike for other reasons. They want more to be seen than anything else. They buy a Harley to prove something or to be hip. That's ridiculous."

"What about the comments," I asked, "that all those folks buying Harleys are just going through a midlife crisis?"

"When I got my Harley, that was something I hadn't done in my life. It was something I always wanted to do, so I just did it. For a lot of people, they get an opportunity to do something. So they do it. It doesn't matter whether they are twenty-two or thirty-two or forty-two or fifty-two or sixty-two or seventy-two. Don't label that a midlife crisis just because it happens at midlife. It could happen at any time. You might be more apt to act on these desires during midlife because maybe the kids are grown and there is more money. But that's not just doing something with Harleys. These are people doing their dream. Doing what they want to do. Maybe earlier, there were other things they had to do, and riding was way down on the list; well, Harley riding just got higher on that list."

"So what does it mean to you to ride a Harley?"

"Riding is a kind of meditative experience. It's similar to scuba diving. You can't talk and you have all this stimulus. You can't talk. You just experience. You are one with the road and the wind. You just see all these beautiful things. This is an important part of the Harley culture. The experience and the bike mean something. Like if you own another bike and its stolen, well it's just money. But if you're Harley is stolen, well. . . ."

Karl rides. He has been riding only a few years, rarely wrenches, and does not fit D. C. Dick's criteria for biker identity. Dick would say Karl has not paid his dues. He has not paid all those prison, hospital, and club fighting dues. Yet he has a love of his bikes that is as sound and durable as that of anyone else on the road. He's a good riding partner. On the road, he's quick, efficient, steady, and reliable. He is most decidedly neither blue collar nor working class. He is international in his background, tastes, and travels. He typifies that new breed of rider that Harley-Davidson has tried, over the past few years, to impress.

This new breed of rider has none of the older, hard-core, biker knowledge at his throttle tips. He comes to it with a fresh attitude and an almost innocent ignorance. He knows the cardinal rule of the road.

Protect your own. But beyond that, he is making his own way in the Harley world unfettered by the mores and rules of the past. This new Harley rider is coming of age with a view of the world that's decidedly different from that of the older riders. While he lacks years of experience, he is nonetheless a serious rider. And most telling of all, he doesn't give a damn what they think of him. He rides, goes his own way, and loves his Harley. He doesn't even care if they call him a RUB.

The newest and last member of Harley culture starts out like a RUB but quickly turns into an OB. Like Karl, the Occasional Biker wants to experience the dream but, unlike Karl, finds out that the dream in his head is very different from the one on the road. The Occasional Biker is a RUB who wants out. He's the guy who puts the "for sale" sign on the bike with only four hundred miles on the odometer. Unlike Karl, who puts thousands of miles on his bike every month, the Occasional Biker club rides. He goes to Sunday brunches and then rides home. He's the one who looks good in chaps but doesn't feel good in them. He loves everything about the bike but riding it. He is sometimes called the Zip Code Rider since he rarely rides beyond his home region.

Ken Siegel is an atypical Occasional Biker in that he rode Hondas during his adolescence. He is also atypical because he still owns a rare model 1956 BMW. This bike, still in good shape, takes primary place in his garage and his heart. His brand-new Heritage Softail, although shiny and beautiful, clearly comes in second. He is a typical OB in his attitudes. He bought the Softail, put around six hundred miles on it, and now is pretty sure he wants to sell it.

Ken, a lawyer, supports a large family, large house, large dog, and large bills, and has little time for riding. What time he does have he prefers to spend with his family. His wife, Rox, is opposed to riding and is vehement in her refusal to include herself or the children in Ken's riding plans. While there is a decided split in family attitudes about adult participation, both are in absolute agreement in their desire to *keep the kids off the bikes.* Both think riding is dangerous for children and do not want their children riding when they get older.

"Motorcycling is way too dangerous to do with your kids. I don't want them to ride. Even though I always wear a proper helmet, leather jacket, boots, and gloves, I still think it is very dangerous. Motorcycles are very risky things to be on, especially when you are a teenager. At sixteen you do stupid things. And the cars do stupid things."

When asked why he bought this Harley, Ken responded: "I got reinspired. I was working with my law firm for Custom Chrome in 1990 and hanging out with those guys, and I liked it. They are bikers, you know—big beards, black vests, classic Hells Angels–looking types.

Big, burly guys with tattoos and all. Well, no one else in my law firm rode. I liked being with the guys from Custom Chrome. It got me interested in Harleys. I decided on the Softail because its style is similar to my BMW. It has the 1950s style."

"Do you enjoy riding the Softail?"

"No—it's a piece of junk. It vibrates. It vibrates so much it makes my hands get numb. It gets to be real bad above sixty. It also scrapes the floorboards and does no serious cornering. The biggest problem, though, is the vibration. It's got really poor engineering. It looks great but it's only the appearance that turned out to be good."

"If it rode better, would you be more inclined to keep it?"

"No. That's a financial decision. There are more appropriate uses of the money at this time in my life. I went only six hundred miles in six months."

"So will you actually sell it?"

"Don't know. It depends on how much I feel I need the money."

"Do you care about the bike?"

"I don't love it. I could *not* part with the BMW. I could part with my Harley and not lose sleep over it. The Harley is replaceable. I haven't even customized it. I just bought it. I thought it would be fun to have a new one. Restorations are real projects and I have no time for projects. I had a good idea what I wanted and I got it. But I am annoyed. There is no excuse for the poor performance. It should be as good as it looks and it's not. It's irritating that for that much money, it uses technology that's thirty years old."

"Why did you buy the Heritage Softail and not a Road King or a Low Rider?"

"I liked the Softail look, the 1950s look."

"Do you think that there's a Harley culture?"

"Oh yeah—definitely. I think that there is more than one. At least two come across really clearly. There are the lawyers and CEOs and other professionals riding. They're middle-aged men with big bellies. Like one of my business acquaintances who's over sixty. He just ordered a Sportster. I asked him if he knew how to ride and he said no. He said he never rode in his life, didn't know how to. I suggested that he take a motorcycle course. Then there are the other ones, the hard-core Hells Angels types. The types with tattoos and beards.

"Oh yeah, other groups. In between the CEOs and Hells Angels, there are the guys who restore the antique Harleys. These are motorcycle people. It's not just a fun fad for them. It is a little bit of a fad for me. But it was built on the foundation of being a motorcyclist. If I had endless amounts of money, I'd keep the Softail and get a new BMW."

Ken Siegel wanted to buy a Harley and his wife agreed. This was his indulgence. The Harley fit into the indulgence framework because it is so impractical.

"Why get it?"

"They're bitchin' motorcycles."

Ken does not see himself as part of the Harley culture. He did not join any group.

"A lot of people see it as a way of life. I'm an atheist, I don't need a religion. I don't feel the need to get involved. A lot of the time the people in these groups just sit around and talk about motorcycles and riding. I want to ride motorcycles not talk about them. They are boring. I never ride with any Harley-Davidson groups."

During some of the interview Rox sat listening. When Ken spoke about selling the bike she nodded enthusiastically. She never wants to join him on the bike. While she did not object to his buying the bike, she thought it a waste of money. He has no time to ride it. He never even rides his BMW.

Ken Siegel, with six hundred miles on his new Softail, fits the general description of an Occasional Biker. He bought the bike because he was lured by its style and looks. He does not enjoy riding it. He resents the riding time, preferring to spend his time at home. He will ultimately sell it. He fell under the sway of the mystique and the hype. As he put it, he was following the fad, and now it's over for him. Harley promises a lot. To some it delivers. To Ken it did not.

Members in this final group within Harley culture, the Occasional Bikers, do not consider themselves part of the culture. They love the Harley hype and style. For some, Harleys have become status and luxury symbols. They are bought, ridden to the nearest upscale bar, and left outside to be admired. These men will be part of the Harley world for a brief time only.

Harleys represent important but different things to each of these men. Dick McKay's got many things going for him in his life. Bikes are one of them. They are and have been an important part of his life. But they are not his whole life. He's a biker, a husband, a father, and a grandfather. He's a retired carpenter and builder. He was raised in an America where a hard-working, working-class man could afford to support a family, own a house, and buy some wheels. He grew up at a time when gender roles gave meaning and strength to men's lives. They defined women's lives too. He knew what was expected of him and was comfortable with both his privileges and his responsibilities. Men of Dick's generation understood that responsibilities rode alongside the privileges of manhood. All the confusions that shaped later generations of men had not shaped Dick. He and Bernie were clear about their tasks and choices. Bernie asserts with pride that she alone raised her children. She stayed home and took care of them. Dick was able to provide enough for them to do that. Most later generations of American men are not able to make that statement. The single-wage household has gone the way of the Knucklehead.

Men of Dick's generation had enough gender building blocks to place their sense of masculinity beyond question. According to James Doyle, "At an early age, these men learned that as long as a male did not act feminine, attained some measure of success in work, provided for his family, stood up for his rights when necessary and was willing to fight if need be, showed the proper interest in sex (always), and displayed a tough and self-reliant manner, he was a man" (1983, 30).

Dick didn't need a Harley to show him how to be a man. There were still enough cultural guidelines for that. He rode Harleys because he wanted to. Women in that generation also rode Harleys. The women, however, didn't always have it so good. For many women the limitations were profound. They built their lives around their families but sometimes the men didn't stay.

Women weren't trained to go it alone. Some women wanted something different from having a family, and this was hard to do. The narrow and rigid gender roles had their strengths, but they also had their weaknesses. They could damage. If the roles suited you, they worked well. If the roles did not suit you, there were problems, and there was very little one could do about it.

For Bernie and Dick, the roles worked. They built their lives upon a complementarity that works to this very day. He maintains his many interests and biking remains an important one. As he puts it, "I grew up riding."

By the mid-forties, times started changing. Guys coming back from World War II wanted excitement. The motorcycle racing circuit took off and men were known for the bikes they raced. With hundreds of motorcycle clubs popping up all over the place, the AMA was busy scheduling races, events, drags, and bike games. One Percenters, Ten Percenters, and Old Bikers took to the roads in record numbers. Riding became a lifestyle. For many of these men, riding a Harley became a rite of passage into manhood. Riding a Harley was the manly thing to do. In many ways Harleys provided a road map to independence and a map of manhood.

Easy Ed remembers, "In 1957, I went alone to California. All my buddies kept finding excuses not to go. Rode my Knucklehead alone at nineteen to places I had never been. Rode to LA right from the middle of the Midwest. Slept in ditches by the side of the road. With my sleeping bag on the bike I could have gone anywhere. But early one morning, when I hit the freeways of LA, I thought, 'Man! This is the hub of the universe.' Later I found Northern California and didn't think LA was so great anymore."

Pablo also remembers, "I've fixed more flat tires than most people have miles. You gain knowledge over a period of time. You gain bike skills. It's something you learn to do well. You get so you can tear a bike down and build it up. That's something you never forget."

For these men, born two and three decades after Dick McKay, manhood had turned from something eased into at adulthood to a prize won through struggle. According to Doyle, "Next to the negative injunction 'don't be like a girl,' no other element is as important and universal for defining a male's sex role as the one that positively charges a male to be a success." Chief among the success markers of masculinity in the past was the ability to support a family. This function is now shared with women: "From 1946 to 1965 a gradual erosion began to undermine the social values that supported men in their role as sole provider for the family" (Doyle 1983, 147).

It is difficult, if not impossible, in most areas today to make a middle-class living on one paycheck. It is just as difficult to achieve a working-class lifestyle. Since economic support, paychecks, and male status no longer symbolize manhood in America, men look toward other expressions of masculinity.

In critical ways, becoming a biker satisfies a number of masculine criteria. It separates the men from the boys. It separates the men from the women. It promotes knowledge, competence, and skill. It provides an avenue by which men can express bravery, male solidarity, and acceptable aggression.

Expertise in a bar fight in defense of a riding buddy is seen as a useful trait. Wrenching on your buddy's bike in the middle of nowhere is acknowledged as a great skill. When money, jobs, and family support, the historical mainstays of American malehood, retreat as markers for adulthood, other markers take their place. Brotherhood in the face of danger, competence on the road, and physical bravery often become those other markers. Harley culture not only accepts these traits, it demands them from the men who enter.

Few women in the early decades of the 1940s and 1950s (there were always some) braved the masculine road. Clubs denied women membership status, and interested females got pushed to the rear of the bike. The bikes started changing as well. Before World War II, the bikes were lighter and easier to handle. With the building of more powerful Harleys, the weight, the kick start, and the price started working against women riders. By the time *The Wild One* played in movie theaters, women riders were rare and at risk. Men could build their identities around biking skills, and biking became a masculine preserve. There were exceptions.

"I had no problem with women riding," claimed Pablo. "I can be a bit chauvinistic, but I try to be liberal minded. At first, seeing women riding was a bit tough to swallow. But now I find it a blessing. I can ride how I want to ride. With Jayne riding her own, I can do what I want. Their only problem is their inability to keep up. You can quote me on that. But at least with women riding, I don't have a woman bitching and moaning in my ear and telling me to slow down and putting her feet down when we stop. I hated that."

Only in the last ten years has Harley, once again, made a pitch to women. The formation of Ladies of Harley was the first overture. It was aimed originally at women passengers. Its primary goal was keeping women interested in the Harley world. It was created to keep them happy so their husbands could keep buying Harleys.

The second overture came with the introduction of the Hugger. This 883 Sportster has a lowered seat, buckhorn handlebars, and a somewhat smaller frame. Since many women have problems with the larger frames of the Big Twins, the Hugger was designed to accommodate a woman's body. It worked. It is still large, heavy, and difficult to ride, but compared with the other Harleys, it casts a decidedly smaller shadow. It has developed a reputation as a "woman's bike."

As more women enter the domain of traditional masculinity, male images are once again realigned. Some men are having trouble coping with this encroachment. If part of male identity is forged around riding, then a woman riding her own can cause problems. While women remain on the rear, the older definitions hold. But as soon as a woman shifts to the front seat, a whole set of behaviors shift with her. Biking has never defined femininity, traditional or otherwise. Women retain their feminine image and identity in spite of their riding, not because of it. How women cope with the realities of the road is specific to each woman and has sparked some serious controversy in the Harley world, as I discuss in the chapters below.

It is within the last two decades that the New Bikers, RUBs and OBs have emerged. Old Bikers have returned. The Evo engine was just too good to pass up. They didn't have to spend all their time kick starting and wrenching, kick starting and wrenching. New Bikers entered the fold. They had always wanted Harleys anyway. Milwaukee finally found a way to bring them in.

They created a better bike. They built a bike that did not leak all over the garage. They built a bike that looked like the bike all the New Bikers wanted when they were boys. RUBs arrived. They didn't worry about wrenching since most could afford to pay someone else to do it.

What RUBs wanted was a good ride. Harley finally produced one. RUBs were used to demanding value for their bucks and performance from their vehicles. RUBs also wanted the style, the pizzazz, the chic of riding Harleys. Those who turned from RUBs into Occasional Bikers appreciated the great resale value of used Harleys. Many found to their pleasure that they could sell their bikes for more money than they had paid for them. Those who discounted the joys of riding were thrilled at the joys of reselling. They sold their bikes for profit.

6

Women Jamming the Wind

"Mastering a Harley is as American as self-reliance and independence."
"Unless you're a woman."

The female riding world, unlike the male world, is made up of women who ride and women who passenger. Sometimes women do both, but that's pretty rare. Unlike men, women are not readily defined by class, age, style of riding, or how many years they've been riding. Women who ride defy the categories that can be used to divide men so easily into separate bundles. While typically white and heterosexual, the riding woman can be working class, professional, or a full-time stay-at-home mother. She can be well educated or a high school dropout. She can be rich or poor. What these women all have in common is their love of bikes and their defiance of female stereotypic behavior. None of these women play it safe. None follow the path of female socialization into timidity. All these women are bold. Each is bold in her own way.

Women who passenger are different from women who ride. Women who passenger are usually thought of primarily in terms of their sexuality because of their association with wild men. Any woman who does such a bold and dangerous act as riding the wind behind a questionable character must surely be nothing less than a *sexual outlaw*. She is the slutty seductress adorning the pages of biker rags. She is the naked calendar cutie leaning voluptuously against the hard and stark machinery of the motorcycle. She has already broken the rules of "normal" propriety; who knows what other rules she will break? Who knows how she will act? She is society's wicked woman and every young boy's secret wet dream. While she is many things in America's collective mind, she is considered beyond redemption and polite society.

Women who ride are different from women who passenger. Women who ride break even greater conventions. These women refuse to ride

88

on the back of the bike. For all the censure received by the sexual outlaw, she is at least following a recognizable gender role. She rides the rear. The woman who rides her own bike is not behaving like a woman at all. She is in charge of her own bike. She makes her own destiny. Women in America have not been raised for this. The riding woman is seen as a *gender traitor.*

All women in the biking world experience various levels of disapproval. Usually, the lure and love of the bikes, the men, and the community is strong enough to compensate for that disapproval. According to male writers (Wolf, Thompson, and Hopper and Moore), women are peripheral to the biker world. Necessary but peripheral. They are also classified in relation to men, rather than in relation to bikes. Indeed, male writers of motorcycle culture have not considered women as riders at all.

Wolf devotes only one page of *The Rebels* to women. According to Wolf, women who participate in the outlaw biker world are passengers and fall into one of three major categories: "broads," "mamas," and "ol' ladies":

> These categories are fundamentally distinct statuses and represent different ways that women relate to the club and to its members. "Broads" is the general term used to refer to a wide range of women who drift in and out of the sub-culture. It is an introductory stage of social interaction with one or more members on a casual and usually temporary basis. "Mamas" are women who maintain an informal affiliation with the club as a whole. This informal affiliation includes social-sexual interactions with the members and, in some clubs, an economic arrangement. "Ol' ladies" are women who have established a long-standing personal relationship with an individual member. An ol' lady may be the member's girlfriend, covivant, or wife.
>
> The women in these three categories play sub-cultural roles that meet distinct male needs and result in different types of male-female relationships; from "loose broads" and "mamas" who often become the passive objects of displays of machismo and sexual gratification, to "ol' ladies" who are respected as long-term personal companions and loved as the active partners of club members. (1991, 133)

According to Wolf and all male writers before him, male bikers view women only in relation to their man; they are all seen as "loose broads, " "mamas, " and "ol' ladies. " While all passengering women are, indeed, dependent upon their riders to bring them into the culture and into the wind, once there, they are not merely the passive recipients of male desires. The male writers are wrong. The women all have their own agendas and their own strategies for survival. Some may ride in with one man and ride out with another. Some may drive to an event with a girlfriend and leave with a biker. Some may arrive with a lover, break up during the run, and bus it home alone. There are no rules about women within biker communities. But there are a number of loose categories. Passengering women fall into three major categories: Biker Chick, Lady Passenger, and Passionate Passenger.

The Biker Chick earns entrance any way she can. She's the woman usually thought of as the "biker's bitch." Easy to pick up, easier to lose. She has only a precarious hold upon the culture. Her entrance, like that of other passengering women, is dependent upon a man. Unlike most other passengering women, she rarely has a special man. She is most frequently on her own in a culture that takes advantage of women on their own. She rides the dangerous edge in the motorcycle world. The Biker Chick is the woman who jumps on the back of a stranger's bike. She's the young, tender, and sexy groupie at the biker rallies. She's the hard-bitten bitch on the back taking the brunt of biker frustrations. She's dressed to please. That's her passage into the community. She pleases one or many because that's her role and she accepts it. She's the beer buying, dope carrying, sexual partner who often as not gets dismissed at dawn. Her position is marginal but entrenched. Sometime she is ridden around, sometimes pushed around. She rides the fringes. She is rarely permanently attached to any one man and must therefore be in a position to please a number of men. She's either very young or can't quite figure out another entrance into the community.

The Lady Passenger is the biker's wife, ole lady, or long-term girlfriend. She rides because he does. She enjoys riding but lacks the passion of full-time commitment. She may show great enthusiasm for riding during their courting stage. She may even share some of the excitement felt by her man. Eventually, however, as the relationship strengthens and her home and family commitments grow, she begins to skip more runs than she attends. She becomes the fair-weather, Sunday passenger who accepts the bike as a permanent fixture in her man's life but does not share his passion. She will ride with him, but it has to be a special occasion. Like wives, ole ladies, and girlfriends everywhere, she dresses and acts to please when it suits her. Depending upon the security of the relationship, she makes nice when she has to. Passengering with someone you love is so intimate an act that great emotions follow long rides. You either get along, or you stop riding together. The Lady Passenger is part of the community because her man is part of it. She would leave it if they broke up.

The Passionate Passenger also enters the culture on the back of a bike, but she carefully picks her man for his ability to ride. She *wants* to be in the wind. She lives to ride, just like her man, who makes biking central in his life. She is as passionate about riding as is her partner and knows that she must maintain good relations with him to secure her place on the road. Desiring to be ole lady or permanent girlfriend, she may have to go through a number of men before a relationship sticks. Unlike the Biker Chick, she never enters into cultural events, rallies, or parties as a casual participant or on her own. She is always escorted in and out. Also underscoring her difference from the Biker Chick is her love of the bike, the road, and the wind. She would be a rider if she could. Most Passionate Passengers want the biking experience but lack the confidence to take it on their own. This is a transient state for some, but others ride the rear forever.

Unlike many of the women who ride, the Passionate Passenger usually does not discover biking in her teens. Typically, she comes to it somewhere in her twenties or thirties when her sex-role behaviors are already well in place. She is most comfortable riding in the rear and has a hard time accepting the possibility that she could actually ride her own. The responsibility is too awesome. She sees riding as a fundamentally male activity and she is comfortable with her female counterpart activity. She must continually please her man to keep herself riding, but as a heterosexual woman, she is used to doing this anyway. Passionate Passengers usually try to establish a long-standing, permanent relationship with one riding man. This insures both emotional and riding continuity.

I interviewed only one woman I would call a Biker Chick. That is how she introduced herself to me and the name stuck. She, alone, of all the women interviewed, asked that I not print her name. At twenty-five, she has been around, seen a lot, and is careful about what she says.

"I first saw bikers when I was a little girl, riding in the back seat of my parents' car. A whole gang rode by. They were all flying colors, though I didn't know what that meant then, but I thought they looked scary. They also looked exciting. They looked like they were having fun. My parents' reaction was instant and very strong. 'Stupid bastards, hogging the road. You stay away from that kind of trash,' I was told.

"After that, I looked up every time I heard a bike. None of my high school boyfriends were bikers. My parents wouldn't let me go out with one. But my girlfriends and I used to sneak into biker rallies. By the time we were sixteen we had been to dozens. We always lied about our ages. We always said we were eighteen so the guys wouldn't say 'jail bait' and refuse to pick us up.

"Where we live there are always bike rallies going on. At least one

91

or two times a year there's something happening. As I got older, my girlfriends and I would borrow a van and all ride up together. Some of my friends would stick their thumbs out and hop on the back of the first bike that stopped. I wouldn't do that. I wanted to get to know the guy first. I never told my parents where I was going. They would have killed me."

"Weren't you scared? Scared of your parents finding out? Scared of riding on the back with almost a stranger?"

"You're never scared when you're sixteen. Riding was such a thrill. And besides, by the time I actually got on the bike to ride, I was so loaded and stoned, I could have fallen off and not gotten hurt. And I told you, my parents never knew. I always told them I was over at my girlfriend's house.

"I love riding, but mostly I love the guys. These are men who aren't afraid to show they are men. They aren't afraid to stand up for what they want. They don't take shit from no one. All of my boyfriends, the ones my parents meet, are so boring. I can lead them around by their noses. But bikers are different. They're thrilling. With bikers, I always have a good time."

"How are you treated? Do they ever give you a hard time?"

"Well, if you're looking for me to bad-mouth bikers, you're not gonna get it. Sometimes I did get knocked around, but it was always after I did something. I've got a really big mouth, you know."

"Are you saying that you deserved to be knocked around?"

"I'm saying that we're here because we want to be. Make that very clear. No one ever forces us to be here. All those girls you see hanging around the men! We all want to be here. Make that clear."

"Do you love riding? Will you ever want to be a rider?"

"I have no interest in riding by myself. I like riding behind a man. If I'm on a bike, it's always going to be in back of a man. Put that down too."

Biker Chicks aim to please. It's their entrance into the world they want. They do whatever is necessary to please. They give sex, food, and fun. They also receive sex, food, and fun. It's a two-way road. It's no mystery why the guys are so fond of them. Most Biker Chicks are young, available, and extremely affable. The guy wants a beer, they bring it to him. The guy wants to party, they supply the good time. It fits a young man's dream. (It fits old men's dreams too.) The women give sex, a good time, and no hassles.

"They are fun to be around. They are fun to party with. You can do what you want around them. You can act however you please. They are not going to be offended."

Easy Ed and I talked about his fondness for Biker Chicks. Having been married a long time to a woman he both loves and respects, he added another dimension of understanding to Biker Chick companionability. He also made it emphatically clear that his wife Sherry is not a Biker Chick.

"They come into the life," said Easy, "looking for excitement or a home. They are often young and innocent. Sometimes they are not treated very well. They start out so tender, but after these gals have hung around for a while they can become really hard. Sometimes they come from abusive or bad homes.

"After they've been around for a few years, they get pretty hardcore. They stay at the campgrounds, listening to the raw talk and getting into drugs and booze. They sometimes get knocked around a bit too. They put up with this year after year and keep coming back for more.

"If she got involved with bikers when she was young, she's probably been passed around sexually and doesn't have very many scruples left. She may also be spaced out on drugs. And she may have had the hell beaten out of her. Biker chicks have seen it all. They can be hard as nails, but still be lots of fun.

"In many ways, she's the female equivalent of the outlaw biker. Hit her one too many times, and she'll come back at you with a knife. But they are still fun. Be nice to them and they are some of the best party gals in the world. But I wouldn't want to spend too much time with one. My real preference is for the woman biker. A strong aggressive woman who rides her own Harley and likes to boogie."

In a male world that's fueled by machismo and runs on high-test testosterone, Biker Chicks live precarious existences. While they make up only a small percentage of the female passenger population, they get the most press. They are the ones showing their tits and taking their lumps. They are also very brave. They ride with all kinds of riders in all kinds of conditions. They make difficult choices to be with bikers.

Far from passive, as they're portrayed to be in the male-dominated press and general commentary, these women have made serious decisions about how they want to live. They like the rewards and they tend to downplay the punishments. They like the male attention. They like the party and the good times that go with it. They have been brought up to please, like most other women, and so long as they are young, nubile, pretty, and pliable, they do. It is only after they have been around too long, are no longer young and pretty, that they start to lose favor among the men.

These women, in spite of the precariousness of their position, are playing out the female social role in its most exaggerated form. They are ultrafeminine. If their value goes down as they approach middle age, so does that of other middle-aged women. Their counterparts, the displaced homemakers, share that experience. Women in their middle years who have been abandoned for younger, prettier, and more pliable models share much in common with Biker Chicks. Housewives, however, have the approval and support (in name, if not in reality) of society. Biker Chicks do not. Biker Chicks are on their own.

Most women in the Harley world are not Biker Chicks. Most women are Lady Passengers. They ride because their man rides. They enjoy the people and the companionability of the road. They enjoy the weekends away from the kids. It's fun, and so long as it remains fun, they passenger. When the weather turns cold, the road becomes difficult, and the party ends, these women stay home.

Blondie Dickow, who when I interviewed her had been married only a few months to Denny, an Old Biker, rides when she feels like it. It is a second marriage for both. With four kids between them and a menagerie of critters, their lives are full and happy. When not caring for the ferrets, the cats, the iguana, the tarantula, the dog, or the kids, Blondie passengers.

"I did not ride before I started dating Denny. When I started seeing him, he didn't have a bike. He was between bikes. But I knew he was a biker. I had known him a long time. In Pacifica, we all know each other. It's a small town.

"I guess you could call me a Sunday passenger. I enjoy the bike, but I don't love it. I was in a bike accident so I get afraid. Sometimes I get scared to death. Denny rides like crazy."

"Now that you are married," I asked, "does he listen to you when you ride together?"

"No, he's worse. He will not slow down when I tell him to. He goes faster. Sometimes I get so mad that I threaten to call his father to pick me up. I've never done that but if his father happens to show up, I will jump into the car. Right after we started dating, he bought a Shovelhead. That's the bike across the street."

I looked and saw a beautiful bike with white and blue flames on the gas tank and fender and with a better than average Shovel rear seat.

"After our first real ride on the bike," Blondie continued, "I made him change the seat. We had ridden on the Perkins Halloween Run up to Santa Rosa and I hurt like hell. I was sitting on one of those little pillion pads in the back. I made him take me to Michaels' Harley-Davidson in Santa Rosa and I bought a real back seat. I rode all the way back to Pacifica in comfort.

"Denny's next bike was a full Dresser. I loved that bike. It was so comfortable, I could fall asleep in back. Of course, when I'm tired I can sleep on anything. I once slept on the Shovel. Actually, we were at

Blondie and Denny Dickow (Courtesy of Blondie and Denny Dickow)

Bridgeport and I passed out. Denny had to hold on to me all the way back to our motel. It had been raining all day, I had been drinking shots all evening, and by night, I had to be helped onto the bike. Denny laughs that he should have bungee-corded me on. But when we rode the Dresser, that seat was so big and so safe that I couldn't fall off if I tried. Sometimes I fell asleep, just because the ride was long and I got bored."

95

"That's so amazing to me," I commented. "Ken would love to have me that relaxed. I am the worst back seat passenger in the world. I have to see everything; every bump in the road, every rut in the concrete, every low turn or sharp corner. If Ken goes too fast or turns too steep, I complain. Denny doesn't know how lucky he is."

"Denny's bike is his passion. When I was younger I enjoyed it, but now that I'm back to work full-time, I don't have the free time I used to have. Now I'm focused on the house and the kids. I have more responsibility. It's harder. I work all week and on the weekends I clean house and take care of the kids."

"Doesn't Denny help you?"

"Yeah, right! He doesn't do anything around the house. The only reason he's helping me today is 'cause he spent all our money on a computer last night. So today he's being nice."

"Do you still like Harleys?"

"I love Harleys. I like the noise, the sound, the name, the dominance on the road. I like all of that. And I used to love the people. Now so many of them are a bunch of fuckin' yuppies. They ride because everyone else does. They aren't true bikers. The bikers I've ridden with are heavy-duty bikers. They are like family to each other. They stick together. Now with those yuppies; they are just snobby. Not bikers at all. They wouldn't help you out if you were stranded on the road. They just want to sit around and talk politics. Who cares! To the yuppies, it's all image and show. It's status and new bikes for them. They aren't into the brotherly thing. They won't wait for you or help you. I used to look forward to all those FogHog Sunday rides. Now I won't even go to them."

"What about your kids and your folks? How do they feel about the bikes?"

"My parents were not happy about my passengering, but they love Denny. And I always call my parents up when I arrive anywhere and again when I get home."

Blondie, in her early thirties, is young enough to be positioned between still-youthful parents and almost grown children. She is responsive to both. Denny, in his early forties and male, is less responsive to the opinions of either generation.

"My children just love riding with Denny. Justin, my eleven-year-old, rides with him every chance he gets. My daughter Lisa is twelve and she likes riding too. I never worry about them on the bike. When Denny is riding the kids, he never rides crazy. He goes very carefully and is always aware of them on the back. He's such a good rider that I'm fine with it.

"I guess the thing that hits me about passengering is being so much out in the world. We can go from 110 degree weather to freezing in the same day. You are right out there in the middle of everything. I love that part of it."

Susan Duckstein, another Lady Passenger, is married to Bradley, a New Biker. She also loves riding on the Dresser. It has a big, high, cushioned, protected seat. It's a comfortable way to travel. Plus, she explains, you can't see the speedometer or the road beneath your wheels. Like Blondie, Susan would not be passengering if riding hadn't become Bradley's passion.

"You know men, they get into their toys and their tools. It gets carried over into the bikes. Bradley's always tinkering with the bike. You should see our garage. He's got his *Easyriders* out there too.*

He says he keeps them out there out of respect for me, but I think it's because he doesn't want me messing with them. I don't really mind that he gets them, I just don't want them in my face.

"And you should see Bradley. He walks differently when he's got on his leathers. He's more grounded. He's fashioned some of his riding gear around American Indian styles, like fringes and stitches and hides. I loved it when he made the FogHog calendar in '93. He was Mr. September. I loved it that a picture of Bradley hung in kitchens all over California.

"I remember my first time on the bike. I was really scared. I'm the daughter of a middle-class Jewish dentist and I should have married a Jewish doctor and stayed home and had babies. What am I doing being a social worker without children and riding on the back of a wild man's bike? The determining factor, I realized, was how important it was for him. It's a part of his soul. The bike, for Bradley, is very important. I'm totally terrified, but for him it's a religious experience. When I'm not up to riding, I tell him to go without me. He *needs* to ride. Biking is that important.

"What I like is sitting on the bike, hearing the motor, and traveling with a group. That part is thrilling. What turns me off is white-lining it in city traffic. Or going very fast. I do remember one time, we were riding up this mountain road, and I'm hanging onto his belt. I have no handlebars to hold onto, and we are riding up a fire road on the side of a mountain. It's a dirt road, very steep and no place to turn around. It's narrow and the road has deep grooves in it. I'm so scared that I

---

*Easyriders, a popular biker rag, is considered by most women to be among the most sexist and sleazy of the rags. Naked women draped over almost every bike part product enhances the appeal to men while it lessens it for their wives. It purports to be an "outlaw" publication introducing young men into the "biker" life but the editors could not possibly live the life they write about and still write. It's still by far the biggest and most influential Harley magazine in the industry.

close my eyes and I pray. I'm no good to him if I'm jumping around, so I close my eyes and sit very still. But I have this terror that goes up to my throat and I can't breathe. 'This is so bad,' I think, 'now I'm vulnerable.' When he had to really lean into the turn to get us off that dirt road, I knew what true terror was."

"Susan," I asked, "what are the best times?"

"When it's good, it's like someone opens the door and fresh air is rushing through your brain. It's like I've been set free. I love the mountains and the air and that's when I love riding. I don't like riding the freeways with the traffic on both sides. I keep seeing the cars getting too close, and thinking, 'There goes my legs.' But put me in Tahoe or in the mountains and I'm fine."

"Do you want to ride your own?"

"Sometimes I think that I feel scared because I'm a passenger and I have no control. Wouldn't it be nice to have my own bike? But I never took the riding class, even though I talked about it a lot. Riding is not my first love. It's Bradley's."

"Has riding changed you?"

"I feel like I've been introduced to a whole new world. I've made some wonderful friendships through it. But I was more into it at first than I am now. I have fear as well as pleasure connected to it. I love it because it is *so Bradley*. It's through him that I love it. For myself, it's not an intrinsic part of my soul. I like the gears and the sounds and the motor. I like the image and the feeling of freedom. That part is great. I like the whole Harley thing—the commitment, the mystique, the experience of camaraderie, and the friendships. I meet people I wouldn't have known any other way. They make no judgments about you. We are all in it for the sheer love of riding. It's a different kind of friendship. If I were dating a man now, I'd like him to ride a Harley. I wouldn't rule him out if he didn't, but I'd like it. If he were riding a rice rocket, I wouldn't go out with him. Rice rockets, to me, mean showboating, and I can't stand that. Harley riders love riding and being out there.

"I understand the need in a man to have that kind of experience. I dated a man who was a mountain climber once. He had the same spiritual need as Bradley. I need the kind of man who wants to take risks and be out there and be vulnerable. It's a kind of strength and it's a kind of vulnerability at the same time. It's irresistible.

"And I do think that there's a Harley connection. It taps into a spiritual connection. It's like riding with God. We are soaring with the eagles. It's how we stay in touch with the elements. I mean, there's also the dress and the attitudes and the mystique and the road code, but that's only one part of it. Riding on a Sunday with full gear and lots of friends is like going to church. It's the group's way of getting in touch with God. It puts you into the world of nature and out of this comes love and respect for the living world."

Susan is a Lady Passenger. She rides because Bradley rides. It is a spiritual connection. If they did not ride together, she would find that connection through her bicycle riding. That too puts her in the middle of the natural world. For Susan, the spiritual connection is intimately linked to the wild road, whether that road is experienced through the motorized speed of a bike or the downhill rush of a bicycle.

Bernie McKay, also a Lady Passenger, has been passengering longer than most; she started at age nineteen. She remembers her first rides. They were not with her husband, Dick, an Old Timer. One special boy-friend of her youth rode bikes. She has a lifetime of biking memories. The bike has been a part of her family for a long time.

"At first Dick didn't think I could handle long trips. I showed him. But I'm not like you. I'm not a real enthusiast the way you are. I just like to look around and relax when I passenger. I don't ever want to be the rider on the stupid thing."

"Bernie," I inquired, looking around their garage, "doesn't it bother you that Dick hangs all those pictures up in the garage? I mean, those young women are pretty naked!"

"It doesn't bother me a bit. Just because he's married, doesn't mean he can't look. Just so long as he doesn't touch, it's OK with me. He's not dead, you know. Besides, it's really the pictures of those particular bikes that he loves."

"Yeah, right!"

"No, it really is the bikes. Sometimes he wishes that the women were not plastered all over the bikes so he could see the bikes better. But even if it was the women, what do I care! Riding and being inter-ested in the bikes has kept us young. Dick's going to be seventy-two and while I'm much younger, I'm not a kid anymore. But riding keeps us young. I've seen women even younger than me act so old. You can have some life in you at any age. They should just get up and go. Riding does that for us.

"Friends used to think that this was just a stage that Dick and I were going through. Actually, not just friends, but anyone who heard about us. They would come over and say 'You! You ride a bike!' They're just sticks in the mud. They would say 'Act your age' and I would think, 'What should I be doing at my age?' I think this is great! It keeps us young. We travel with younger people, we go on a lot of friendly rides, and it keeps us spirited. But I don't like what some riders do. I don't like drinking and riding. We can have a drink or two when we get where we are going."

"What do you think about some of the new calendars showing pictures of naked men lounging over the bikes?"

"I wouldn't want to see those pictures. What do they have that I haven't already seen? Besides, I think that's as bad as having those pictures of women all over the bikes. A Harley-Davidson is a U.S.A. bike that has a lot of class. This is a machine that should be treated with respect. It's like a Rolls Royce or a Cadillac. When you put some naked person over the bike, it just cheapens it. You could do that with Jap crap, but why do it with a Harley? The bike is so beautiful, you should let it alone. The machine is a classic. The lines are beautiful just by themselves."

Bernie appreciates beautiful lines. She is an artist of local renown. As a traditional housewife responsible for the raising of the kids, the managing of the household, and the maintenance of the family, she worries about contemporary families. She was fortunate enough not to have to work continually outside the home. She could be home with her two daughters while they were growing up. She took part-time jobs when it pleased her. Dick was able to do what most working men can no longer do. He could, single-handedly, support his family. Bernie had time to develop the home arts that have been lost in most modern households. Not only is she a superb cook, but she can crochet, paint, sew, and garden, and she excels in an entire array of crafts. She's a traditional woman who can ride the back seat of a big bike with the best of them.

"Were you ever afraid?"

"Most of the time I was fine. Dick's a good rider. He has a lot of confidence in himself. I had no fear and it never bothered me even when there was a lot of wind. In the past I was never scared. But then just a few years ago, we went down. Now I'm scared to death of gravel. We were on the side of a mountain in Garberville. It was just before going into the pit at Redwood Run. We went up the side of this hill and we all hit gravel. All five of the bikes we were with. The guy in front of Dick stopped short. Dick had to stop. We lost traction. The wheels are not made for this kind of road. We went down. It scared the hell out of me. 'Hop off! Hop off!' Dick kept saying. But I couldn't. He had to get off first. I was stuck in front of the sissy bar. Dick wanted me to get off on the back but we were too close to the side of the mountain and I was filled with fear. It was a really bad experience. Now I'm always scared around gravel.

"I also don't like going around the cars in traffic. I just close my eyes, keep my head right in back of his, and pray. He goes right through. But I don't trust people in cars. They will turn in front of you and then claim that they didn't see you. We are not that small, you know. Cars scare me.

"I like the way the Harley community has changed. You meet a better type of people. I'm glad to see that most people aren't so sleazy anymore. We don't all have to have that 'bad biker' look. We don't have to wear black leather bras and black leather skirts and see-through blouses. You don't have to look like cheap sleaze. You can dress with style. You can be a classy-looking biker. As a woman, you don't have to look cheap. You can be a lady on the bike.

"I'm always a lady when I ride and it makes me mad to see how we are portrayed. How come they never put people like us in the movies? Whenever they show pictures of bikers, they always make them look like outlaws. They make it look like we are all murderers. Then people get afraid to walk into bars with bikers. But most of us don't dress like outlaws. We don't act like that either. But we are never shown on TV or in the movies. Only the bad images get shown.

"I think riding together is great. It's a good family thing. The bike has been a blessing. With the kids grown, Dick and I have time to ride and it's something we enjoy doing together."

Bernie and I often talk about the differences between passengers and riders. She tells me that she never intends to ride her own. I tease her about it because I would love for us to go for rides together. But she remains adamant about her position. She belongs in the back and she likes it.

The Passionate Passenger differs from the Lady Passenger in her passion for bikes. She is similar to the Lady Passenger in her desire for a long-term relationship with a particular rider, but unlike the Lady Passenger, she is never a fair-weather, Sunday rider. She will passenger whenever she can. Her passion often exceeds that of her lover.

Like the Biker Chick, the Passionate Passenger must depend upon some man to get her into the wind. Unlike the Lady Passenger, she desperately wants to ride the wind. This puts her into a very awkward position. When she breaks up with her biker boyfriend, she must replace him with another biker boyfriend. If she is a Harley woman, she must replace him with another Harley rider. This greatly narrows her field of available men.

Linda Davis, unlike Susan and Bernie, is a Passionate Passenger. Linda lives with an Old Biker and would rather be riding than almost anything else. After she left her last relationship, we talked about the kinds of men she might be interested in. A lot of possibilities arose. Linda was pretty open about what the guy might do for a living. She was pretty open about his age, race, class, and background. She had one criterion, however, that could not be violated. The man had to ride. As a Passionate Passenger, Linda has to get herself in the wind. As a Passionate Passenger, Linda has to be with a man who shares that passion. Linda tells her story in chapter 9.

While Biker Chicks are the most visible women in the Harley world, it is the Lady Passengers and the Passionate Passengers who make up the majority of the passengering community. While Blondie and Susan, both Lady Passengers, enjoy riding, they make it quite clear that they would not be on the bikes if their men had other hobbies. Linda, on the other hand, a Passionate Passenger, would always find a way to keep herself in the wind. Linda would find a way to ride the rear, even if she had to change men to do so.

All passengering women have much in common. All accept one very important aspect of the traditional and stereotypic position of women in society. They ride the rear. They are also marginalized in the sense that they depend upon a male rider to get them into the wind. Most passenger with men. Only a few will travel with women. Like Harley bikers, Harley passengers are mainly heterosexual.

Passengering women all share the dangers and delights of the road but are never acknowledged for their bravery. Within Harley culture, biking women are seen as adventuresome and brave. Passengering women, however, are not seen as brave. In fact, they are rarely seen at all. They are most often considered as just an appendage within the social community. Even wives of long standing remark upon their marginality. And they bitch. Yet, in many ways it is more difficult to be a passenger than it is to be a rider. Giving the responsibility for your life over to another, even a well-known other, takes immense bravery. While the passengering woman does not want the responsibility of riding her own, she does not like to have her position demeaned. She too jams the wind. She too takes her chances with the road and the animals and the weather. And her survival depends upon someone else's skill. She often rides on small, uncomfortable, and dangerous perches. She would like some respect for what she does. She rarely gets it. In the biker world, she is often seen as less than nothing. In the eyes of the rest of America she is a sexual outlaw.

Women riders, like women passengers, fall into three recognizable categories: Lady Biker, Woman Biker, and Woman Rider. None of these women can be placed within the male categories. There could possibly be a few female Old Timers left, but I have never been able to identify or interview any of them. By definition, no women riders could have been One Percenters, Ten Percenters, or Old Bikers. Those cultures did

Linda Davis (Courtesy of Linda Davis)

not permit entrance to women. A few women did ride during those male-only fifties, sixties, and seventies, but they could not have belonged to any biker group. Women riders did not join the riding ranks in any numbers until the late eighties. The loosening of gender roles, the development of the Evolution engine, and the general quest for individual freedom in an ever tightening bureaucratic society have all played a part in increasing the numbers of women who ride.

The women who ride fall into three categories: the Lady Biker, the Woman Biker, and the Woman Rider. The Lady Biker rides but does not wrench. When something goes wrong, she expects male assistance. She may ride like the wind, but she remains dependent upon men for her bike maintenance. She has no bike smarts and does not want any. She most frequently presents a sexy-looking demeanor and "plays" the female role, especially while riding the bike. She uses gender-specific behavior when riding with men. A typical Lady Biker has one or two female riding buddies, but her main riding companions are male. She makes nice. She expects male help when she needs it. And she gets it.

The Woman Biker rides and wrenches, takes care of all her own mechanical needs, and expects to be treated as an equal by men. She can tear a bike down, build it up, and participate in all aspects of bike maintenance. She asks for no special consideration and gets none. She may present a variety of demeanors, anything from sexy broad to hard-living biker, but she never makes nice. She makes a point of being straightforward and tough. She expects to be taken on her own terms and on her own merits. She does not play any female-specific role when riding. She takes pride in her rejection of female stereotypes. She takes no prisoners. Like the Lady Biker, she usually prefers to ride with men.

The Woman Rider stands midway between the Lady Biker and the Woman Biker. She rides, wrenches only a little, and expects help when serious breakdowns occur, but does not use feminine wiles to get herself out of trouble. She holds an anomalous position within the female riding world. She is neither sexy lady nor tough broad. She doesn't wrench, but she doesn't make nice either. This can present some severe problems if she's stranded on the highway. She can play female-gendered roles when necessary but chooses, most of the time, not to. While dressing with less deliberate allure than do the Lady Bikers, she does not wear chain grease with pride. Unlike the two other groups, Women Riders actually prefer to ride with other women but, like women on the road everywhere, will ride with mixed groups whenever necessary.

The following women all ride the wind.

Jayne Kelly de Lopez, lawyer, mother of six, rider, married to Pablo, is a Lady Biker. Blond, stylish, sexy, and gorgeous, she pays careful attention to her looks. While she has been riding over thirty years, she has never, ever picked up a wrench (or any other bike tool). Her first bike, a chopped Panhead, was inherited from a boyfriend. He was killed in a car accident and his father chose to give her the bike. She was pregnant with his child and needed the money. But instead of selling the bike, she decided to keep it. "It looked like fun, so I learned to ride." This was the first of Jayne's six pregnancies and her first Harley. All through her twenties she rode. She had babies and she rode. All her kids grew up with a riding mother.

"My kids ride. It scares the hell out of me, but I'm not a hypocrite. That's the hardest thing about being a parent. Not being a hypocrite! I come from a long line of brave women, even though my mother prefers not to know when I ride. I take after my aunt. At seventy-nine, for her birthday, she parachuted out of an airplane."

"Were you always so brave? What made you ride Harleys?"

"Well, there was a period in my life where I rode a Honda Interceptor. I liked it. I loved the speed. It went really fast. I also rode dirt bikes. But I got a Harley as soon as I could. As soon as I had the money, I got a new Harley.

"The Honda was just for getting around. Harleys are a way of life. You can't be a biker on a Honda or Suzuki. They just don't demand respect. Don't underestimate the intimidation factor of a Harley. Don't forget that Harleys are *the American bike*. They represent the very symbol of the pioneering spirit. They are much more than a bike. Most of the riders help one another, actually give a damn about each other, and share a common bond. That's being a Harley rider."

"Jayne, you're a big-time lawyer, for God's sake. How did you make riding such a strong part of your life?"

"I always loved being different. I grew up in New York City and all the interesting badasses rode motorcycles. I went out with lots of guys who rode. Then I met my first husband and he didn't ride. Then I met my second and he didn't ride either. Then I met Pablo. Now I represent a lot of bikers in court. I let the court know that you can be a really good parent and still be a biker."

Jayne not only rides, she has turned her riding into a personal and professional motif. Her office is filled with biking symbols and pictures. She will often ride to court hearings. She is known around town for her motorcycle ways. It's part of her image.

"Most people I know are fascinated by bikes and also terrified of them. There's something very raw, rough, and basic about biking. Most people don't want to admit to themselves that they are attracted to that kind of raw power. Bikers are raw but we are also real and direct. We are direct almost to a fault. We do not bullshit. I know that I embarrass people with my honesty.

"Harley culture is a search for community. We want adventure, a good party, acceptance by other bikers. We love living on the edge. Most people are afraid to do that. A lot of people don't want to admit that this lifestyle can be fun. Take my tattoos. I got my first one at sixteen. It's an ankle tattoo. I've turned it into an ankle tattoo bracelet and keep adding tattoo charms to it. I got my second tattoo on my ass. It's a snake and a rose. One of those long-stemmed pink rosebuds that's very pretty and very feminine, but you have to be careful, it also has thorns. I also have this rattlesnake. It demands respect but it won't strike unless you attack it first. My fourth is an eagle tattooed on my upper right shoulder. The last two were both done by Lyle Tuttle. He's great."

Jayne didn't become a lawyer until she married her second husband. As the wife of a very successful accountant, she was able to attend law school and raise children. Describing herself as ambitious and aggressive, she said she was always attracted to Harley culture.

"When I met Pablo, I knew this was it! But he was married, and I was married and it went against my politics to run around with a married man. But once I met him, I was dead. I'm dead serious, first time I met him, I fell head over heels in love and I wanted him. I couldn't wait even six months. Right after we met, I got divorced, he got divorced, and we got married. It was fast like lightning.

"I always rode, but I was not part of the biker culture until I met Pablo. It was not a major part of my life. Now I have five sons who all ride and one daughter who rides a moped. I'm very satisfied with the culture. I'm part of it. I love it. Bikers are basic people. They are direct, straightforward, and clear. Most lawyers are always full of shit. There's no honesty there. No one ever says what they are really feeling.

"One of the things I love about riding is the ability to communicate when you are on the bike. We are very approachable. Riding around here last spring, I was dressed in my biker clothes, and this nice family of yuppies walked by. The older folks were a bit wary, but the young kids smiled and said hi and gave me a wave. Especially the little girls! They love seeing a woman on a big bike.

"Another time I was riding in the city when this ancient Chinese woman came up to me and said, 'Good, very good.' We shared a wonderful moment."

Jayne rides with Pablo and in mixed groups where there are usually far more men than women.

"I haven't had much luck riding with women. Once I was riding with a bunch of women, and they left without me. Another time, I went to the bathroom for water and I was left again. I have much better luck with the guys."

Jayne with her blond hair, tricked-out bike, six kids, and biker husband is a San Francisco celebrity. She's also something of a legend.

"I do a striptease act in front of the courthouses. First I throw my riding gear into the saddlebags. Then I pull out the high heels, purse, and legal file. Next comes the makeup and hair fix. All this gets done using my rearview mirror. I do have to be careful about fixing my face before entering the courtroom. I can't let them see me with any dead bugs plastered to my forehead.

"I gotta tell you about a true story that happened to me one time in court. It started with a routine case and ended with a Wild West ride for high stakes. Winner take all.

"The trial had been going on for three days and it was bad. It was a family divorce and they were fighting over everything from the kids to the kitchen sink. It was an acrimonious, bitter battle with little kindness and less humor. We were all exhausted from the fierceness of the anger. We were down to the wire. It was late Friday afternoon. Everything had been divvied up but one remaining item. They were arguing over a grand piano. How much was it worth and who was going to get it?

"The judge was exasperated. The other lawyer and I were exhausted and it looked like this case would go on forever. The judge informed us that we would have to return Monday morning if we could not resolve this piano issue immediately. We were desperate. I looked over at the other lawyer. He's a cool guy. I knew that he rode a Harley and I also knew that he didn't let a lot of people know that he rode. He was discreet.

"'You got your Harley here?' I asked him.

"'Yeah,' he whispered.

"'What do you say we race for it,' I whispered back to him. 'Winner take all.'

"He thought I was kidding, but I told him to ask his client. He asked her. He represented the woman and I represented the man. She figured that her lawyer was an easy winner so she said, 'Yes, race for the damn piano.' My client knew that I rode, so he also said, 'Yes, race for it.'

"Then we both asked the judge. We told him that we wanted to race for the piano because it was judicially expedient. It would save our clients a lot of money if they settled the case now rather than having to return to court the following Monday. It would also be a hell of a lot more fun than further arguing. It was put into the court record. The party whose lawyer came in first would receive the piano at no cost. Winner take all. All agreed. The case would finally be over.

"The judge said there was no way he was going to miss this show so the entire courtroom emptied out to watch the match. We trooped out to the parking lot. We decided to race from one stop sign to another and back again. Fortunately for us all, there was no traffic in front of court at that time of day. Dramatically, we revved our engines. The flag was a dropping of the law files.

"It was an easy win. I was riding halfway back before the other lawyer reached the first stop sign. My client was overjoyed. The other lawyer and I gave each other high fives and the judge cracked his first smile of the day. Now any time I'm handling a difficult case, the judge will lean over and whisper to ask if I'll race for it."

Jayne is a battling lawyer and a biker with bite. She is one of the Lady Bikers who make this community so interesting.

Marjory James is also a Lady Biker. Unlike Jayne, she is a recent rider. She was comfortable on the back of her boyfriend's bike but thought it might be fun to ride her own. Now she rides a green Shovelhead that gets almost as much attention as she does. Marjory has been the poster "girl" for more articles on bikers than she can recall. With her remarkable good looks and youth, her face adorns everything from calendar pictures to local newspapers. For all of that, she is new to riding and new to the biker world. True to Lady Bikers everywhere, she uses her saddlebags to carry clothes, condoms, hairdryer, and booze. Nary a wrench in sight.

"I remember the first time, just a few years ago, I went on my first toy run. I had no idea what I was doing. I went in tennis shoes and no helmet. It was freezing. I had to borrow my date's duster just to get home. I actually started riding to please Tim. He was my boyfriend then. He bought me a big bike. While the idea of riding my own scared me, I knew the basics. But I really started because Tim wanted me to.

"Then I got into it. My ego got involved. I saw other women riding and I thought, 'If she can do it, I can do it.' But I found the bike really heavy. It was OK while I was riding, but when I had to stop, the weight was terrible. The first time I put it down, oh my God, I couldn't believe the weight. Since then I've put it down eight or nine times. I did not drop it. I laid it down. There is a difference. I only crashed it once. You remember, that time at camp."

I did remember. I remembered how scared we all were for Marjory. She was riding side by side with Tim. Suddenly she went down on a patch of gravel. She went down hard and wound up in the emergency room. She lost much of her memory, broke quite a few bones, and scared the shit out of all of us. She recovered, got back on the bike, and has her own war stories to tell.

"I got too cocky. I was riding side by side and staying too close in the turns and leaning too far over the lip of the road and finally went over onto the gravel. I saw the hole and the rock and that's it. It stopped me. The bike hit with enough force to turn the handlebars around. I remembered nothing for days afterwards. I could have broken my neck but I landed on my face. I'm still scared. The bike and I both flipped over and over, and the bike landed just inches from me. I wasn't wearing a helmet and when I got out of the emergency room, I got a ticket for going bareheaded.

"It took me six months to get back on the bike. A year later, I was riding to Bridgeport and going over all the high passes. And I'm afraid of heights. But still, there's so much I do not remember about the accident. I think that the brain really knows but fools me into forgetting. If I remembered it all, I probably wouldn't ride again.

"I love riding. Before I met Tim I didn't give a damn about bikes, but now I would ride regardless of who I was with. I like the wind through my hair, and don't forget the attention. It's great for my ego. No one ever gives me a hard time about it."

"Are other women given a hard time?"

"Some are. It all depends upon the attitude you put out. Having a Harley goes along with the attitude. I have my Harley personality. I have a closet full of Harley clothes. But I am very feminine. Even though my Harley look appears tough, I can still be girly. You know, nose in the air, aloof, ultrafeminine, acting better than everyone else. My Harley side does tend to bring me more down to earth. I am able to take care of myself, feel stronger. My Harley personality says 'I can think for myself.' I think that women get so much attention when we ride because it's like we are doing the masculine thing. It's not expected. It's expected that we will be passengers and when we're not, it's a surprise. Being a passenger is a whole different story. That's a very feminine position. You just kind of belong to the rider.

"Riding is great but it's hard. My bike vibrates a lot especially when I have to go a long distance. It's not an Evo. It's a Shovel and it vibrates like hell. But it's easy to fix on the road."

"Do you ever fix your own?"

"Are you kidding? There's always some guy around to help me if the bike breaks. And I ride mainly with men. I don't really have any female riding buddies. The guys are great to ride with and they all wrench."

Lynn Farrell is another kind of Lady Biker. A recent rider, she has the distinction of having owned and run the biggest, baddest biker bar in San Francisco. Morty's, a family-owned business, was not always a biker bar. She and her brother tried a number of different motifs before they settled on bikers.

"We tried everything. We had male strippers. We had female strippers. We had private parties. We had comedy nights and alternative theater. We had thrasher bands. We served food and, of course, there was the bar.

"One night a couple of guys showed up on their bikes. This gave me the idea to put a few flyers out at bike shops. Soon we had biker night once a month. If someone showed up on a bike, they got in without paying the cover charge. I put bike parking in front of the restaurant. I let bikers store their gear in my kitchen and use the side door.

"Soon we became known as a biker bar. We became a hangout for all kinds of bikers. Mainly Harleys but sometimes Jap bikes too. We started holding ABATE meetings there. We started political rallies from the bar and held benefits for any number of people. We did a real service for the community. We did benefits for accident victims as well as ABATE runs. I started advertising in the local newspapers. I ran ads in *Thunder Press*. That was the best deal for our money. Everyone reads *Thunder Press*. Morty's got integrated into the biker community. Through Morty's I got into the biker world. Morty's became famous.

"I would stand at the door and welcome each biker in. But I'll tell you, I was constantly doing behavioral management. Think about it. All those drunk bikers! People who drink eventually do some pretty dumb-ass stuff. I was chief bartender and bouncer.

"You saw all different kinds of people at Morty's. Mainly, though, it was neutral territory. All the clubs used it. We had many different patch holders. The H.A.'s were there in colors. So were the Survivors and the Vietnam Vets and the Iron Souls and Hells Bells. All different HOG chapters came, and even the Sons of Hawaii drank at my bar. During biker night I noticed patches from everywhere. But there was no fighting. Contrary to what everyone imagines, there were no brawls. It was very noisy—bikers are loud—but no brains were bashed. And I saw it all. The last two years I ran the whole place by myself.

"I joke about having to do behavioral management but it's true. Guys are always doing such dumb things around Hells Angels. Some stupid jerk would like go up to an Angel and pull him by the sleeve and say, 'Hey, you really a Hells Angel?' Like that's pretty dumb. The H.A.'s wearing his colors and this bozo is giving him a hard time. I was always getting in the middle of those kinds of things. Those guys have a short fuse, so I was kept really busy.

"I finally sold the place. What a relief! It feels like such a weight off my shoulders. Business was only really good on the weekends. And only ten percent of my customers drank ninety percent of the booze. Most everyone else had coffee or Calistoga. You can't stay in business with those kinds of orders.

"Besides, there's a real contradiction here. I was in the business of selling drinks. But I knew that these guys were all riding and I didn't want them to go out and ride drunk. They were all on motorcycles so I'd worry. No, I'm not sorry I sold it. I feel free."

"You do know, Lynn," I interjected, "that the whole biker community is sorry that Morty's got sold. It is no longer a biker bar. There is no place like it in all of Frisco."

"I know, but let someone else do it. I'm tired."

I visited Lynn in her small apartment in the Mission. With its beautiful yard and wonderful view, it makes a cozy San Francisco home. Besides the string of crescent-shaped lights running over her living room window, she has a great string of red heart-shaped lights framing her bed in the adjoining room. This was clearly a woman's living space filled with a mixture of the intimate and the practical. The computer in the kitchen balanced the biker pictures in the living room. Lynn is not an old-time rider. Lynn is a novice, and I immediately sympathized with her learning pains. Having already been in an accident on her 883 Sportster, she was slowly making her way back from a broken arm and bruised confidence.

"I never used to like bikes. Back in high school, I thought that all bikers were scum. If someone had said, even five years ago, that I would be riding my own bike and be secretary of a local club, I'd have said they were crazy.

"But one day at Morty's, while we were still looking around for the right clientele, this drop-dead gorgeous biker comes in. Five minutes later his rider girlfriend joins him. I look at her and I think, 'If she can do it, so can I. If she can ride, I can too.' She wasn't super big or strong or muscular. She looked like the girl next door. And I thought, 'Yes, I can do this.'

"And then I thought, 'I really like these people. I want to hang around with them.' I wanted to go to the events, but I could never find the right person to take me. I wanted to passenger but I couldn't find the right rider."

"Lynn, you've got to be kidding."

"No, I couldn't get a date out of Morty's. Either I'm butt ugly or the guys were just too intimidated to date the owner."

Far from being butt ugly, Lynn, in her mid-forties, is sexy, appealing, and very comfortable with her looks. This is a woman who never lacks for male companionship. In fact, her motto is, "If you can rope me, you can ride me."

"You mean you never passengered with anyone?"

"Well there was this one biker. One guy I did meet at Morty's. He was a good rider but he scared the shit out of me. He had an FXR that went like a rocket. No sissy bar on the back. It was scary as shit. I remember one night we were riding together and he stopped the bike and told me that I wasn't riding the right way with him. He said that I had to cram myself right up behind him like we were glued together. Then when he leaned I had to lean with him all the way. I was like a monkey on his back. Then we rode. He went over steep grades, around buses, white-lining it everywhere. It was so scary. I thought, 'He's gonna kill us both!' He was right about one thing. I did need to ride my own. I needed to get myself to the events."

Lynn was outspoken about her riding problems in a way that is foreign to most riders. She didn't hide, mask, or downplay her fears. She let it all hang out.

"I think there are a lot of women like me. I'm scared shitless. Lots of times when I ride I think, 'I'm gonna die—Oh God, I'm gonna die! Why am I out here doing this? Am I crazy?' I know women who get diarrhea every time they go on a ride. I know myself, the night before a run, I don't sleep. Will it be windy? Will the weather be unbearable? What if it rains? Then I think, 'Yes, yes, let it rain. Then I don't have to go on this run.'"

"Does your daughter ever get upset with your riding? Does she get scared for you and want you to stop?"

"My daughter Chandra calls me biker mom. She's twenty-two and she would like to ride but I would kill her if she tried. She's got a kidney transplant and she's just too vulnerable. She wants to ride but her immune system isn't up to it. There would be too much stress on her if she rode. But she's OK with me riding. She doesn't worry about me on my Harley. I've always been kind of wild."

"Since you're a novice rider," I asked, "how do you get to all the different events? I'm still scared to ride any long distances. I've just learned to deal with bridges and tunnels, but my maximum mileage is about 150 miles a day."

"Oh, that's not hard, I trailer my bike to the different events and ride when I get there."

"Do you ever get any flak for that?"

"I used to but now I tell them to fuck off. Last time I looked, this was still America. If I want to trailer my bike, I will. I'm a charter member of WHORE. That's *We Haul Our Rides Everywhere*."

Lynn appreciates her position as a Lady Biker. She makes it abundantly clear that there is no grease under her fingernails. She calls herself a lipstick biker.

"To hell with all that dust and dirt and wind and bugs in your teeth shit. I'm a fair-weather rider. Riding in the rain is too risky and I can't stand the wind. I need optimal weather to ride. I really respect women like Marjory and Jayne but I never push myself the way they do. I may be envious of them but I don't want to be like them.

"My favorite ride is the Laughlin River Run. That's just over the border in Nevada. All the Hollywood types show up. It's all glitzy and social and filled with celebrities. It's *the* celebrity run. I love all the bikes too. They are so beautiful. Almost all of them are trailed in. People down there don't ride their bikes, they trailer them. They only take them out to ride down the strip. They wouldn't take a chance on their bikes getting dirty.

"And we stay at the best hotels. That's the kind of run I like. Everyone looks so good, all dressed up like that. Remember I don't rough it. I don't do campouts. It's camping to me when there is no mint on my pillow. But then again, I grew up in Marin. All you city folk seem to need to camp out because you grew up in concrete. I'm used to nature. We had a whole backyard full of it."

We talked about the things she's seen during her ownership of Morty's. She knows the biker world. She had a lot to say.

"You know what pisses me off? I get so tired seeing women on TV always getting stereotyped on those shows. The biker-chicks-from-hell type of shows. Like that's all we are. It gets me mad.

"But I also get mad at lots of women in the biker community too. I have a problem with the Women Bikers. They are tough broads. They are hard cases. I get really fed up with them always trying to be so politically correct. It's so boring. Last year at the Love Run, one of those broads had a fit because some of the girls were showing their tits. She said, 'That's what I hate. I've fought so long to change all that. It's disgusting.' Screw her. If a girl wants to show her tits, that's her business. I say if someone wants to show her tits, that's her right. I can't stand this politically correct shit. Maybe those tough broads can make some new kinds of rules but they don't have to put down the old ones. Those women have too much testosterone for their own good.

"I think that I'm an artistic, fun-loving, intelligent, feminine woman. I am a sexy girl too. I like it. I don't want to be seen as a grease-under-the-fingernails, cigarette-puffing, masculine, foul-mouthed woman. Some of these tough broads are testosterone laden.

"But I'm not a bimbo. Being feminine has nothing to do with being a bimbo. There are bimbos everywhere. They are in every community. I just like to be around men. I really like being around the guys. I am real flirtatious.

"I love riding, but the bike is not the major part of my identity. It's

113

not my center. It's not my core. I like to go to the events but I am not attracted to most of the men there. I especially don't like the ones who are as greasy as their bikes. I want someone who can get dressed up and go anywhere. 'Cause I can. I want someone who is socially presentable with a lot of ambition. I want someone who is busy doing his own thing and leading his own life. Oh, and he has to have money. And be good in bed too.

"I like having relationships with bikers, but if I met a guy who I really loved and he said *get off the bike*, I would. I've been single for years. Not that I've had a lack of sexual partners. I'm a sex goddess, as you can see. Yes, you can put that down. But I do not want any commitments. I like going around with all these cute young men. Just no commitments please."

Since Lynn and I differed on this major point, I asked again about her choices. She resolutely refused to form a single lasting relationship. In spite of her lip service to true love and her willingness to leave the bike for a guy, she doesn't seem ready to settle down. She says she sees too much of men at Morty's to think too highly of them.

"Men are scum. Don't you know that? They all think with their dicks. They see something they like and their dicks get hard. They all fool around. They are all unfaithful bastards."

Lynn says this, then laughs. She speaks with the easy voice of a woman who loves men both because of and in spite of their behavior.

"Lynn, how can you say that? There are lots of faithful guys."

"Bullshit. Trust me. All men fool around. They may say they don't, but put any one of them in the right circumstance where a woman comes on to them and they will. Especially if they think no one will ever find out. I told you, men are scum."

Again she laughs. Without a man around, Lynn would be like a fish without water. Men are her medium. She gets off on the attention, the affection, the energy, and the sex.

"I know. I get approached all the time. All the guys love to come on to me. I must be putting out those pheromones. When I'm in a serious relationship they come on to me less often, but even then it happens. And those guys are all married too. Their wives would shit if they knew about it."

"OK, Lynn, I'll concede this point. I do know that lots of times I'll go into a bar and see Ken surrounded by a number of groupies and I get pissed off. So I just elbow my way in, take his arm, and make it real plain that we are a couple."

"That's just my point. He wouldn't move if you didn't wade in after him. I'll bet you go to all the big events too. Just so he won't be available to other women."

"A lot of the time, sure."

"I told you, all men are scum. We shouldn't have to watch them all the time. That's why I'd rather just fool around and have fun."

Lynn has lived a number of lifestyles in a number of places. She has always been comfortable around alternative cultures. It has been her preference.

"I'm very straight you know. I do no drugs and I don't drink. And that's pretty funny 'cause I am always around people who do both. I used to be a radical in the sixties. But as I get older, I find myself changing politically. I am almost a Republican now. I used to think that bikers were really radical people. When I found out how conservative they were, it surprised me. Especially when I read all the ABATE literature and how they are backing so many Republicans for office."

"But that makes sense, Lynn. The Republican party does claim that it stands for independence and self-help and small not big government. Bikers like that. Not to mention, more Republicans are for gun ownership and against the helmet laws than Democrats."

"Sometimes it's really hard to make some political choices," Lynn continued. "Like what to do if the candidate is antihelmet, which is good, but is also antiabortion, which is bad. I can't understand how a party that says it's for independence and individual freedom can be against abortion and a woman's right to choose.

"I do like the changes that I've seen in the biker community. At Morty's I've seen it all. There is a new commercialism among the new riders. Lots of people ride now because they want to be part of the culture. Having a Harley is having a ticket to the party."

"What if you were living with a guy who rode? Would you have been content to remain a passenger?"

"I think that I would still have wanted to ride my own. I don't think the guys really like hauling someone around all the time. Also I would want to see if I could do it. I still would want to get my own bike. I need the freedom to act as I please. At the last Love Run when Bruce Springsteen was performing, I threw my bra on stage. Then I flashed every one. I love the culture. I like the bikes. But my major hobby is men."

While there are remarkable differences between these women, differences of age, temperament, achievement, and choices, there are also similarities. Each Lady Biker expects to play gender-specific roles. She uses her dependence upon men to get herself out of a jams. If her bike breaks, she expects a man to fix it. When the times get tough, she says "Help!" And, of course, she gets it.

Women Bikers differ from Lady Bikers in some critical ways. The first is attitude and the second is mechanical ability. Women Bikers expect to be treated as equals on the road. They do not look to men to bail them out of difficult situations. And, of course, they wrench.

Sherry Terpstre is a Woman Biker. She rode the day after she had her baby. When questioned about how she felt, she answered with only one word: "Sore."

Nicknamed Shovelhead Sherry, she rides a 1974 FXD Shovelhead, one of the rare Harleys that have both an electric and a kick start. "It fires up nice," she remarked, "but it must be tuned up real good to turn over on the first kick."

In an interview in *Hogpen* (December 1994), the newsletter of the northern Nevada HOG, she talked about her life and her riding. For family she counts two sons. For pets, a lot of tree-eating gophers, a couple of rattlesnakes, and all the crows that eat her fruit. She lives on a twenty-acre Silver Springs ranch where "the women are tough and the men good-looking." But she can't find any, she notes. She is an impressive six feet two inches tall. She claims that she can always touch the ground when seated on her Harley—an ability a lot of women wish they possessed.

Always a Harley enthusiast, she fell in love with bikes the day her older sister started dating a biker. He arrived for the date dressed in slicks, the greasy pants of an experienced mechanic. He took her for a ride. The next day he came back dressed up. He had cut his hair, slipped into a suit and tie, and come to court her sister. "It must have worked," Sherry recalled. "She married him."

Her brother-in-law taught her about bikes. He taught her respect for the machinery. He taught her to wrench. She learned how to change points, fix a tire, and build and rebuild her bike as many times as it needed. For parts she uses her '49 Chevy truck. She's been riding and wrenching for twenty-five years.

She's heard, more than most riding women, the very mixed compliment offered by men when they wish to present high praise. She's been told that she "rides like a man."

Like Shovelhead Sherry, Pat Tompkins is a Woman Biker. In her early forties, she's been riding for over twenty years. She started riding for the very best of reasons. As she puts it: "I got tired of kissing a guy's ass just to get a ride. One of the guys promised he'd give me a ride if I did his laundry. Another asked for something else. I said, 'Fuck you, I'll get my own bike.' And I did. I got a '61 Panhead.

"I just got on the bike. No classes. Nothing! I had been riding behind friends so I knew how bikes worked. Next bike was a Sportster. I bought this one 'cause my next boyfriend had a problem with my riding. The Sportster was less intimidating than the Pan. Eventually I married the guy and gave up the bike. He never loved it. He just used it. So the bike went. For fifteen years I stayed with that man. When we split, I was devastated.

"After about three months, I looked around to see what would make me happy. He left in April and by June I was looking around to see what I wanted to do. It took me a couple of months to be brave enough to say, 'Yeah, I can get my life back.'

"I took a friend to Michaels' in Santa Rosa, you know, the Harley shop there, and he rode some bikes around the block. My friend was a mechanic and I trusted him. This time I bought an '88 Sportster.

"And I practiced, and I practiced, and I practiced. It took me six months of riding alone before I felt ready to ride with anyone. It took six months before I felt that I could handle the bike. Initially, I was scared. But I respected the bike. It was tougher than I was. All those married years I wanted to ride and didn't. Now I could. I traded him for the motorcycle. I should never have chosen him in the first place. I should have chosen the bike. All that time I was being someone I'm not. Never again. I can't be something I'm not.

"When I started riding there were only a few women riding. I wore no helmet and had two long braids and wore headbands. In those days, the guys were really resentful. Once at a stop sign, my bike went over. Some guys came over and stood around watching me try to get the bike up. They didn't even help. Finally I got the bike on its wheels and the guys just stood around and smirked. Then the bike was flooded so it took the next half an hour kicking it to start it.

"Mostly I ride alone or with close friends. Most are men. I've been around bikers all my life. These people you meet at HOG meetings are not bikers. They ride Harleys but they are not bikers. Bikers ride. Bikers always ride. Cars are never the first or the best option. I ride in the rain. I don't like it, but I ride. Riding lets me let go of all the other pressures in life. It presents a whole different reality. I lose myself in it.

"Like I said, those HOG members aren't bikers. They don't know the first thing about motorcycles. I don't respect guys who don't understand their own bikes. I have some pride 'cause I work on my own bike. I know how a bike should be fixed. Even if someone else has to work on my bike, I stay with it. I am always learning.

"The bikers I grew up with had to learn to fix their own. If you don't have a lot of money, you learn and love doing it or you stop riding. More than one time, I've been riding with the guys and I'm the first one under the bike wrenching. The guys I ride with are no longer intimidated by this."

Pat doesn't ride with just anyone. She's real careful about her companions. It's part of her respect for herself and her bike and part of her feelings about riding.

"I want to know the skill level of anyone I ride with. I say 'Show me!' I can prove my skill, now prove yours. The guys I ride with can fix their own. That's why I prefer to ride with them. I know some women who ride, but I usually like the way the guys ride."

As a computer consultant who owns her own company, Tompkins West, Pat is used to being very direct and making big decisions. She makes her own money, makes her own way, and takes no shit. She would not be with a man who did not ride.

"I don't want anyone to adapt to my lifestyle. I don't want to adapt to any guy's way of living either. Any guy I go out with has to ride, and ride a Harley."

"Don't you think this is a bit extreme?"

"No, not at all. If he didn't ride a Harley, he wouldn't understand my obsession. I love Harleys. I've never ridden a dirt bike. I've never ridden for speed or status. I love to cruise. I've never even been on a Japanese bike. I love how a Harley sounds. The louder the better. The rumblier the better. I like the feel of the bike. I also like the attention that a big, loud motorcycle gets. I'd be lying if I said I didn't like the attention.

"But most of all I require respect. I am not an airhead. I take pride in my skills. There is substance there. I'm not just some woman who wants to look good on a bike. My ex wanted me to go around in dresses and six-inch heels and play the airhead. That's bullshit. You are whatever you want to be, but you are also what you wear. That ex of mine wanted me to act in ways that just aren't me. Lots of guys like the idea of an airhead woman. You know, the guys who fall all over themselves when Ms. Harley-Davidson comes into a room. They all rush to get the door for her or get her autograph. I mean, will you guys get a grip? Get a grip on your dicks for God's sake."

Pat was clear about what she liked in men, bikes, and behaviors.

"I like guys who can get dirty. Suits are not sexy to me. I grew up in Alaska and I like things pretty natural. What could be better than dirt? It washes off. When I'm working on the bike, I'm covered with grease all the time. And I'm happy."

During this interview, one of her boyfriends who was with her at the time couldn't resist adding a comment: "You'd see her come in all covered with dirt and sweat from some bike she was fixing. How could you not love a woman who's covered with dirt and soaking wet!"

While she was sergeant-of-arms of a local HOG chapter, she had quite a lot to say about the membership. Sergeant-of-arms is traditionally a male position. It's usually taken by someone very big, very strong, and very tough. The main role is that of bouncer, law keeper, and knife holder, and Pat's ability to win and hold the position was a

118

first. Pat isn't quite as tall as she looks. At five foot ten, she appears bigger. Even though she is slender, she casts a large shadow.

"Most of the guys in this group are wannabes. You know, weekend warriors. They dress in the Harley regalia but it's really playing dress up. They've got the bike, but something's not right about this picture. They can barely turn their bikes around. They just go to rallies to hang out. They are not there to ride. They are a bunch of dweebs. These HOG groups are not bikers at all. They ride Harleys but not one of them knows their way around a wrench. The people I ride with can wrench. Maybe some of the HOG guys will learn and that will be good. Good things can happen.

"One of the good things that has happened lately is that we all go to coffee houses instead of bars. It's a blast. Here are all these big, bad bikers looking for the best espresso in town. It's a good thing too. I've seen a lot of bad stuff happen when you drink and ride. Since most of the guys I ride with have blue-collar jobs, drinking used to come with the territory. But we now go to coffee bars."

Pat talked about Women Bikers, women's role in the biker community, relations with LOH, and her ideas about femininity.

"When my bike broke down in Mexico, I had to ride the back seat to go and get help. It was very uncomfortable. In general, I wouldn't be comfortable riding on the back at all. I know too much. I want to be in control, be in command of the bike and my own destiny. If I am going to crash, I'm going to do it.

"I never liked LOH. Ladies of Harley! What is that? It's separatist. We don't have a Gentlemen of Harley. There are no Men of Harley. I ride. Guys ride. What's the difference! I just want it to be equal. I don't want to belong to a separate group. I've worked all my life just to be equal. When you go to a run and you see a wet T-shirt contest, I want the guys to take their pants off and have a wet whatever contest. I don't want to keep separating the sexes. The guys have such a hard time understanding this.

"Femininity is such a hard thing to define and even harder to deal with. Society defines feminine as having qualities of weakness and gentleness. It's also seen as being delicate. By those standards I am not feminine. But I believe that society has an antiquated definition. I believe that that's the definition applied over a generation ago and it does not apply now. Women in our generation have redefined what we are and what we are supposed to do. We are who we want to be. We are moving away from set roles and labels. We can define ourselves as we wish. The genders have moved closer together. We can all be aggressive and straightforward about our sports and about ourselves.

"Twenty years ago, women like me were automatically assumed to

119

be dykes. In fact, a few of my girlfriends and I used to joke about it. When ever we went into Dudley Perkins, we knew the guys were all taking bets on whether or not we were lesbians.

"Guys see a strong, independent woman who also is a good biker, and they don't know what to think so most of them jump to the conclusion that we must be dykes. I have a lot of friends who are gay. Who you sleep with has nothing to do with riding a bike. Old antiquated labels again. No basis in reality. It shouldn't matter if I was or wasn't a dyke. That shouldn't have anything to do with how I ride. The statement you make in a bedroom has nothing to do with the statement you make on a bike. I don't fit the definition of how they think a heterosexual woman should act. But who cares! I am not delicate, weak, or modest. By that definition, I am not feminine. But screw that definition. By my own definition I am. Feminine is just being yourself. Not playing any role, not turning people off by your aggressiveness but being aggressive if you want. If you respect people, you won't turn them off. If you turn out to be competent and aggressive it's OK. Both genders carry characteristics of both masculine and feminine traits.

"In the past, women weren't allowed to show their masculine side. Men weren't allowed to show their feminine side. But now both men and women can show both sides of their personalities. To do anything less is to compromise yourself. All of us are people who have many, many facets. Don't tell me that I'm accepted. Show me!"

Pat and Sherry aren't the only Women Bikers I talked to. Lynn Walker, although different from Sherry and Pat, is in her own way a Woman Biker.

"I'm a lesbian. I'm afraid that I'm going to fit the stereotype of the lesbian with the motorcycle. The first lesbian I met in college had a bike, so I thought, 'Ah ha, that's what lesbians do, they ride bikes.' When I came out, I got a bike.

"I was nineteen when I decided that I was a lesbian. One month later I bought a 350 Honda. I found that I really liked to ride. It's so easy—you just jump on the bike and go. Besides, it fitted into my image of the lesbian biker. A woman who was strong and independent. Also, living in the city it was the perfect transportation. No traffic jams to worry about. No problems about parking. In Europe it's seen as normal transportation. Everyone has a bike or a moped. It's economical.

"Of course, there are so many different types of riders and they all have different images. There's the whole James Dean Hollywood image. Then there's the outlaw types and all the different classes of motorcycles riders. Everything from the crotch rocket eighteen-year-olds to the Hells Angels. Then there's the HOG chapters and then there are the big butch leather dykes. And, of course, now there's the techno-rider. People who are into the science of riding. Lots of BMW people are in this category. Those people are into technology and data processing. Since I ride both my Harley and my BMW, I seem to fall into two groups. The BMW crowd is more yuppie and, unlike Harley yuppies, these folk like to ride. They are definitely the Silicon Valley. But we all love those curvy roads and like to go as fast as we can.

Someone once said that the difference between a Harley run and a Beemer run is that Harley folk ride to the run to party. Beemer folk ride to the run to ride. For the BMW crowd the run is only the start of the next ride.

"Harleys are for cruising. On a Harley you ride down the highway fast as long as you are going in a straight line. But forget about the curves. My Softail is customized a lot. I lowered it and raked it. It handles well on the freeway. It sounds good, looks great, and I look hot in all my fringe leathers. It's a great image.

"Harley culture is something you can wear like a hat. I think Milwaukee has done brilliant marketing. They tell everyone that when you buy a Harley you not only get a motorcycle, you get companionship, a group to ride with, a lifestyle to enjoy. You get all that and instant friends. You get to look cool too. The fact that everyone can customize their Harleys just the way they want them speaks to the desire for individuality and similarity at the same time. It's also going to the extreme. Let's face it, Harleys are extreme.

"I ride a bike that matches my style. I don't define myself as masculine or feminine. Everything is relative. I prefer, as a lesbian, more feminine women, but I wouldn't say that I feel butch. Even though I wear leathers, ride motorcycles, have tattoos and all that, I don't conjure up the picture of a butch when I think about myself. I'm just me. No labels."

Lynn Walker, Woman Biker, rides and wrenches. She prides herself on her ability to do both. The women in the next group do only one of these activities. They ride. They are the most recent additions to women in the wind. They are Women Riders. They have something in common with both Lady Bikers and Women Bikers. Like Lady Bikers, they do not wrench. Unlike Lady Bikers, they do not make nice to get their bikes fixed. Like Women Bikers, they want to be treated as equals. Unlike Women Bikers, they are unable to repair their own bikes. They fit somewhere between the two other groups.

Sharon Turner epitomizes the Woman Rider. Self-sufficient, competent, and independent, when not riding she works as an operating-room nurse in a VA hospital. She knows bikers (literally) inside and out. She is so committed to riding that she does not own a car. Rain,

Sharon Turner (Courtesy of Sharon Turner)

wind, sun, or fog, she rides to work on her '93 Softail Custom. Blond, slender, and soft looking, she does not fit the stereotype of a serious biker. Sharon, however, is a serious rider. She travels both long and short distances on her bike and has passed on her love of riding to her oldest child, her daughter Heather. This year, they are riding to Alaska.

"I thought I hated motorcycles when I first saw them. I thought they were dangerous, ugly, and not any part of my lifestyle. I did not know anyone who rode except for my daughter's boyfriend (when they were both sixteen), and that was not a relationship I encouraged.

"Then this young man came to show Heather his new Kawasaki, but she was not home. He was so pleased with the bike he offered to give me a ride. To my enormous surprise, I accepted the ride and loved it. It was exhilarating. It gave me a wonderful feeling to have all that air in my face. It was so exciting it brought back the memories of how much fun I used to have when I rode my little moped.

"After a few more rides, I decided to get my own bike. I did not want to passenger. Since I couldn't ride, when I finally did buy my 650 Honda I needed Heather's boyfriend to pick up the bike and ride it home. After that, we would drive to a safe area and he would sit be-hind me while I learned to ride. I never did take a class. I just practiced by myself until I got it. Many, many miles of practice later, I made it to a highway. Since I never knew anyone my age who rode, I always rode alone. I remember I had just turned forty when I rode from Redding to the coast and back. It was a weekend ride. I found it amazing.

"Believe it or not, I used to think of myself as a very dependent person. I always lived with someone. I was never really on my own. There were the kids and several husbands. I was always with others. Someone was always around to tell me what to do. I saw myself as a wife and devoted mother, dutifully taking care of my family.

"When I moved to San Francisco, after my kids were grown and my first marriage was over, I put my bike away. Then I married Jim, my second husband, and he did not ride. He refused to have anything to do with the bike. Besides, the hills in San Francisco seemed a little intimidating.

"When Jim and I split up, I finally got back on my motorcycle. I joined the SRRA [Sierra Road Riders Association] and started riding with them. I wanted a bigger bike and began to look around. Right away I liked the sound and the looks of the Harley. I liked it that all kinds of people rode them. The BMW, which I also considered, didn't have the sound or the feel of a Harley. They also didn't look comfortable for touring. I knew that I wanted to tour. When I felt that I was ready for a bigger bike, I knew it would be a Harley."

Sharon rides but she does not wrench. She can do small things like change a battery or a tire, but that's pretty much it. When she bought her Harley, she joined the Golden Gate Chapter of HOG.

"I loved the meetings in the basement of DP [Dudley Perkins]. I loved sitting among all those bikes. It made those meetings special."

"Do you consider yourself a biker?"

"I would never call myself that. I do consider myself an enthusiast. Bikers are, you know, the ones who carry chains and have tattoos all over their bodies, like in *The Wild One*. But I am part of Harley culture. Harley culture is made up of all those people who know how wonderful it is to be in the saddle of a really good bike. I even considered joining a few other groups."

"What happened?"

"I went to a meeting of SFMC and I was the only woman there. I know that there are women members, but the night I was there, there was only me. It felt very male and very exclusionary. I felt that it was a male fraternity, with a no-women-allowed atmosphere."

"What about your daughter riding? I know your son doesn't ride, but Heather does. Do you feel uncomfortable about it?"

"As a mother, I get nervous sometimes. But other times it's great. I do get very concerned for her safety. Actually, I get more concerned for hers than for my own. But I feel confident of her riding abilities. I know that it is an awesome responsibility. But here I am, I ride. How could I want to deny that to her?"

"Do you feel feminine when you ride? You ride a big bike. Is that ever an issue?"

"I see myself as feminine. To me that means I enjoy the feminine side of myself. I enjoyed all the nurturing parts. I liked being a wife and I liked being a mother and raising kids. I do not see riding as being inconsistent with being feminine.

"Out there on the road, I see lots of men and they are always very helpful and concerned and kind. This is their way of taking care of their feminine side. They wouldn't see it that way, but I do. I feel that I can express my feminine side by all the nurturing I still do. And I can express my masculine side when I am out there on the road riding my motorcycle. I'm taking the bull by the horns, so to speak, and the bike by the handlebars. I need to take care of both sides of my personality.

"I do really wish that there were more women riders. You do see more women riding all the time, but I'd like to see women my age riding. Since I just turned fifty, I notice that most of the riders are younger. If older women could just shake loose some of their old attitudes about riding, they would have a grand time.

"Women get hung up a lot. Most women don't have the moxie to just get on a bike. Women need to learn to take control of their lives. Older women are very dependent and give up a lot for men. They let men make their choices for them. So many women are just too timid and too intimidated to do what they want to do. They wait for permission to do what they want. And you know that most men will never give their wives permission to ride a motorcycle.

"For these women, life is just going to pass them by. One day they will look back and be sorry for all the opportunities they missed. They will be sorry that they did not take their chances. There is a wonderful quote on my refrigerator door and I truly live by it. It says: 'A person will be called to account on judgment day for every permissible thing that he or she might have enjoyed but did not.' I love that saying. I truly do. Life is meant to be lived and for me that includes riding my bike."

Sharon Turner started riding in her thirties. Debby Lindblom, also a Woman Rider, has been riding since she was twelve. She juggles home, kid, husband, law career, and riding into one very crowded life. She is also the inspiration behind many riding women. As an LOH officer one year, she was personally responsible for helping seven women learn to ride. Between practice rides, baby runs, and scoots to munch and brunch, we were cajoled, teased, pulled, and blackmailed into riding. Debby has so much personal charisma, clout, and spirit that we all fell into line when she organized an outing. If it were not for her, half the women I interviewed would not be riding today. She is a woman to be reckoned with. We sat in her apartment, strewn with children's toys, as we poured our ice water from her famous refrigerated vodka bottle. When I first walked in, Debby welcomed me with the most astounding greeting.

"You look like a big-bike woman now!"

"What?"

"You have the look of a woman who rides a big bike. It took you a long time to look like that. You must be really loving your Low Rider."

"Deb, what the hell are you talking about?"

"It's wonderful. It's your personal bike power. It's in your face and the way you move and the way you wear your jacket. It's the set of your forehead and the firmness of your step. You have a biker's face. I wouldn't mess with you. There's a real tangible difference. You're a woman with a big bike. You are out of your riding adolescence and ready for your Low Rider."

"Well, I have made a quantum leap. I can now go over bridges and under tunnels, and the bike feels right. I think I have become that most disgusting of creatures, a *big-bike chauvinist*. When I rode my Sportster, I hated big-bike chauvinists. But now that I own my own Big Twin, I can really appreciate the difference. This bike is so steady and strong. It makes all the difference in the world."

"You are right. Harleys are perfect and now that you are a Big Twin rider, you won't ride anything else."

For many long moments, Debby and I traded tales, gossiped about old friends, listened to each other's domestic stories, and talked bikes. She had just returned from Bridgeport and was truly troubled. She had had one of those riding experience that most of us dread. It happens, but we all dread it.

"I had my first roadkill. It wasn't on the freeway but on the top of a mountain pass. I was winding around the curve on this two-lane road when I killed my first critter. It was a little chipmunk. This chipmunk was in its own world. I was the intruder. The critter was just using its own paths, enjoying its own life, not aware of me at all and I killed it.

"There I was, riding in the natural world, in the middle of Mother Nature and feeling very lucky to be there and lucky to have the ability to reach that world, and I killed an animal in its own home. I am a murderer. I killed somebody in its home. After that I felt haunted. You know the biblical injunction 'an eye for an eye.' It would have been justice if I'd died too. So I am going to stay off the bike for a while."

"Deb, this is terrible."

"I heard the sound of its death. Both wheels bumped over it. I had a hard time making it home. I was the intruder, the invader."

"Motorcycles permit you to get the awesome sense of Mother Nature." I was agreeing with her. "No question about it. All bikers get close to the natural world. We all love it. Some of us don't talk about it, but we all feel it. But our love and respect for the world of nature has its painful price. The price is roadkill."

"Eventually bikers get callous over roadkill. Most have to or we'd feel guilty all the time. But right now, it still feels terrible."

Debby then began to talk about her background and how she came to biking.

"I had all the small-town advantages. You know, the nice house, clothes, food, piano and ballet lessons, sit-down dinners at home. It was a real stable environment. But it was a small town. In many ways we lived in complete ignorance of the outside world. We were isolated. I grew up so internal, I didn't perceive the real world for a long time. I was a dreamer. I was not a very social person. I never had more than one or two good friends at one time. They didn't know any more than I did.

"Then I got pregnant. In very short order, I was thrown out of high school, forced to marry, and moved to another town. Everyone told me I was a failure. They said I would never amount to anything. I was pregnant at fifteen, married at sixteen, and divorced at twenty-one. All I kept hearing was: 'Oh, what a pity,' 'Such promise!' and then the ever-present 'Oh what a slut!'

"I wound up in a miserable marriage, on welfare (both with and without him), homeless, and finally sheltered in a housing project with an infant. But I had the American Dream. I really did. You know, 'Anybody can become anything in America.' I believed it. I wanted to become a lawyer. And I did.

"One step at a time I did my dream. I worked. I managed. I did manual labor. I waitressed. I took any and all kinds of jobs. I paid my dues. I paid my bills. I got into college and eventually, I got into law school. Everyone had said that my life was over. That's bullshit. But I bought into the system enough to want to prove them wrong.

"I also owe a lot to the times. It was the seventies in Northern California. It was the age of self-help. There was self-enlightenment and opportunity. So when my daughter Jennifer was nine, I went to San Francisco to start the long journey through school. In 1988 I graduated

Hastings Law School. It was a proud moment. It was also a poignant one. I worked graveyard shifts, doing security, while attending law school. This degree did not come easy or cheap. I always appreciate my education, but I am constantly aware of what I had to go through to get it."

Debby now works in a law firm that values her not only for her competence and skill but for her sensitivity and humanness. She has the kind of client rapport that comes from experience. She has been there. She knows about hard times, adversity, and triumph. When asked about her riding she grew enthusiastic.

"I knew right away that I wanted to be a rider. I am a terrified passenger. I have never passengered for more that two miles total. So for me, it was rider or nothing.

"I started with a 250cc bright yellow scooter. I had been on a Honda 50 but that was when I was a kid. I took the learn-to-ride course 'cause I wanted to learn how to shift. With the scooter, shifting isn't necessary. But my goal was to get a Harley. I rode every day. I took that scooter out in rain and sun and I rode until I felt comfortable. Then I started shopping for a motorcycle. I went to Dudley's every day but they didn't have just the right bike for me. Then a friend in Modesto found the bike I wanted. It was an '87 Sportster and I bought it outright. For a while, it stayed in Modesto.

"For months I traveled to the bike to ride. There was no real traffic and I practiced and practiced and finally, three months later, I rode the bike home to San Francisco. I pushed myself. As soon as I got home from work I would get on the bike and practice. Thank God for the FogHogs and [Mike] Molinari and your husband Ken and Dick Croft. All those folks were so supportive. They took me under their wing. Remember when Ken rode with me all the time? I would go so slow on the road, but he would stay right with me to make sure that I was all right."

I did remember. Ken would ride with Debby as his road buddy. Ken rode slow enough to keep Debby secure. This kept me secure. Since at that time I was passengering, I had a real vested interest in his going slow.

Debby, during her two-and-a-half-year tenure as an LOH officer, sparked dramatic and radical changes in the organization. She sponsored so many rides, drives, events, parties, and meetings that we all needed a separate calendar just to plot our LOH activities. She bullied us into riding. She made us face the wind and ride the back roads, and finally she led us out onto the freeways.

"I loved LOH. I loved the women. It was a female society. What a hunk of power. It was wonderful. All those fantastic women. The realness of those women. The companionship. The directness. All of it. The women were so open and genuine and real. No one pretended to be anything they were not.

"They were women for themselves. They were not being women for men. I'm not talking about sexual preference. I'm talking about personality. Some of the women were lesbians. Most of the women were not. All the women were strong and brave and up-front. It was the power of the women that made me want to come back to the FogHogs. I signed up for life membership.

"The newsletter also affected me a lot. I had never read anything so unedited and open. When the conflicts between the old timers and new people arose, the newsletter covered it all. It was like a family working out its problems and accepting all opinions. And God knows all the opinions were in there. I also loved writing for the newsletter and since you and Ken edited it, I could always get published."

Debby made a big and lasting impression on the both LOH and the newsletter. But she would have ridden with or without the organizations.

A year and a half after joining the FogHogs and LOH and buying her Low Rider, Debby married Usaia. She did not give up riding. Usaia, who was from Fiji, was not used to motorcycles. He rode on the back of her bike to a number of runs but it was clear from the start that he would have preferred to ride his own. Debby rode a big bike, but Usaia is well over six foot and needed more space.

"I rode after I returned from Fiji. I kept riding two months later when I got pregnant. I rode all through the pregnancy. I remember riding quite pregnant with Usaia on the back, and Reg wanted to put a picture of us in *Thunder Press*. I didn't mind riding with the group but I was embarrassed by being the center of attention. I was also flattered. But I guess it is unusual to see a woman nine months pregnant and still riding. It's even more unusual to see a woman packing her man. You know I rode to work the day Joe was born. I rode home in labor and they were strong contractions. That was an interesting ride. I went back to work two days after the delivery and rode the bike again one week later. I rode the Low Rider 'cause I wanted that wide, comfortable seat. I wouldn't have gotten on the hard Sportster seat for anything.

"My best fantasy is that Usaia will learn to ride and the three of us will ride together. I don't want to pack him. It's more work packing than riding solo. He's big. He weighs over two hundred pounds. I would like us to each pack just a kid (I want another baby now), and we could go everywhere. We would ride to the Grand Canyon, Yellowstone, the Badlands, everywhere on the bikes. I would want to take the bikes overseas and tour Australia and other lands on motorcycles. I want my kids to grow up knowing nature the way I learned it. From a bike. I want my children to experience riding through a rainstorm *and* into a sunset.

"But I'm not sure what to do when they become adolescents. I am afraid of their teenage years. It's hard to be a teenager in America. I'm afraid for them on bikes, in cars, and in schools. I think we may send them back to Fiji for those critical seven or eight years.

"There are other aspects to packing as well. You have to be very responsible and responsive when you are packing. You have to make sure that your passenger is comfortable and safe. When I ride alone, I just have to keep myself alive."

This appears to be a uniquely female perspective. I never heard a single man talk about passenger comfort or safety. I never heard one male voice concern about passenger feelings. I know that some of the men may share Debby's views, but if they do, they *never say them in public.*

"After Joe was born I found that I didn't want to take some of the risks that I took before. I have much more responsibility now. Joe is an infant and Usaia would have a hard time making it alone in a strange country. I still ride, of course, but I do take less risks. That wonderful trip that I took to the Grand Canyon last year down Highway 50 was so treacherous that I wouldn't do that now. Also I wouldn't ride alone like that again. Not while I am still so needed."

Debby rides with abandon and flair. In her shocking pink jacket and white helmet with black ribbing, she does not present the typical picture of a biker. She can be seen for miles around. She is a great one to follow in a crowd because it is impossible to lose her. Deb has never been accused of being a follower of fashion. She leads the parade.

"Debby, you are a riding woman. Do you see yourself as a biker?"

"No. Out of respect for bikers, true bikers, I don't call myself that. True bikers, those who started early and earned that title, should have that title to themselves. I take the title 'rider.' That should be PC enough. To be a biker is to have paid the kind of dues I haven't paid. I respect those who have made biking their lives. They can tear a bike down and build it again. I can't do that. I respect their skills and their lives. I am a rider.

"I am not a motorcycle enthusiast. I am not a Sunday rider. I bought my Harley to ride. I did not buy it because it was the 'in' thing to do. Most enthusiasts would be as comfortable on a Gold Wing as a Harley. I don't want to ride a bike that can go in reverse.

"Bikers and riders are both hooked on riding. I love being on the bike. I love riding the weather, being in the eye of Mother Nature's power. Last week, I left my helmet at the office and I had to ride home without it. I rarely wore a helmet before that stupid law passed. I had forgotten how wonderful it feels with the wind rushing by. I hate the terrible restrictions of all that gear around my face and head.

"Being a rider is part of what I do. I have a piece of my identity tied up in it. But only a piece. I am a mother to Joe, a wife to Usaia, a mother to Jennifer, a grandmother to Victor, a lawyer, and a rider. Women cross the boundaries a lot more than men. A Shovelhead woman will ride with another woman whether she rides a Honda Rebel or a BMW. We are more willing to go beyond the boundaries than men. But all bikers will stop to help others stranded on the road.

"We all help each other. There are a lot of good things in the biker world. That's why I get so displeased when people stereotype us as bad people. We are pictured as drunks or stupid or crass. I don't want to be categorized as that kind of person. We are people who appreciate freedom, the outdoors, individual pursuits, self-expression, and nature. We are willing to cross lines. We are not concerned about what other people say we should do. But most important, we appreciate our abilities to think for ourselves. We appreciate self-expression. Riders are extremely sensitive to Mother Nature. In another time we would all be riding horses over this country. Or we would be sailors riding the waves. We are adventurers, explorers, travelers. In this time, in America, this is the way we are able to express these feelings and longings. Every time I am out on the road, I wish I was on my bike. That is when I am happiest."

Like Debby, most of the women she has helped to ride are also happiest when we are riding.

Each group of riding women holds different views of themselves as riders and as women and of their roles in the biker community. For example, while Debby, a Woman Rider, finds LOH useful and necessary in her journey toward riding confidence, Pat, a Woman Biker, is offended by the gender separation within LOH and is sensitive to the implicit assumption that women riders are less competent and road wise than men. Jayne, a Lady Biker, also scoffs at LOH, chafing under the implied slight to women's riding abilities even though, unlike Pat, she would never consider wrenching.

These three groups are rarely good friends. They may ride together, but they have profoundly different approaches to riding, wrenching, and "correct" female behavior. Women Bikers look with a good deal of contempt upon Lady Bikers but reserve judgment for Women Riders. Lady Bikers are seen by Women Bikers as taking unfair advantage of their female anatomy. Women Bikers want to be accepted as bikers on a single standard of excellence. They see their gender as irrelevant. They want to be judged by the same standards as men.

Lady Bikers tend to ignore and sometimes pity the Women Bikers, whom they feel have both bad attitudes and bad taste in clothes. Recognizing women's one-down position within the rest of society, Lady Bikers see nothing wrong in exploiting gender-specific behavior when it suits them. If it works, if it gets them what they want, so be it. It is the way of the world. They use what they've got. And what they've got is a strong sense of style and the knowledge that men, especially biker men, find the mixture of hard-riding woman coupled with feminine demeanor irresistible.

Women Riders tend to remain neutral in the dance between Women Bikers and Lady Bikers. They can be accepted begrudgingly by both groups. Women Bikers forgive Women Riders' lack of wrenching skills because they do not fall back upon "feminine wiles" while on the road. They never act the Queen Bee. Lady Bikers forgive their lack of the use of "feminine wiles" because Women Riders usually dress in gender-presentable ways. They don't show up covered in tranny oil or brake fluid. At the same time, because they don't make nice, they are no threat to the sexy position of the Lady Biker. They will not take male attention away from her. Women Riders can be comfortable companions for both Lady Bikers and Women Bikers. They threaten the sensibilities of neither group. Since all groups are composed of strong-minded, highly spirited, individualistic women with different approaches to riding, they bond infrequently, but ride together as necessity demands.

Each behavior is an adaptive response to male road culture. Within Harley culture, all three groups tend to be more hetero than lesbian, but not exclusively so. It is not possible to tell a woman's sexual orientation by which group she rides with. Unless she is observably out, flies a gay liberation flag, or wears the lavender triangle of gay liberation on her clothes, her sexual choices are undetectable. Most assume that the Lady Biker because of her sexy clothes and make nice attitudes is heterosexual, but she may not be. Most assume that the Woman Rider is also heterosexual because of her neat, presentable appearance and lack of wrenching skills. She may or may not be. Most assume that the Woman Biker is lesbian because of her mechanical abilities, her refusal to make nice, and her up-front attitudes. Like the other two groups, she may or may not be. It is this group that most puzzles biker men. When meeting a woman in this category, men often take bets on her sexuality. They are often wrong.

All biking women break the stereotypes of gender-specific behav-

ior. Even Lady Bikers are riding in the wrong seat. Society expects that
if a woman is on a bike at all, she will ride on the back. The back-seat,
supportive, auxiliary role is the anticipated female role within the
biker world, just as it is within the rest of American society. All riding
women break this stereotype. They break it, however, in different ways.

The Lady Biker breaks it by giving strong mixed messages. The
contrast between competent rider and helpless mechanic is a difficult
one for male bikers to ignore. This is a highly successful strategy. She
breaks the stereotype by riding but reinforces it by being unable to
change a battery or fix a flat. Women Bikers break the stereotype in
both their riding and their wrenching. This is why they are so often
thought of as lesbian within the male biking community. They do not
depend upon men for any of their riding needs. This strategy works
because of the extraordinary competence of these women. The Women
Riders break the stereotype in that they ride a motorcycle. They are
willing, however, to accept assistance from men even if they pride
themselves on *not* using their femininity to get it. The biker code of
ethics, the one that offers assistance to any downed rider, is sufficient
to get them through most hard road times. This strategy works because
while they do not make nice, they do not rebuff assistance either. Both
the Lady Biker and the Woman Rider permit men to play the socially
accepted male role of helper-protector when they are on the road. If
the bike breaks, he is permitted or implored to fix it. Women Bikers
do not, of course, do this. They permit men no entrance. They signal
no female vulnerability. The male bikers must accept them on their
own terms or not at all. They reject all the stereotypes.

Women who ride, no matter how well or how long, get *themselves*
into the wind. They throw a leg over and take off. All three groups
share a profound love of bikes, the road, the culture, and the community. Some riders start young. They grow up knowing that they want
to ride. Some come to it later in life and endure many struggles earning
their entrance. Still others take up riding after years of riding the rear.
They may have loved passengering, but after their fifth breakup (with
biker boyfriends) they decide that the only way to stay in the wind is
to do it themselves. But no matter how they get themselves into the
wind, these women share the common bonds of all women on the
road. They share the dangers, delights, and desires of the road. With
or without their acknowledgment, they share a sturdy sisterhood. In
the eyes of General American Society, however, they are all gender
traitors.

Biker Chicks, Lady Passengers, Passionate Passengers, Lady Bikers,
Women Bikers, and Women Riders make up the female part of the

Harley world. These groups differ in their attitudes toward riding, and in their relationship to bikes, bikers, and the riding world in general. These distinctions, however, do not reflect differences of women's riding skills or abilities, nor do they reflect women's passengering skills.

A Lady Biker can be a very good or a very poor rider. What makes her a Lady Biker is her perception of herself within the Harley community and her insistence on male support. A Woman Rider can also have any level of skill. What distinguishes her is her attitude toward the road, the men, and her relationship with her bike. She may need help, but she does not ride to be rescued. The Woman Biker, by definition, is a good rider. She doesn't get into that category until she can wrench and ride well.

Women who passenger vary as much as those who ride. While the Lady Passenger and the Passionate Passenger have considerable leeway in their abilities because of their long-term relationships with men, each may be a good or a poor passenger. She may know how to lean into the curves and ride the rear lightly or she may sit like a sack of sludge. How proficient a passenger she *must* be depends upon the patience of her man. The Biker Chick has fewer options. If she is a poor passenger, she runs the risk of being left at the side of the road.

For every woman who rides, there is a separate story. For every woman who passengers, there is another one. For the few women who do both, there are multiple tales and fearful contradictions.

7

Sex and Gender

"So you think you know what femininity means? Try riding a Harley."

Women have always defined femininity for themselves. Men have always defined it too. It's part of what culture trains us for. Often the definitions do not agree.

"My butt hurts. My butts really hurts. I'm not going to be able to walk or sit down."

Debby shouts this bit of information to me as we stop at a red light on the way to Apple Jacks.

"My cunt hurts too," I shout back. "My cunt really hurts. I'm not going to be able to walk or sit down either. Hey Deb, how many men do you think ever get to say that while they're riding?"

Stopped at a red light in the middle of a feeder highway to Sky Londa, we rock with laughter. Each time we yell about some female complaint, Ken, our riding companion and my husband, rides a bit faster. He definitely appears to want to get away from us.

"Well, a guy *could* say his cunt hurt," I continue, "if he were packing and treating her like shit." The light changes and we take off down the highway.

We two are riding buddies. If it weren't for Debby, I wouldn't be riding. A lot of women have helped me gather the courage to brave the bike, but Debby most of all. We women, we are not raised to ride. Riding is so contradictory to the traditional forms of femininity that finding women on the road at all is truly astounding.

"My God! It's turning into a run. I'm not ready for a run."

Debby raises this issue for the tenth time since arriving at Mike's house. We've ridden for thirty minutes just to get there. There are ten bikes and twelve riders all facing us in the driveway when we arrive. Deb hasn't been on the bike since her long ride to Bridgeport and is feeling uneasy. We had both expected a nice little putt to Alice's Restaurant. We did not anticipate more than three or four friends showing up. Debby is reluctant to continue.

"Can't back out now," I growl. "I am not—repeat—not going to be the only woman rider with this bunch."

Now it's not always so bad being the only woman rider. In fact it can be downright invigorating. But if you are the only one, you had better be able to outride all the guys. If you are the only woman riding with a group of men, they must damn well be forced to eat your dust. I know lots of women who can do this.

Sharon can take off at unclockable speeds and be racing down the highway before the guys have shifted into fourth. Kit can outride any man around. Road Captain to a bunch of unruly riders, she rode alone to Alaska. I have seen Jayne keeping up with Pablo at impossible speeds.

But when you ride the way I do, you need lots of special favors. You need everyone to take unlikely roads, ride at lower speeds, and be prepared to wait at turns. For this you need other women riders along. For this impromptu run, Deb and I get special favors. The men modify the route, the speed, and the destination. Ten well-seasoned male bikers, two women passengers, and Debby and I take off from Daly City on a gorgeous Sunday morning. It is our first riding day after three months of rain and we are raring to go.

In many ways, it's a typical run. Left in their dust, we two are lost after ten minutes of riding, having made the wrong turn onto the wrong highway at the wrong exit. We are rescued by Denny and Blondie, who are riding backup. They formed a search party to find us. We would have found our own way back, but it was really nice knowing that our friends were looking. Also knowing how spooked I get on Freeway 280, Denny rides ahead, keeping the speed down to an unbelievable fifty-five miles per hour, and I have the first enjoyable freeway ride of my life.

Once off the freeway and well into the mountainous, curvy roads of the Sky Londa hills, Denny and Blondie maintain a rear position and just dare any of the fast-moving cars to ride up my rear fender. I'm slow on curvy roads too. Since Denny rides a full Dresser and is bigger than his bike, he provides the perfect backup. For years, Denny was sergeant-of-arms for a local club and nobody ever messed with him. As I said, he's real big. He has formidable features and sports a variety of tats and some wicked earrings. When he's not being wonderfully nice to novice riders, he can also be real mean. And if there is one thing you do not want, it's having Denny get mean. Denny's, an Old Biker, and can fix anything on wheels. For Debby and me, he is the perfect escort. Blondie too is pleased. It is one of the rare times that Denny's ridden slowly enough to allow her to get a good look at the scenery.

Yelling words of encouragement to each other, we women make it to Alice's Restaurant in record time. We stop for food and drink. Half of us eat breakfast. The other half drink breakfast. Then off to Apple Jacks for some more companionable drinking. Debby and I clump in together. Two women riders in a sea of testosterone. There are several women passengers, and I notice, for the first time, that Deb and I separate ourselves from them.

Sitting on those great, log-carved chairs on the porch of Apple Jacks, beer bottles in hand, we watch the riding world hurtle by. All the world's motorcycles are out today. With our feet up on the railing, our backs against the wall, we view the forest just beyond the road— the oaks, pines, redwoods—and we compare notes. We swap stories. We remember rides we have loved and runs we have missed. Debby remembers how she almost had her bike stolen and the fear she felt along the highway. Her bike is customized. Lots of chrome. Chrome ornaments the instrument covers and swing arm. The bike is tastefully, not gaudily, chromed right down to the tappets. I too remember. Later, I will recount my rare moment of biker bravery.

"It was right here, sitting just like this," I recall, "that Margo and I talked about your trip. Because of your trouble in Nevada, we decided that if we ever traveled alone, we would pack weapons."

Debby sits very still for a few minutes, looking out at the passing bikes, and tells me the whole story for the first time.

"I was in a tiny, tiny town in the middle of nowhere Nevada. The next town over was a plateau and mountain range away. I was ninety miles from the closest town and I had to stop. I had no choice. I had to gas up and eat. I decided to park where I saw two motorcycles in front of a restaurant. They were rat-bike Shovelheads and real beat up. Spray-can paint jobs. Nothing about them was upscale but they were not outlaw bikes either. They were just beat-up old Harleys. I related to this 'cause as a child I knew lots of people with just those kinds of bikes. I thought it would be a friendly place to be.

"Boy was I wrong. I pulled up, parked, and was starting to get off the bike when two young guys came out and started right on talking about my bike. 'How'd you get such a nice bike?' 'Who you with?' All the time, they were circling around me. The whole place was deserted. It was just my luck, in this wilderness, to run into scooter trash. You know, guys riding rat Harleys who steal bikes and bike parts for themselves. Guys who give solo Harley riders a bad time.

"'I see you're from San Francisco.' They did their gay number, like

136

only fags live in San Francisco and you're just a woman from a faggot town. 'What gives *you* the right to ride a bike like that?'"

I remembered that Debby had taken her long, solitary trip on her new Low Rider just before she met up with us in Bridgeport. She had traveled through Nevada and Arizona and Utah.

"These guys didn't think that I deserved that bike. I was sure that one of them was going to try to take it away from me. Just then one guy's girlfriend came out to the edge of the sidewalk and admonished them. She told them to back off and 'to leave the woman alone.' She said, 'All the more power to her and leave her be.' The guys, keeping their egos intact, backed off with comments like 'It's not worth troubling with.' Then they left. If that woman hadn't come out when she did, I'm sure they would have tried to take my bike.

"Well, I couldn't just leave. I had to get gas and food. So I went down the block, ate fast, gassed up, and left. I remember I had iced tea, filled up the water jug, took two pieces of bread and cheese, and split. It was about five in the afternoon and it was windy with rain clouds filling the sky but I wasn't going to stay there. I went 120 miles further and didn't stop until I saw a HOG bike."

"Deb, what's a HOG bike?"

"You know. A '92 Evo with saddlebags and chrome and helmets with chain locks. Someone had put $20,000 into that bike and it screamed HOG rider. I was never so relieved in my life. The rest of the trip was OK."

Debby had been waiting to take that trip for a long time. She had bought the Low Rider for just that purpose. Debby already owned a much-loved Sportster, so her new bike was for adventure.

"I had wanted a long ride for years. I ordered the Low Rider with the intention of making that ride. I rode through canyon lands from Reno to Monument Valley, from the Grand Canyon in Arizona to the backlands of Nevada and finally met up with all of you at Bridgeport. I rode over 4,000 miles. Most of it alone. In one day I rode about 628 miles. It was great. But I wouldn't ride alone like that again."

It's easy to reminisce at Apple Jacks. There is something about the booze and bar quality of the place that makes for good stories and tall tales. My story was much simpler than Debby's. My story began and ended in five minutes and took place in a local Frisco backroom bar. I was in a meeting with twenty other women riders. We had gathered to discuss runs and were relaxing around the long table with drinks and smokes. The bikes were all parked outside in the street. Suddenly a woman from outside yelled, "A man's messing with the bikes!"

Startled silence. Then action. We all, to a woman, rose, grabbed our bottles, and rushed outside to defend our bikes. As I rushed outside with the others, my only thought was to protect my beautiful bike from some marauding male. I had no plan and it didn't occur to me to have one. I had a bottle in my hand and genuine anger in my heart. What we found was a solitary deliveryman trying to maneuver his truck around the parked bikes so he could make his delivery. He had made the mistake of trying to push one of the bikes out of his way. This gave him the appearance of trying to take a bike. His face registered extreme shock when he saw twenty enraged women bikers bearing down upon him. He leaped to his truck and, from the safety of the locked cab, explained and apologized for the misunderstanding. He left immediately. We returned to the meeting.

Only later did I realize that had there been a confrontation, I wouldn't have had a clue as to what to do. I am not a street fighter. In my most radical youth, I fared very badly in battle. I have never trained in self-defense, and I am a coward. And at my age, this behavior is ridiculous. Upon reflection, the whole event is hilarious. Yet if my bike were threatened, I cannot say I would not rise up again to defend it. There is something quite primal about protecting your bike.

Tired of sitting, and having satisfied both thirst and tired muscles, Deb and I are ready for the road. The men, of course, are not. They wish to stay, so Deb and I make our way back to Frisco. We are so proud of ourselves that we stop for ice cream sundaes along the way. Our first ride after a winter of dormancy. We have managed the road, the wind, and the gentle jabs from the men, and we vow to ride again together soon. Women riding buddies create a strong bond. It is a bond worth exploring.

Women bikers. Women riding buddies. Women's passenger clubs. The very words bring up mixed images. Women riding motorcycles? Early in the twentieth century it was pretty common. In the recent past it was almost unknown. Today it raises eyebrows if not noses. In the early days of biking, women rode. Nothing special. Women just rode. Milwaukee created an organization for them and featured women in many of their ads.

Men and women both rode motorcycles; it took daring to do so, but women as well as men have this characteristic. From the late forties on, things changed. The biking woman became the biker's woman. Known as the "bitch on the back," she rode only with her man. The biker was male and the woman's place was behind him in the bitch seat.

The bitch seat, usually small, extremely uncomfortable, and precariously perched (almost as an afterthought) both actualizes and symbolizes the woman's position. She is both necessary and peripheral to the biking world. She is accepted as a subordinate sexual companion and is sometimes replaceable and nameless. She is the biker's groupie who drives to the bike rallies, sneaks into festivals to provide food, drink, and sex, and is often dismissed at dawn. If she loves bikes or bikers and survives the biker's bitch stage, she could settle down with a biker. He would invariably expect her to fulfill her female role within the male biker world.

In every era and in each generation, there were, of course, extraordinary and remarkable women who rode motorcycles. They rode independently in their own way and in defiance of the stereotypes. Sometimes they rode with men. Sometimes they rode with other women. But most often they rode alone, choosing a solitary and unforgettable path. They became the stuff of legend but they did not become the leaders of this generation's remarkable biking women. Perhaps they were too few in number or too individual in their tastes and choices. But for whatever reasons, and regardless of how exemplary their behaviors were, they remain outside the main arena of women and motorcycles.

Women who ride today are a relatively new phenomenon. There are many groups, clubs, organizations, and chapters of riding women, and they grow stronger and larger each year. In Santa Cruz, *Thunder Press* supports a twice-a-year event called "A Gathering of Women Motorcyclists," and last year it pulled over two hundred women to the run. There are women's motorcycle festivals, parties, rallies, and gatherings. The only entrance requirement is the bike. Women can ride or passenger, although most who participate in these events ride their own.

The women at these events cover all parts of the riding continuum. They are rich, they are poor. They are young, they are old. They are hetero, they are lesbian. They are urban, they are rural. They are working class, they are professionals. They are big, they are small. They are mothers, they are childfree. They have mates, they are single. They all, however, share some traits in common. Whether they ride in the front or on the back, they have all challenged the historical roles of women in the biking world. None of them are bitches in the back.

In this context, *all* these women have broken with stereotypical femininity. All these women have rejected, consciously or unconsciously, the written and unwritten rules of female behavior. Yet they all consider themselves feminine. The women have their own definitions of feminine.

They have rewritten the rules. And they must. For all these women hold anomalous positions in a dangerous and predominantly male world. In this world, the language, rituals, and rites of passage have been male defined, and all women bikers ride the roads at risk.

The world at large never sees the major differences between male riders. We know that the Harley world alone is divided into at least seven recognizable categories of male riders. And that's just the Harley world. Different kinds of bikes attract different people, and while all have much in common—love of the road and the need for the kind of freedom the open road provides—they have many differences. While Harley riders consider themselves the kings of the road, that's a self-image and is not shared among other riders. Biking folk protect and defend each other, but the divisions run deep.

Sports-bike riders, riders of the very fast and colorful Hurricanes and Ninjas, who are usually young and hip, tend to regard Harley riders as middle-aged, rough, old-fashioned, and hard-core. Harleys are seen as loud, troublesome, and poorly performing bikes. They are seen by Yamaha, Honda, Suzuki, and Kawasaki sports-bike riders as down and dirty bikes. Members of outlaw clubs, of course, ride Harleys, and this continues to contribute to the hard-assed Harley image.

Those who ride European bikes—Moto Guzzis, Ducatis, and BMWs—usually separate from both other groups in terms of class, money, and style. Riders of these bikes typically refer to themselves as motorcyclists rather than bikers and reject the working-class sensibilities of the other groups. Then there are the dirt bike riders, the racers, and solo riders of all types. They cross all lines and affiliate with many different groups. Sometimes they go it alone.

All groups are snobs. All groups are held together by both positive and negative forces. High on the negative list are public attitudes and sanctions against bikers. These range from social disapproval to legal oppression. Having the laws of the land work against you creates strong bonds among different groups. High on the positive list are shared love of the road, a common language, journals, and events.

But the world at large never sees major differences between male riders. All male riders are seen as "bikers" and as potential members of an outlaw club. Here comes *The Wild One* again. The riding clothes help reinforce the stereotypes. Most bikers ride leathered up, but a large number wear black leather on almost all parts of their bodies. From the leather jackets to the leather chaps, all this leaves a distinct impression. It may look like something out of the Wild West, but it is functional riding gear. Nothing survives a spill so well as leather. Nothing protects against road rash like leather. Other functional articles ride the belts of bikers, from the ubiquitous knives to chains and keys. It all looks formidable but it works.

Riding down the road in shades and leathers creates that distinctive image. And it is a male image. While it is extreme, it does no fundamental damage to the acceptable stereotypic male look. The male is still, basically, in pants, jacket, and boots. Masculinity in all its traditional forms has been upheld. In fact it has been pushed to its limits. It appears as an exaggeration. Here he is presenting the qualities of strength, ruggedness, and toughness. The look promotes the in-your-face attitude held by some bikers and *believed* to be held by all of them. The world expects bikers to be crass, crude, and boorish. The general public would not be surprised by a nose-picking, publicly fornicating, street-pissing biker. In fact, such behavior would only reinforce the already negative stereotype.

Since the forties, bikers have had bad press. Some of it was deserved. Most of it was bullshit. The public has this strange love/hate fascination with bikers. As a symbol representing both the unknown and the unallowed, bikers make a great study in contrasts. They are seen as the heroes of the id and villains of civilization. As rampaging rogue males, raping, marauding, and pillaging. As men who are "manly" enough to grab what they want and thumb their noses at the forces of law and order. Here comes the ole outlaw again. Supermacho masculinity on the loose. Keep the women and children inside!

There is just enough truth in the myth to keep it alive. There is so little truth in the myth that folks within the biker community think it's a hoot. But they still play off the myth. Bikers are not above using the badass stereotype to their advantage to get fast seating in a local bar, quick service at the gas station, and groupies at gatherings.

Bikers serve as forces for both hatred and wish fulfillment for the general public. Biker stereotypes are largely myths, but they serve a function within the larger society. Most Americans are uptight about sex. Bikers are seen as superstuds. Most Americans feel locked into shitty jobs. Bikers reject such obligations. Most Americans feel trapped. Bikers ride free. Most Americans feel afraid in their homes. Bikers fearlessly ride the open roads. In short, many Americans think that bikers can do what they themselves wish they could do and cannot do. In an uptight, rigid, scared, overburdened society, bikers are a symbol of freedom. Most Americans both love and fear freedom. Both emotions are part of our cultural heritage. Freedom represents the wild, the uncontrolled, the unsafe, the untamable, the unknowable, and the irresistible. In a fearful, insecure country, riding a speeding motorcycle down a winding road is a courageous act. Most Americans will not commit such an act. Many Americans wish they could. Because they don't, they punish those who do.

The punishment takes many forms. Attitudes and behaviors toward bikers reflect part of this punishment. To many Americans, bikers are scum. The persistent "wild one" image is part of it. The behaviors toward bikers are another part of this punishment. The laws grow more restrictive and punitive every day. From the inappropriate and dangerous helmet laws to even more threatening legislation looming on the horizon, bikers carry the burden of America's anger. Bikers are convenient scapegoats. Most Americans feel trapped. Bikers ride free. Punish the bikers!

The contradiction between myth and reality is becoming more apparent. Even when the Harley world consisted of only Old Timers, One Percenters, and perhaps some Ten Percenters, the stereotypes had only a little bit of truth. But since the addition of Old Bikers, New Bikers, Rich Urban Bikers, and Occasional Bikers, the stereotypes hold less and less.

The last four groups all share the same responsibilities as the rest of America. These bikers ride both sides of the road. They go to their jobs, pay their bills, raise their kids, and pay their mortgages and their taxes. In short, they are dues-paying, hard-working citizens. They *do* differ from other Americans, but the differences express themselves in their love of their bikes and the risks they are willing to take in the pursuit of riding. The difference is that these bikers have taken some time out to pursue their dreams. These bikers take both their riding and the rest of their responsibilities seriously.

If the world at large has trouble seeing the differences among male bikers, it has no problem recognizing women. In fact, gender is often the only difference acknowledged by the general public. Women bikers are seen not as gang members or living reproductions of the "wild ones," but as either sexual outlaws or gender traitors.

The female biker, either rider and passenger, is seen as risky and tough. She is so outside the norms of even multicultural femininity that almost anything is possible. She breaks the patterns. Who knows how she will act? She is unpredictable. She is dangerous. The general public, much like the historically male-oriented biker world, believes that females, if they belong on bikes at all, belong on the back.

But a woman passenger who willingly participates in such a dangerous and wild activity as biking must certainly be no less than a sexual outlaw. She is the quintessential sex object beyond redemption and certainly beyond acceptable society. She is the slutty seductress gracing every garage calendar and the breast-braced bitch advertising bike parts. In short, she's odd, addled, and permanently in heat. But while the public has contempt for the woman passenger, real scorn is reserved for the woman rider.

The riding female is stereotyped as gender traitor. This woman refuses to accept the gender rules that place her on the back of the bike.

She rides her own. She has dared to enter the masculine preserve that most men in America are too wary or afraid to enter. Both the woman rider and passenger, like all male riders, brave the risks of the road. All deal with the wind, weather, traffic, animals, and unpredictability. But the woman rider goes it alone. She is in charge of her own destiny. She has taken an assertive and risky position. She must maneuver both the bike and the male riding world. Some bikers accept her. Some don't. The general public, however, categorizes her as a dyke and dismisses her. These stereotypes of biking women as sexual outlaws and gender traitors are as ridiculous and wrong as the stereotype of all males as the "wild one." But they persist in the minds of nonbiking America.

Women did not start riding in large numbers until the mid-eighties, a period that coincided with the manufacture of the Evolution engine. Here was a comfortable bike that could be ridden without wrenching. Gone was the kick start. Gone were the oil, gas, and grease drips. But the bike still had to be modified to fit most women's bodies. It still had to be lowered. The seat still had to be repositioned. The frame still had to be raked. Yet overall, it worked and women rode. Eventually, Milwaukee came out with the Hugger. This 883 Sportster is low framed, smaller, and so well positioned that most women can stand flat on their feet while straddling the seat. By the mid-eighties, some women were making real money and some of them were buying Harley Sportsters.

Who was riding? The public saw only the tough, the troublesome, and the dyke. In reality, women from all social, cultural, and regional areas started riding. Hetero women who had been passengering for years suddenly had the urge to move up to the front seat. Lesbian women who had considered biking too campy and stereotyped suddenly started riding. Even male anthropologists noticed the phenomenon.

According to Wolf:

> The newest and fastest-growing phenomenon on the asphalt highways of contemporary North America is the solo female rider. Every year more and more women are turning to motorcycles and motorcycling on their own. For the purpose of mutual companionship and support these sisters of the highway have begun to organize themselves in groups that are independent of males. The following is an excerpt from a letter to the editorial section of V-Twin magazine. "Our name is Against All Odds MC and our patch will consist of the Queen of hearts playing card in the background. In front will be two dice showing three and four circles representing the number seven. We will hopefully show that women can ride motorcycles and still be ladies and that we actually have brains in our heads, not mashed potatoes." (1991, 131)

Wolf goes on to add:

> In addition to the emergence of individual clubs, there is a growing number of national associations for women motorcyclists, such as Women on Wheels, Leather & Lace ("Ladies of the 90s,—Leather stands for our inner strength, Lace depicts our femininity"), Women in the Wind, and Ladies of Harley. In 1986 *Harley Women*, published by Asphalt Angels Publications, Inc., emerged as a magazine "dedicated to all women motorcycle enthusiasts." An increasing number of women bikers are also taking an active role in political-rights organizations such as MRO (Motorcycle Rights Organizations), ABATE (Pro-choice helmet legislation) and AMA (American Motorcycle Association). (1991, 131)

But when Wolf writes about the outlaw clubs, his descriptions of gender and women bikers change.

> The reason women do not ride their own motorcycles or become club members in the outlaw sub-culture does not relate to lack of interest, ability or desire. Rather it is because the fabrication of male and female gender identity and roles within the sub-culture requires female partic-ipation only in a marginal and supportive manner. A man's image of "machismo" (dominance and aggression) is achieved in part by con-trasting it with a women's image of "femininity" (subservience and pas-sivity). From a comparative perspective, gender relations defined by outlaw motorcycle clubs are not a radical sub-cultural departure from but rather an exaggerated statement of the traditional values that have dominated North American society for several centuries. (1991, 132)

Among the outlaws, according to Wolf, men and women's relation-ships mimic in exaggerated form the rest of society. Outlaw bikers' ole ladies may be seen by American culture as sexual outlaws but clearly not as gender traitors. They ride the back of the bike. They are tradi-tionally feminine.

It was a blow to much of the riding male population when biker babes became bikers. How individual women decide to ride is differ-ent for each woman. There are as many biking stories as there are women who ride. Each woman has her own tale and her own triumph. Biking women are each different, yet they share some remarkable traits in common. Every one of them had to manage to fit her female self into a male-biased world. Every one of them had to overcome the negative images of the broader society. Every one of them had to redefine femininity.

Traditional masculinity in American culture has been described in various ways. A man is tough, strong, independent, capable of making quick judgments and actions, self-sufficient, and competent. These traits are absolutely consistent with riding a motorcycle.

Since the resurgence of the feminist movement in the late sixties, the negative side of masculinity has also been described. A man is aggressive, domineering, overbearing, abusive, needs to be always right, is rarely swayed by his emotions, and is willing to go it alone. These traits too are absolutely consistent with riding a motorcycle.

Most of the time and in most cultures, masculinity is defined in relation to femininity. Masculinity gets some of its meaning in contrast to femininity. To be a man is to have a significant number of masculine characteristics *and* not to possess feminine ones.

Traditional femininity in American culture has been described in various ways. A woman is soft, gentle, nurturing, emotional, caring, and responsive. She is tender, conciliatory, and willing to negotiate solutions. These traits do not promote biking competence. By themselves, they do not prepare a woman for the road.

The negative side of femininity, since the late sixties, has been well explored. A woman is small, petite, dainty, subservient, passive, ineffectual, and submissive. She is vulnerable, weak, unsure of herself, and has a great need for group approval and love. These traits are absolutely inconsistent with riding a motorcycle.

If femininity is frequently defined in opposition to masculinity, then a woman must possess a number of feminine traits and *not* possess masculine ones.

Contrary to these popular stereotypes, most people in America have a mixture of both masculine and feminine feelings, behaviors, and traits. It is the proportion that is significant. Very few people possess almost all the traits of one group and almost none of the other. Most of us are blends. We identify with the core principles of our gender and then we branch out to include aspects of the opposite one. (Cross- and trans-gendered folk, however, may have other identifications.) While the core principles of masculinity and femininity differ somewhat from group to group, there are some common beliefs. Men are seen as strong and action oriented. Women are seen as nurturing and gentle. Men who ride bikes are seen as exaggerating their gender. Women who ride bikes are seen as denying theirs. They are gender traitors.

How does a woman who participates in the riding world combine biking and a vision of femininity? She changes the meaning of the word. She changes the concept. She changes the societal definitions. All biking women to some degree have revised, modified, and redefined the word "feminine."

"The word 'feminine' has been abused. I like to think that I'm feminine—soft, sweet, and all the nice things that go with being a woman. It's a term that's been misused by the press. We are seen as bitches on wheels, and we're not."

Jayne Kelly de Lopez shares these views with me one sunny San Francisco day. We are comfortably seated at her law office when Pablo comes in with their lunch. Since I have forgotten to bring mine, we all share. Pablo, Old Biker that he is, mentions that he had difficulty at first getting used to Jayne's riding. She is the first woman he has been with who rides her own. Now he considers it an asset. He strongly approves of the way she looks and the way she expresses her femininity.

"I like the fact that women and men are different," Jayne continues. "Feminine is different. It's a softer way of dealing. I like to think that I'm feminine. I don't like the concept gotten from the women's movement that women should be aggressive. I want to be soft and strong. Femininity has been used for a long time as a derogatory term and that is ludicrous. Feminine is lots of things, including making cookies all day Saturday 'cause your kid is in Chicago and lonesome. It's a good thing too. I'd hate to give that up."

Jayne, who promises to throw the biggest party in San Francisco next year when she turns fifty, is an interesting study. Like all biking women she is amazing. She has also had her share of difficulties along with accomplishments. She is the mother of six kids, runs her own law practice, and continues to maintain a good marriage with Pablo. She rides a big bike. Her brand-new Low Rider has already been modified to heighten its power, its rumble, and its angle. Jayne favors ape hangers and loves giving her bike a chopped look.

Debby Lindblom has to think about femininity. It is too big an issue to be discussed right away. Also a lawyer, she works for a private firm, rides to work, and has a reputation for both fairness and toughness.

"We all know the stereotypes of the feminine. Some are good. Some aren't. They are nurturing, caring, sweet, quiet, demure, loving, and gentle. Then there are the other things. The things we are supposed to do like cooking, cleaning, and the rest of it. On the bad side, there is the idea that we are submissive, and oh yes, there is PMS.

"Those are the stereotypes. But for me feminine and masculine have become so blurred that I really only use these definitions in the stereotypical sense. It may all be an artificial dichotomy. I don't really believe in it. Masculinity is also just a stereotype. It's a false dichotomy. We are all just people. The masculine stereotype is just as bad as the feminine one.

146

"I consider myself to be both feminine and masculine in both stere-otypic senses. I am a woman, female and feminine. But in my personal-ity, all the lines are so blurred that I don't believe there really is such a separation. It's a creation of language. You create a distinction that may not be there at all."

I asked Deb how she arrived at these conclusions. I wanted to know when and how she started seeing people as possessing a whole mixed bag of traits and not merely the expressions of societally given ones.

"I learned really early that masculine and feminine didn't apply to people. They were just words. People were different. When I was really young, I knew that I wasn't dainty or teeny tiny like a ballerina. I also wasn't muscular or strong like a weight lifter. I wasn't dainty, never have been. I wasn't muscular, never have been. But I am a person. So I knew the categories were wrong."

"But Deb, these are just words. When did you really start feeling that the differences were false? When did they make you take notice of them?"

"I noticed the behavioral difference for the first time in fifth grade. I was told that I shouldn't sit cross-legged 'cause I was a girl. Then when I was around eleven or twelve my mother made me stop riding our motorcycle. My foster brother was allowed to continue but I had to stop. We had one of those really little Honda 50s. It was such a thrill! I must have fallen down hundreds of times but I always got up want-ing more. I loved riding. Loved it! Then my mother stopped me from riding and let my brother continue. We were the same age. This was the first time that I was confronted with one of those girl/boy things. In most other respects my mother told me that I could do anything. I believed that girls and boys could do the same things. But not with riding. My mother said I couldn't ride. I left home a month after my sixteenth birthday."

Linda's view of femininity is considerably different from both Jayne's and Debby's. She's an Old Biker's ole lady and has been passen-gering for many years. It is her intention to learn to ride.

"Feminine is a good word. But it's not just something that women do. It's not just something that women are. The word isn't just applied to women. Everyone has their feminine side. It's the nurturing, loving, feeling, social part. Some people have it developed more than others. Some people have it less developed but everyone has it. It's like yin/ yang. Masculine and feminine each form a part of a total person. Women usually have more feminine parts and men more masculine ones but we all share both parts.

"I feel very feminine when I'm on a bike. Being on a bike is about expressing feelings, it's letting those feelings out and being comfortable with myself. It's when I get the chance to be in touch with that part of myself when I feel free, wonderful, and alive."

"Linda," I asked with real curiosity, "what about the men? Do you think that they let their feelings out?"

"I know that this is totally the opposite of the stereotypes but I think that men are at their most feminine when they are riding."

"Linda, are you out of your fucking mind?"

"I know the stereotype of a biker is supermacho, antifeminine man, but all the men I like most, who I have ridden with, get most in touch with their feminine side when they are riding. When they are on the bike they are experiencing their feelings and they are part of the world around them. They are in touch with themselves and it's wonderful. It's the best part of them. It's what makes them so much more attractive to me."

Kit Walker had a very different response from Linda. Good friends, different views.

"The most attractive thing about femininity is its strength. I don't find weakness attractive. I see myself as feminine. That means more sensual, refined, and sensitive. It's a very good trait. I see masculine as more gross, sexual rather than sensual, and definitely less refined. I don't usually define myself as masculine or feminine. Everything is relative. But when I slip into something silky at night, I feel very feminine."

Susan had to get back to me with her views on femininity. She felt it was too big a topic to just talk about. She had to think about it first. Later that day, she called back.

"To begin with it's the gentle side of your spirit. It's the softer side of your spirit. It doesn't have anything to do with looks or gender. It doesn't have anything to do with how I relate to being a passenger on the back of the bike. It's a self-definition. I could be doing anything and I could still feel the feminine side of me. It's me having the experience of femininity. Now, as a passenger in Harley culture, some of the time I feel like a nonentity. Like I'm Bradley's appendage. But I always carry my sense of femininity with me no matter what the outside world sees. One part of my being, the internal, and spiritual, is a part of my femininity. I have no doubt about who I am as a woman. I have no doubt about who I am as a person. Femininity is one part of it. Bradley is a man who is in touch with his feminine side. And I love him for it. It's his spiritual side.

"When I'm riding my bicycle, I get in touch with my power. Riding my bicycle makes me feel like the eagle on the wind. It's not masculine or feminine; it's just a wonderful experience. You get all your senses heightened. It's like—Oh my God, why didn't God give us wings? We keep wanting to grow them. We keep wanting to fly. In my generation, we see masculine and feminine in everything."

Susan's generation came of age in the seventies. She's in her early forties. Married to Bradley, she passengers with him and wants to ride her own. Bernie, on the other hand, came of age in the fifties. She passengers with her husband Dick and has no intention of ever moving to the front seat of the bike. Bernie's definition of femininity is as reflective of her generation as Susan's is of hers.

"You can be feminine and still ride on a motorcycle. Someone is feminine who is very ladylike. This is the opposite of being a rough person. It is a good term. You can be brave but not tough. You can be feminine no matter what you look like. You don't have to be petite. You can be fat and still be very feminine. It means nice tempered."

While Bernie was giving her definition, Dick called in his: "It's women who wear dresses, have neat hair, and don't chew tobacco."

We both laughed at this, but it highlighted an important point. Bernie did not see the clothes as making someone ladylike. To her it was temperament and manners.

Women who ride are seen by the general public as gender traitors. Women who passenger are seen as sexual outlaws. None of the women interviewed hold anything even remotely resembling these views about themselves. What they have done is to redefine the concept of gender to fit their biking behaviors. All the women expressed feelings of femininity. Their definitions varied considerably from Debby's behavioral androgyny to Linda's yin/yang interpretations. They varied from Susan's idea of both masculinity and femininity existing in varying degrees in us all to Kit's view of femininity as sensitivity and strength.

Stereotypic femininity pivots between feelings and behaviors. What all the women did was to take the concept of femininity out of the behavioral realm and place it squarely onto feelings. Femininity became defined by how women felt, not by how they acted. Even Bernie's definition of feminine as meaning ladylike comes closer to how a lady feels than to how she acts. By divorcing femininity from behavior, biking becomes just another activity. It neither promotes nor rejects the feminine. If femininity is seen as an internal feeling rather than a particular behavior, than a strong, competent women pushing around six hundred pounds of steel and chrome would not be seen as a contradiction.

And while Jayne focused upon baking cookies for her kid, it was the underlying feelings of the act, not the act itself that was important. Soft and gentle become positive feelings, not behavioral weaknesses.

In fact, soft and gentle, along with caring and sensitive, become strengths. Thus, the concept of the feminine is not a tight shoe to be forced upon women's feet but a loose-fitting robe, large and light enough to allow all sorts of interesting possibilities. It is also a leather jacket, boots, and chaps to keep out the wind.

In the women's biking community, the concept of gender has been transformed. Femininity has been seen as a positive force allowing the best of feelings to emerge. The behavioral component has been completely eliminated. It is not what a woman does that makes her feminine; it is how she feels. Femininity has lost its restrictive and dependent component. Thus femininity can be seen as absolutely consistent with biking.

None of these women credit the women's movement for their ability to ride. They take their entrance into the male biking world as acts of individual bravery. And they are. Yet there is a hidden element here. The early feminists, whom so many women bikers wish to distance themselves from, helped pave the way for today's riders. Those old-time, serious, relatively rigid, fighting women now in their fifties and sixties identified gender problems, rallied for women's rights, won the freedoms now taken for granted, and cleared the path for a redefinition of femininity. They may have made femininity temporarily a dirty word, but they set the stage for its reinterpretation.

There is a wonderful song by Holly Near that best sums up this historical blank that many younger women draw when contemplating feminism. The song is about an old-time woman. She sits on her porch rocking while the younger, troubled woman confides in her. The old-time woman takes the young woman's face in her hands and says, "If I had not suffered, you wouldn't be wearing those jeans, being an Old-Time woman, ain't as bad as it seems."

I hear that song and I think if my entire generation of feminists hadn't been such hard-nosed, hard-assed, hard-working, civil-rights pushing, abortion-rights gaining, humorless bitches, there would be damn fewer women in the wind today.

8

Rites of Passage

"Sure, we do everything on the bike. We live and we die on it."

Much of what makes a culture viable, what makes it survive over the long haul, is the attention paid to the routine functions of life. Birth, death, and the ordinary rites of passage affirm and reaffirm a community. Harley culture is ritual rich and ritual proud. Having attended a number of weddings, a few funerals, and one birth, I have noted a number of patterns. Always, the bike is front and center. Even in the birthing room, where it was not possible to take a motorcycle, the bike was never very far away. The new mother had ridden to work that very day.

THE MARRYING KIND

It was a beautiful wedding. The bride wore white leather, the groom wore black leather, and the bike was polished to gleaming. The ceremony took place at one end of a one-street town. The revelers lined the entire block. The wedding took place during the annual Bridgeport High Sierra Run.

It was typical Bridgeport weather. It stormed over the passes and snowed for fifty miles in all directions, and the visibility was zero. A number of men, experienced riders all, had gone down in the passes.

We arrived in Bridgeport late, hungry, cold, and very wet. Bradley saved us camping space at Twin Lakes, just twelve miles out of town. Ken and I made camp among the rest of the sodden crew. Three Wheel Steve, arriving with no accommodations, crashed with us. Tired and cold and miserable with altitude sickness, I crawled out of the hut the next morning to discover a bright, clear, exquisitely beautiful day. We were in high country. Gone were the foothills; this was the real thing. Over 7,000 feet up, we were nestled in a forest of evergreens. The site, with its tiny wooden huts and rustic cabins, was a camper's delight. A small army of brightly colored two-person tents dotted the campground, and small fires were already sputtering among the tenters. Snow-capped mountains, higher than one could lift a neck to see, towered above us and the air smelled of trees and lakes and flowers and wood fires and cold, cold snow. The little restaurant at the edge of the campground was crammed full of frigid bikers. We waited our turn for food.

The ride from Twin Lakes campground to the town of Bridgeport follows one of the country's most beautiful roads. It winds around mountain lakes, plunges down two-lane roads, and ends with incredibly tall mountains on one side and High Sierra meadows on the other. Quiet cattle graze in the meadows while deer race in the distance. As Ken and I flew down the road I knew that I would never be able to fully describe the importance of this riding experience. This must be experienced.

Riding gives us access to a world that can be experienced no other way. The bike provides an entrance into that world. This day on that small two-lane road to Bridgeport, Ken and I shared a high-country meadow. We were sharing the trees and smells and clear, clear air. Even Ken's Beast silenced its customary roar in the presence of such a world. For once I didn't complain. In all my urban existence, I had never experienced the awe of commonplace mountain meadows. With tears streaming down my face, we rode into town.

Bikes open a special kind of entrance into the natural world. For tent campers, backpackers, day walkers, mountain climbers, and sturdy hikers, the bikers' entrance must seem strange. Since we go where the roads go, travel at fast speeds, and scare woodland creatures away with our noise and our fuel smells, we must seem like improbable nature lovers. Yet all bikers talk of their love of nature, of the wonders we have seen and of the incredible beauty of the land.

Riders become quite eloquent when sharing their experiences of the natural world. Riding gives one kind of access into the world of air and wind. It gives us access to deserts and mountains, forests and cliffs, gorges, valleys and meadows. The bike is transportation and entrance at the same time. For those who do not hike, climb, or backpack, it is the only way in. Cars, while serving as transportation, go from place to place but shield you from the very world you wish to enter. Called cages, cars keep you away from the action. Even open-topped cars, while permitting the wind and sun to enter your domain, nevertheless shield you from the immediacy of the surrounding world. Cars prevent intimacy. Inside a car you're flesh encased in steel. On a bike you're flesh combined with steel. Flesh and steel are one. Both experience the immediacy of the moment.

The combining of flesh and steel defines the other events of a biker's life. At Bridgeport there was the wedding. The ceremony was simple. The guests, all three thousand bikers, participated in the exuberant pageantry of the event. The bride and groom, leather-dressed to kill, rode up and down the main street while an army of bikers cheered. After several laps around town, the newlyweds took off with a roar. We all celebrated. People who knew the bride and groom told elaborate stories about their meetings, courtship, and prospects. Other folk remembered weddings they had been to and brides and grooms they had known. The words passing between us quickly became the stuff of legend: an oral tradition in formation. Years later, during chance meetings, faraway friends would begin sentences with "You remember, it was the year of the Bridgeport wedding. . . ." The experience had passed into folklore.

Tired and in love with the country, we returned to the campground. That evening we were fortunate. We were able to remain in our small wooden hut. The hut was closed on three sides. It consisted of one very small interior space plus bathroom. The fourth wall was a window covered with only thin mosquito netting. The hut lacked the luxury of a pup tent, but it had a bathroom and gave some privacy. It was a fine night to party.

And party we did. After visiting with the rest of the riders, friends and strangers alike, we retired to our hut replete with armfuls of emergency rations. We munched. Food lay everywhere in reckless abandon. By the time we retired, we had eaten our way through half of it. The rest lay scattered around the hut.

She came somewhere late in the night, following her cubs. For a few minutes I had been watching incredibly cute bear cubs playing amid the tents and garbage cans. I hadn't given a thought to mama until she arrived. Black and heavy and as big as a cow, she walked with none of the playful charm of her offspring. All of a sudden I remembered the literature about camping and bear safety. All the booklets said "Do not keep food near you." We had the entire hut littered with sweet-smelling junk food. "Do not provide easy access to your accommodations." We had half a wall covered with nothing but fine mesh netting. As mama bear lumbered closer and closer to our hut, my blood froze. We were going to die. I had not the slightest doubt about it. I should have listened when my Sierra Club friends talked about hiking and bear safety. But since I never expected to come face-to-face with a real live bear outside of a zoo, I most often zoned out when they started on their precautionary tales. I should have listened. Now we were going to die.

Very, very quietly I crawled over to where Ken, oblivious to it all, was sleeping soundly. "Ken," I whispered, tugging on his sleeve. "Ken, Ken, there's an enormous bear out there and she's going to come in here and kill us. We've left food everywhere. Ken, Ken, wake up. There's a bear out there!"

Rolling over, opening one eye, and responding between clenched teeth, he answered, "What do you want me to do about it?" and promptly fell back to sleep.

The next day we took off for town and I rented a motel room in Bridgeport. It cost a fortune but I didn't care. Mama bear had decided to munch on something other than us. That night we were not her dinner. I was not going to give her a second chow call.

Besides weddings, the Bridgeport run is famous for its raffle. Each year one or more Harleys are offered as prizes. Each year some lucky raffle holder claims the ultimate prize. Bridgeport opens its doors to bikers and bikers open their hearts. All buy raffle tickets, and the proceeds help support town organizations.

One year the money went to build a local hospital. Another year it went to a medical clinic, the fire department, and facilities for the elderly. All raffle helpers were volunteers. Bridgeport weddings are high points. Bridgeport raffles are routine. It's part of the spirit of reciprocity. It's part of the desire to give something back to a community that welcomes bikers.

Wedding are the high points of biker events, but not all of them take place in the country. One very impressive wedding took place right in the center of San Francisco under the dome of the Palace of Fine Arts. Again there was the requisite leather clothing, the sound of the engines drowning out the preacher, the smell of the gasoline mixing with the magnolias, and everyone pretty pleased with themselves. We rode to the wedding, hugged and kissed the bride, smacked the groom on the back, and cheered the new union.

THE BIRTHING OF BABIES

Biker births are rare. For obvious reasons, most bikers do not give birth to babies. Most bikers are men. But every now and then, an extraordinary woman emerges. The woman I have in mind is so rare and special most would assume she was quite mad. Mike Molinari calls her Wildwoman. Others call her Superwoman. I call Debby Lindblom friend.

All through her pregnancy she was told to stop riding. Anxious friends, cautious doctors, and strangers in the street all warned her off the bike. Through it all, she rode. Through her first trimester when she barely showed, she rode. Through her second trimester with her belly starting to balloon out in front of her, she rode. Through her third trimester when she was so big that it was difficult to fit between the seat and handlebars, she rode. Up until the day of delivery she rode. "Only time I ever felt good," she would claim. "Only time my back didn't hurt or my feet weren't sore." She said that riding was good for the growing baby. And we never doubted her. She rode 650 pounds of Low Rider on the day she delivered ten pounds and eleven ounces of a robust healthy boy. A baby biker.

We were all there in that birthing room. Her husband Usaia, her daughter Jennifer, her trusted friends, assorted hospital staff, and her grandson Victor. "Push, Grandma, push" came Victor's rallying calls as Debby struggled to give birth.

Pushing forty, as well as pushing out a baby, with many years between her two pregnancies, Debby was determined. Four days later, she was back at work and riding. Debby is a Frisco legend.

THE WOMEN'S ODYSSEY

Between the birthings and the dyings, the weddings and the ceremonies, comes the odyssey. Men go on trips. Men go on runs. Men go on rides. Women go on odysseys. It is a female rite of passage. It's a proving time, a coming-of-age event, and a ritualized passage into adulthood. We women take to the road and we do it alone. Sometimes a single female companion goes along, but that is rare. The trip, this odyssey, is the testing ground for the woman biker. We go off by ourselves because we must. We must prove, mainly to ourselves, that we can manage the road. Debby rode through the deserts and mountains of the high country. Sharon took off to Sturgis and never stopped until she had covered half of the United States. Margo, with the companionship of one girlfriend, rode to Colorado and back.

The experiences are all different. They reflect the differences in the temperaments and personalities of the riders. They reflect the differences in the routes and routines. They reflect the differences in the times, the bikes, and the luck of the road. Yet they share some remarkable similarities. All the women are testing their ability to survive.

Being a biking woman is working against stereotype. Tradition kicks us in the rear when we leave the rear of the bike. Little in female socialization prepares us for the rigors of the road. The knowledge of mechanical repair or the smarts to survive are typically male traits. All women making the odyssey are testing their skills against the dangers of the known and the dangers of the unknown.

The known dangers are formidable. Women riding alone along America's highways are vulnerable to all the problems that face men riding alone. Robbery, assault, and violence are part of the American scene. But women risk added dimensions of danger. Women risk rape. Women are especially vulnerable. It is assumed that men, while growing up, will learn forms of self-defense. Men who travel the roads find ways of self-protection. Weapons and physical agility and strength and widespread protective human networks provide men with some measure of safety. Someone hell-bent on assaulting for profit usually leaves the touring male biker alone. In general, bikers have a reputation for both meanness and toughness. This is excellent road protection.

Women lack rep. Women are seen as easy victims. In the mind of the assaulter, women are targets because they can be outrun, outridden, outfought, and outfoxed. Some women may not fit this stereotype, but in general, women do not learn the "arts" of warfare in routine ways. Training in these arts is not usually part of a women's tool kit. When a woman takes to the road, she faces the common dangers of the road. Plus she faces the dangers of her femininity.

Double jeopardy. The odyssey causes women to take precautions. Sometimes that means packing a weapon. Other times it means going with a girlfriend or having designated and expected stops along the way. Sometimes it means psyching yourself up for emotional protection by thinking only "good" and "protective" thoughts. The following women all went on odysseys. With one exception, they never packed a weapon or charted expected stops. They did, however, rely heavily upon thoughts and attitudes.

Margo Bouget's odyssey took place on her modified Hugger tricked out to look like a cross between a Heritage and a Fat Boy. That trip covered 3,200 miles and she partnered it with a girlfriend. While she had no significant hassles along the way, she did experience one good scare.

"On a back road in Nevada, near a penitentiary, next to a sign that read 'Do Not Pick Up Hitchhikers,' me and my girlfriend had to stop for gas. There was this guy in a white truck who saw us stop there, and he followed us for about thirty miles. He kept accelerating right on my tail. Each time I would move over to let him pass, he would slow down. When I speeded up, he would again be right on my tail. He kept this up all the way until we got to the next interstate."

Margo's eyes light up when she talks about her odyssey. She rode through Arizona, New Mexico, Colorado, and Utah before turning back home to California. She had no network before the trip but she forged one on the road.

"During the trip, when we came to Silverton, Colorado, we were helped by a real, rugged-looking, old-time biker named Flash. He and his buddy Barron were part of the High Plains Drifters. They gave us wonderful hospitality. They let us camp in their backlands and invited us to their July parties in Silverton. They couldn't have been more decent. They opened their homes, helped us service our bikes, gave us road tips and directions, explained the routes, and headed us toward wonderful scenery. We also got to attend the very best Fourth of July party. It was a trip of a lifetime."

Margo's networking, good spirits, and overall good-naturedness kept her and her buddy safe for this trip. Other women employ other methods when they travel.

Sharon Turner bought her daughter Heather a brand-new Sportster. Mother and daughter would ride to Sturgis together. Sharon is an experienced and fearless rider. She owns no car, commutes on her bike, and travels everywhere on it. Grocery shopping and laundry pickup are done on the bike. She rides in the rain, in the wind, in sickness and in health. On her '93 Softail Custom she rode cross-country with one girlfriend. She traveled from San Francisco to Tennessee, north to Wisconsin and across to Minnesota, over to South Dakota, and home again.

"I was never hassled by anybody on any of my trips. I only got good vibes from people. I never had any problems anywhere I went. On my first trip across the country I took a stun gun with me. They were not illegal them. You didn't even have to register them. But it was just too much trouble. If I ever needed it, it would have been too difficult to get it. It was never handy. But I never had occasion to use it. After a while, bringing it seemed kind of silly. But then, I have never felt uncomfortable on the road. It's part of learning to take control of your life."

Pat Tompkins is a biker, a woman biker. For eleven years, due to an unfortunate marriage, she did not ride. She and her husband split and she returned to the road. In 1992 she bought a Sportster, a Softail, and a '53 Panhead. When asked why she had to have all these bikes, she said they all had different purposes. In eight months she traveled over twenty thousand miles. She cranked both her Softail and Sportster down, shortened the shocks, and negated the suspension.

"They all ride really hard. I've always liked a hard ride. I didn't want to feel like I was riding on a sofa. I'm in really good shape. I work out and have an athlete's body. So when I ride, I want to feel the motorcycle on the road. I want to feel all the bumps and ruts and ridges. The eleven years I didn't ride, I wasn't in good shape. I was miserable. Once I started riding again I took much better care of myself."

"When you did all that riding alone," I asked, "what did you do to take care of yourself? What if you broke down? What did you do for protection on the road?"

"The bike breaks down, I can fix it. If I'm on the road and my bike breaks, I take care of it. I grew up in Alaska; I can take care of myself. When I'm on the road, I get respect from everybody. It's a matter of pride."

"How did you get to these attitudes? They're unusual for women. Even biking women."

"My friends in Alaska are really raw bikers. They are into the club thing. They are old bikers. When they are not working on a job, they are working on their bikes. They're in the trades. Not career oriented. They are mechanics, electricians, carpenters. They prepared me for the biking experience."

"Which is?"

"When I'm riding, I want the rain and bugs and wind on me. I don't even like a windshield in front of me."

"What keeps you safe on the road?"

"I know how to ride. I know how to wrench. And I don't ask special favors of anyone. And I have attitude."

Pat, at five foot ten, presents a formidable figure. Margo, at five foot two, presents a very different kind of figure. With masses of long curly black hair, violet eyes, and high-heeled boots, Margo has an image that contrasts sharply with Pat's lean, muscular, and spare one. Sharon, at fifty, with short blond hair and a sturdy but fashionably lean frame, looks as comfortable pouring tea as pumping gas. Sharon, Margo, Debby, and Pat all went on odysseys. All of them showed concern for road safety. All of them shared the view that the road held serious dangers. Each coped with these dangers in her own way. Since none of them took weapons (except for the stun gun on Sharon's first trip), they all relied on particular states of mind to see them through. Margo relied on her interpersonal skills and networking. Debby was lucky. When she was threatened with a potential bike thief, the guy's girlfriend intervened and Debby counted her blessings. Sharon, after a short time with a stun gun, relied on good vibes. Pat counted on attitude. All attributed their safety records to good karma.

Women who ride are extraordinary people. According to Margo, they have a wild spirit. She sees riding women as throwbacks to earlier times. Women riders break out of the traditional mold very early in life. And they keep on breaking out. They have interesting lives. They live lives of high adventure. They go to the very edge. Sometimes, they go over it.

THE YEARLY RUNS

The Carson City Run has been around for a long time. Bikers come from all over California and Nevada to attend. The lucky ones stay in fancy digs at South Lake Tahoe. They ride over the mountain for the festivities. For most, though, Carson City, with its cheap motels, honky-tonk atmosphere, and close proximity to Virginia City, provides an ideal location with all the action needed in one place.

Bikers converge on this cowboy gambling town to spend a weekend doing heavy partying before departing with light memories and lighter wallets. Bikes line the streets, cruise the highways, roar up the hill to Virginia City, and park in front of every motel in town. The Virginia City atmosphere at the Bucket of Blood Saloon, the camel races, and the smells from hand-dipped chocolate provide the day's entertainment. The moonlight rides up and down the mountain grace the evenings with enchantment. When you're riding two-up, snuggling close, gliding without lights along the moonlit roads with a softened throttle, the night-blooming flowered air has a mystery of magic.

There are routine rituals of renewal. Friends meet with old friends. Lovers arrange trysts. Long, long nights are spent around parking lots swapping stories of the glory days. Lies are retold.

Bikers love to hang out in parking lots, and Carson offers more parking lots than any other city of its kind. Pull three chairs out of a motel room, place them next to several parked bikes, break out the Jack Daniels or Wild Turkey, and you've got a party. All night long, people will be coming and going. New recruits will arrive as the old ones stagger off to bed. The sweet-pungent aromatic smell of grass mingles with gas and oil and grease. This is a gathering in time. This is a time to rekindle old relationships. This is a time to get laid.

On a run, bikers ride hard, party hard, and still have enough energy left over for sex. Many a couple have gone to bed wearing just bare skin and chaps. Having survived another day on the road is reason enough to celebrate. Having so many friends in such close proximity raises the celebration level.

My first Carson Run was special for all the usual reasons and for a few unusual ones. Ken and I had the phenomenal luck to be rooming right next to D. C. Dick and Woody. Two old-time Ten Percenters, two founding members of the FogHogs. These guys knew their way around bikes.

Well into the night we talked. Sitting on a narrow strip of concrete between rooms and bikes, we drank and talked in an atmosphere stilled of mufflers, carbs, and cams. We staggered into our rooms late into the night.

159

About 5:00 A.M. I heard the sound of shouting. I raised the (stiff with dirt) curtains to see a hair-raising sight. Four teenage boys were backing up a large truck. They were shouting directions to each other and it looked like they were heading right for Ken's bike. The Beast was sitting directly in their path. Waking Ken was out of the question. He was sleeping off his partying. Shoving at him with all my strength produced only an incoherent 'Huh!' Dressed in four seconds, I ran out yelling at the kids to stop. It was a big truck. It was a tight parking lot and they were trying to turn around. They had one straight shot out of the lot but they apparently didn't want to take it. They wanted to turn around and head in the opposite direction. Unfortunately, the Beast stood directly in their path. Equally unfortunate was the state the boys were in. They had been partying as hard as the bikers. We were in for trouble.

Just when I figured that the Beast was going to die, Woody opened his door to check out the commotion. Mostly undressed for bed, with his long gray beard, wild long hair, and total body tattooing, he must have looked like an apparition to these young and drunk boys. They stopped in their tracks. The truck stopped. Their shouts stopped. Their very breathing sank to a whisper. Woody sized up the situation instantly and drawled in his soft, still voice, "Hey Barbara, you want I should shoot them?"

It took less than ten seconds for those boys to jump onto the truck, gun the motor, and leave the parking lot by the straightest route out of there. They did not wait around to see if Woody was packing. They just split. And all things considered, it was the wisest thing they could have done.

THE CAMPOUTS

Runs are special. But campouts are sublime. We camp below the snow line. We camp near Santa Cruz in the incredible woodlands of Big Basin. There are no bears. This year, though, there is some talk of cougars. We camp far away from all the other campers. Every year the management of Big Basin places us as far away from civilization as possible. We camp next to wild meadows. We camp next to groups of slow-moving, fearless deer. This is their home and they know it. The bikers are entranced. One part of our group whispers 'Bambi' while the other part yells 'Dinner!' We camp under huge redwoods. We camp in woods that seem as though they've been around since before the animal kingdom rose from the sea. We camp in the wilds with outhouses for toilets, spigots for running water, and mosquitoes for pets.

To backpackers, this is tame stuff. To mountain climbers, this isn't

Ron "Woody" Woods (Courtesy of Noel Paraninfo)

even the wilderness. We did, after all, get here on the backs of bikes. We did get here through dirt roads and gravel paths. To the *real* outdoors person, this bit of nature is cultivated and domesticated. But to city dwellers who never expected to see an unpruned tree, this is heaven, indeed.

And we change.

The woods change us. We arrive full of reverence for the natural world. We arrive filled with awe and wonderment. This lasts about an hour. Then we make this part of the wilderness our home. Two-person tents go up, portable chairs come out, firewood gets gathered, and food is prepared. Soon, all is mundane except for the critters, the trees, and the shifting, sliding smells of the outdoors.

The woods change us. Gone are our urban ways. Bikers in nature are a fearful sight indeed. This is no fitness crowd. Riding is hard work but it is not a hard workout. Upper-body strength is developed but total body fitness is not. The aerobic, muscle-building, body-slimming effects of other sports are absent from the biking experience. After all, you sit on the bike and *it* does the work. The power is in the engine, not in the rider. Add to that the penchant to drink as much beer as possible, move as little as possible, and eat everything in sight. Eventually most bikers develop the infamous biker stance: big bellied, bow-legged, broad shouldered, and muscle dense.

Do all bikers look like this? Of course not. But a surprising number do. This is not a culture that promotes physical fitness. There are individuals who take good care of themselves. Individuals who work out and jog and diet and go to a gym. There are isolated accounts of bikers who are strict vegetarians, teetotalers, gourmet coffee drinkers, or exercise buffs. I can even name some in each category, but this is more the exception than the rule. The contemporary physical fitness movement is largely youth oriented and middle-class based. The bikers I travel with are predominantly working class and middle-aged. Hard-working folk do not feel like going to a gym after working at construction sites or climbing roofs to install electrical systems.

Office workers feel the need to move their bodies after having spent hours at a desk. Management folk need to stretch and run and jump. Plumbers, truck drivers, cops, and painters want to take it as easy as possible. The physical urge to move doesn't grab in the same way. Often it doesn't grab at all.

Then there is the matter of looks. Men get no points for looking fit. Guys get no flak for flab. An individual may decide to diet, exercise, and abstain from drinking as a personal push toward a more healthy existence, but the subculture neither supports nor discourages this choice. Big, massive guys, massive with muscle or fat, are fully ac-

Campout

cepted. With no cultural incentives to trim down and cut back, middle age runs its course and many bikers sport that special biker look that much of middle-class, youth-oriented, trim-obsessed America has learned to hate.

Overweight and underfit, the men of this hard-living culture push their pleasures to excess. Avoidance of pain and promotion of pleasure is a far more accurate description of the goals of this group than is the deferred gratification of the golden mean. The men will eat, drink, and screw as much as possible. When they can.

Bikers, along with the rest of America, have a double standard when it comes to looks. Men can be fit or fat, large or mega-large, sturdy or slender, or just plain plain. Men have choices. Women do not. Women are expected to be "attractive." Most women make concessions to standards of weight control, flattering clothing choices, and "attractive" presentation of self.

Women who passenger feel more pressure to conform to routine community standards of prettiness than do women who ride. Having a man (rider) to please is part of the passenger's job. As is true for women in the general culture, the emphasis is on being slender, appropriately dressed, and carefully made up. Fashions for women passengers shift from region to region, community to community, but women

163

tend to uphold the local fashions when possible. It is very common for women passengers to look as sexy as possible while riding the rear. It makes their men look good. While men get no points for fitness and no flak for flab, women do.

At biker rallies there are wet T-shirt contests for women. Men compete more frequently in contests for the most extensive tattoos or piercings. Recently, women too have been competing in the tattoo contests and men have been competing in wet shorts. But traditionally, the emphasis has been on women's youth and innate good looks and on men's acquired characteristics.

When women break the "looks" rules and go against the grain, they are choosing to defy biker cultural standards. Women riders are more apt than passengers to wear whatever they please, rather than what makes them "pretty." Since riding is already in opposition to traditional femininity, women tend to make their own rules even when it comes to looking good. They use their own definitions of the term "good." As riders, they are not dependent upon men to get them into the wind.

Campouts produce a strange mix of machinery and nature. Bikers, out of their natural domain—the domain of garages, gas stations, and asphalt—change. It is a time of license. The old rules of behavior are relaxed. Play becomes even more important. There is an emphasis on practical joking. It is a major form of play.

Middle-class America is leery of practical joking since to succeed a joke has to transgress upon someone's rights and privileges. There are both psychological and physical transgressions inherent in practical joking. Middle-class America views this with alarm.

I love listening to the tales of pranks past. The time when the shitter was turned on its side with one of the guys trapped inside. The time when the tent was rolled down the hill, much to the consternation of the biker sleeping within it. The time when one of the members snored so loudly that his tent, with him inside, out cold, was dragged to the far reaches of the campsite. He spent the entire next day trying to figure out how he got there. The time when several guys picked up a friend's motorcycle and carried it over the ridge and buried it under some bushes.

For practical joking to succeed, it is necessary for the people involved to be friends. Try playing jokes on relative strangers and someone could get seriously hurt. This explains some of the functions and fun of the practical joke. It tests and affirms the bonds of real friendship. It also pushes the boundaries of what is considered fun. The butt of the practical joke usually does not appreciate the joke at the time of its occurrence. It is a measure of the friendship that he or she accepts it. It is also a measure of that person's character. To be considered a good sport means that you can take practical jokes in stride. When they happen to you, it may not seem funny but it is funny to everyone else. If you're good-natured about it, the rest of the group is permitted to laugh and you can be assured of getting your turn next time around.

License takes other forms as well. On one campout we were so far out in the woods that we thought we were completely separated from neighbors and immune from contact with them. This belief permitted us to be as loud and vocally offensive as we pleased. We yelled, pounded on logs, listened to a car radio at top volume, sang at top voice, and participated in other annoyances with great pleasure. As the night progressed some of our dope- and booze-thickened voices grew louder and more obnoxious. One by one our companions, lovers, and mates drifted off to the tents, while a few of us remained to serenade the night.

First the rangers came. They voiced their initial complaint. Cease the commotion. Others were trying to sleep. Extreme distance from other campers was not sufficient to shield them from our foul behavior. Even having a cop in our ranks was not sufficient to stem a reprimand.

The second time the rangers came we hooted their approach. Beyond reason, we were asserting our rights to be troublesome loud-mouths. Only a few of us remained stationed around the campfire. Only a very few were prepared to go down screeching.

With astonishment, I recognized myself among the few. I was behaving in ways that I would have profoundly objected to in anyone else. My husband, in disgust, had long since gone to sleep. He missed the fun. He missed my narrowly escaping being brought up on charges of drunk and disorderly conduct in a wooded campground. He missed my confrontation with the park police over my right to be an asshole. Luckily, our cop friend got us out of the jam.

In the morning, which dawned cold and damp, we crawled, half dead, out of our sleeping bags. One of the early-to-bed folks was singing "O Sole Mio" at the top of his lungs. Keep him up at night, would we! He'd show us.

"Coffee's on! Coffee's on!" He kept yelling.

As we crawled out of the tents, he informed us that coffee was indeed on. All we had to do was ride into town to drink it.

BIKERS FUNERAL: THE FINAL TRIBUTE

Biker funerals are affairs of the soul. They are testaments to respect, finality, and affirmation. Friends gather, bikes and bodies in full gear, and ride from the memorial home to the grave site. When a patch holder dies, the entire club turns out for the funeral. When Dudley Perkins Jr. died, most of the motorcycle-riding police force created a motorcade as a final tribute to this extraordinary man. Biker funerals are impressive; they contribute to a reaffirmation of the culture and are a constant reminder of how close to the edge we all ride.

A member of our group died and we wished to give him a biker farewell. Since Ken's bike was down, we both had to ride my Sportster to the procession. At that time the Sportster had not been equipped with passenger pegs, legal rear seat, nor other items of passengering safety. But to show up in a car was unthinkable. We two-upped in the longest, saddest, quietest ride of my life. Forty Harleys rode through the San Francisco Mission on the way to the funeral parlor. The streets of San Francisco had borne silent witness to many a biker funeral and on that day the FogHogs paid a last tribute to Ken Mosely.

After the services, we gathered at a local bar and drank to his memory. We told elaborate tales of his riding abilities. We swapped stories. We mourned our missing member as we reinforced our ties to the living. Grieving, mourning, and remembering stamp the realities of life and death into our souls and into the community. Doing this as a group reinforces the group identity, reaffirms our commitments to each other, and lets us face the unfathomable aspects of death. We may grieve in silence and in solitude but we mourn in common.

The bikers I hang with are "old-time" people. They appreciate family life and have a wide tolerance for family makeup. They appreciate riding with friends and participating in community activities. Births, deaths, marriages, ceremonies, and rituals are taken seriously. The looseness of the community reinforces and does not weaken its ties. This is a community that crosses economic, class, race, and gender lines. The bike, as symbol, icon, transportation, and greatly loved machine permits us to cross those lines. The bike provides the solidarity glue that cements us as a community. The bike provides the activity, the interest, the conversational topics, and the shared language that bind us together. The bike brings us together. Without it, some of us would remain friends. But without it, most of us would fragment into our separate worlds. The extraordinary strength of the bike lies in its ability to forge a community out of disparate folk *and* keep it going.

9

Family Portraits in Duplicate

"There's nothing like a Harley to bring a family together."

There are no typical riding families. There is nothing routine or ordinary about bikers. Each person, each bike, each family has its own style and story. Recognizing the arbitrariness of the label, let's look at the following families who ride.

Robin is ten years old. She started riding at four and a half and will proudly tell you that she rode with her dad all the way to Bridgeport. She did this when she was six. This difficult, ten-hour trip has left many a passengering ole lady exhausted. Not Robin. She is experienced and casual about her abilities. She passengers on motorcycles. She rides horses. She gets in the wind, any way she can.

"I first tried it out when I was four. My dad rode me around the street. He taught me to hold on to his back and balance myself. He also gave me a strap to hold on to. I always held on. I never let go."

"Were you scared?" I asked, remembering all of my early experiences.

"No. My dad let me start riding when I was real little but we didn't go on the highway until I was at least six. I was never scared, but I remember once, I was singing to music and wiggling all around on the bike, and my dad told me to stop because I was making the bike move all over the road."

This last remark was accompanied by a giggle and a swift look toward her mother. Robin lives with her father and his girlfriend in San Francisco. She also lives with her mother and her mother's boyfriend in Oregon. They share her. I have known Robin for almost five years, gone on many a run with her, and was delighted when she consented to talk to me about her life. At ten she is into her long-legged "coltish" stage, staggeringly beautiful and totally poised. We both recalled the time I had sent a picture of her and me on a Trike to the magazine

Harley Women and had seen it published in the Kids' Korner section. We also remembered the time she posed with KrisAnn Whiteley, a former Ms. Harley-Davidson, and the two were featured in the 1993 FogHog calendar. Robin has grown up in the Harley world. We had expected that Robin would run for the title of Ms. Harley-Davidson when she was old enough. We all thought she would be a natural. When the contest was disbanded, she was disappointed. So were we all.

The Harley-Davidson Motor Company had been getting flak about the contest. Some men and women were complaining that it was a sexist holdover and should be terminated. There were mixed opinions. The contest was eventually dropped, to the great regret of many Harley riders. A number of women have voiced their complaints over the abandonment of the contest. Comments ranged from "It's a fun thing to do" to "Why doesn't Milwaukee have a Mr. Harley-Davidson to reign alongside Ms. Harley-Davidson? Then we women would have someone to vote for too." None of us doubted that if Robin ran, she would win. Her Harley experiences alone put her right up there. At Bridgeport she had successfully climbed a slippery greased pole and won the contest, out-maneuvering a whole group of older kids. She kept most of the prize money too. Her leather vest proudly sports HOG colors and she passengers with complete confidence.

"I ride horses now," she confides, "'cause my dad was in a motorcycle accident and isn't ready to ride yet. I still ride with Mike when I stay with my mom in Oregon, but I don't get a chance to ride on the bike as much as I used to. I love riding horses. I am more in control when I ride a horse. It's different than a bike 'cause you don't have to bounce around if you don't want to. With a horse, I do the riding and no one is there to tell me what to do. I did get scared on a horse once. My old, old horse, she went over a jump and then she stopped and she threw me off. She only bucked one time but she stopped short and I went over her head and over the fence. I was OK and so was the horse, but I was scared."

I asked Robin if she intended to continue riding.

"I'm gonna ride a bike and I'm gonna ride a horse. I like them both in different ways. I love trail riding, that's my favorite. You never have to worry about cars. When I grow up, I want my own horse and I want my own Harley. I still want to be Ms. Harley-Davidson."

Robin's mother, Linda Davis, left the room before the end of interview. Then she returned and told me her story. Born and bred in the Bronx, she arrived in California in the early seventies. Now in her forties, she lives in Oregon with an Old Biker. She had fallen in love with bikes from the very beginning of her California experience.

"When I first came to Berkeley, I was only eighteen. Walking down the street, a guy on a bike came up and offered me a ride. I went."

"Just like that?" I asked. "How was it?"

"I was both excited and scared. We rode back to the place I was living. There were bikers staying at the house. My son Sean was only a year old and some of the people in the house were watching him. It was a communal house in San Francisco so there were lots of people around."

"What was the place like?"

"There was a war going on in Vietnam. There was also a war going on in San Francisco. Some of the guys staying in the house were from the Gypsy Jokers MC and they were hiding out from the Hells Angels. They had some bikes hidden upstairs in the bedrooms. They had rolled the bikes up the stairs. They hid out with all of us for a while."

"Do you still see them?"

"No! Who knows where they are now. Who knows if they are even alive."

"Did you have a lot of problems having a baby with you?"

"Yes, but I wanted him. I didn't marry his father. I was only sixteen when I got pregnant, and the welfare authorities wanted me to be a ward of the state. I would have had to give him up for adoption or have him taken away from me, so I ran away. They would have taken away my baby. I guess you could say that I had already started to do things that were *not* down the mainstream path. I had a great willingness to be different. I wasn't afraid of difference. I was from the Bronx."

"Was this your first experience with bikers? When you came to California?"

"When I was pregnant with Sean and crashing and squatting in different apartments on the Lower East Side, I had a run-in with the landlord. I was a pregnant teenager and the landlord came in and told me and the other people there to get out. There was a group of bikers staying in another apartment in the building. They were from a Texas MC. The president of the club came down to our apartment and told the landlord that *he* should get out. I remember the president of the club real good. He wasn't very big but he had an enormous presence.

"Next day we all went down to say thank you to the MC president. We had taken acid. I didn't know then not to take acid when you're pregnant. When I saw the MC president he was so beautiful. He had rainbow colors all over him and he was radiant. I remember saying, 'Is it true that you bikers kill people?' They just laughed and laughed. But they never answered. They always treated me as if I was their baby sister. They always treated me really, really good but I never rode with them."

"Did they seem different from the other people you were with?"

"They were bikers. We were hippies. They were dressed in leathers and had long hair and beards and lots of tattoos. They acted really tough. They wouldn't let anyone get away with anything but they were also really sweet. They were very nice to me."

"Well," I asked, "if you didn't start riding with them and you only rode once or twice in San Francisco, when Sean was a baby, when did you start loving bikes?"

"I didn't really get into riding until I was with my second husband, Robin's father. By then, I was an ICU nurse and pretty much anti-bike. I had taken care of lots of downed bikers. Lots of brain-dead people. I was very negative about bikes. But I was cajoled. I gave in. My husband really wanted a bike so we went to DP [Dudley Perkins] in '89 and bought a Heritage Softail. I paid the down payment. Then I went for a ride. I got on, rode around the block, and got off right away. I was absolutely terrified. Then he put Robin on the bike. She was almost five. I could see that he went slow for her."

"If you were so scared, how come you let Robin ride?"

"You know Don. No one could tell him anything. He wanted her to ride and she loved it, so I gave in. I would drive the truck and follow them. He got the bike in '89 and joined the FogHogs right away. We separated and then got back together again. We went to Sturgis that year. He rode the bike, I drove the crash truck.

"Then we got involved in the FogHogs and that was very good. Even though the first time I saw the men, I was really nervous. They looked like huge guys in black leather and I feared they were all Hells Angels. But when I met the guys it was different. Everyone treated me very nicely. That was the year we went to Bridgeport and Robin rode with Don. While we were there, I asked him to take me on the back for a little ride and it was nice. But it didn't continue to be nice. He always wanted to ride too fast. He liked to ride that way. So he would always take the bike and I would always drive. That way I could still participate.

"The trip to Sturgis was great. I met some wonderful women and we would sit and talk and visit. Some of the women dressed me in riding gear so I could passenger for a while. They loaned me boots, helmet, gloves, jacket, and scarves. I was all dressed up like a biker and Don and I rode together at night with a full moon in the mountains and it was so beautiful that I couldn't get over it. But then we went on the highway and that was the hard part for me. The wind was so bad I couldn't breathe. I went back and forth between excitement and panic. Then one of the women I met told me about finding the sweet spot."

"Linda, is that like a biker's G-spot?"

"Very funny! The sweet spot is the spot that you find where the wind goes around you and over your head. You are on the bike in the wind, but you can breathe. You use the guy's back to shield you from the wind. And it works. When we were in Sturgis, I rode around on the back of the bike and it was fine.

"When we got back from Sturgis, I joined the FogHogs and was voted in as secretary. I almost always took Robin to the meetings. She was like a club mascot. I got more and more involved in the biking community but I still didn't ride. I only passengered with Don some of the time. I never really liked riding with him. Then we broke up."

"Wasn't it awkward? Don was the member, you were only an associate member. He had the bike but when you two split up you stayed on in the club and he left!"

"At first it was really very awkward. I didn't know if anyone would want me to stay. I didn't ride. I was at first very embarrassed and afraid that I would be a burden to everyone. Then Noel Vivian made his famous comment and we all laughed and I felt better."

"Noel Vivian made a comment?"

"Yeah, you know. He said that I could ride with everyone. I could ride with all the guys. He said, 'We will all give you rides. We will all pass you around like a cheap dollar bill.' And I knew that he was joking and being nice and so I started riding with other riders. They were my friends.

"I first rode with Mike Molinari, the director of the FogHogs. It was great. We went down the road all relaxed and leisurely. I remember looking at the speedometer and seeing that he was doing eighty and I realized that I was not scared. I thought, this is wonderful. I was so happy. I had finally crossed a line. I could passenger. I loved it. Before that ride with Mike, I knew I loved the bikes and the people, but I was really scared to ride. When Don and I split up, I started riding with other men and discovered that I really loved riding in the wind. That riding season I rode with at least a dozen guys. All friends. I never slept with any of them. I was very proud of that!"

"Why didn't you sleep with any of them and why were you proud of it?"

"I didn't want to complicate things with the FogHogs. They were my riding group. They were my friends. We would hug and shake hands and hug again but it remained friends."

"Why?"

"I was walking a really thin line here. There were a lot of risks. I didn't want the other women pissed off at me. I didn't want to risk the women being really mad if I rode with their husbands. I also didn't want to risk the guys getting mad and fighting over who I rode with. But mostly, I didn't want to risk being thought of as a biker's whore. When you are a single woman and you are riding with a lot of different guys, there is always talk. I didn't want any of the talk making me seem like a whore. This was my social group. I wasn't going to lose them by breaking my own rules. I wanted to keep riding. And I rode on the back, so I had to keep on good relations with everyone."

"Why did you have to keep riding?"

"I loved it. Lots of people will tell you stuff about riding, but there is lots of things they will not tell you. The bike vibrates. It's a great sexual feeling. I've ridden with lots of guys on lots of different kinds of bikes and it was all great. I never had an orgasm while riding but it's real sexual. Don't let anyone tell you it's not."

"Did you know, Linda, that Bradley calls it the Milwaukee vibrator?"

"Well it is. Most of the time I go into a different place in my head when I'm on a bike. I'm sitting on that seat yet I'm flying. I close my eyes and I feel like I'm in a bubble. I feel absolutely safe. It's almost like dreaming. It's hard to explain. I'm not asleep. But almost. It's like being hypnotized.

"Then there are all the smells. Everything feels so close and good. You are surrounded by pines and flowers and woods when you ride in the country. You become part of everything you ride through. The man I live with feels this way too. But mostly the men don't express it the same way.

"Riding with people you're friends with is wonderful but riding with someone you love, someone you are really close too, is even better. You see something wonderful and point it out to him and he sees it too. You both see and feel it at the same time. You both share that beauty *at the same moment.*

"Also, I love the smell of the grease and oil and I love the sound of the bikes. I love to go on rides with someone I love because we can get really close. I can get totally relaxed and let myself drift into the ride. I also get to experience this wonderful bubble of safety where I am secure and nothing can hurt me.

"When we ride in groups, it's a different experience. You smile at each other. You talk across the road, you yell to each other and play games. Remember on the Love Run where we kept handing each other the camera? We took pictures while we were both on the back of the bikes!"

"Yes, we were riding so fast and so close I was afraid that we were going to drop the camera. But we did take wonderful pictures."

While Linda and I talked, Robin played and her ole man lounged

172

outside. Since they all loved to ride and I thought of them as a biking family, I asked them about Harley culture. Linda thought for a while and then responded.

"I love it when we are riding in groups, dressed in all our colors. It feels like a culture. When we stop for lunch and go to eat we all look so good. That's when I feel included, accepted. This is the culture I love. We all look so spectacular that *you know* we are all getting off on it. When we go stomping into a restaurant and all the other people there look at us, they are thinking we are bikers. They are thinking about all the stereotypes about bikers, and I think that's special. Those people are thinking that we're the biggest sex dolls around."

"Linda, that's playing to all the stereotypes."

"I don't care. Those stereotypes can play against you but they also can work in your favor. Everyone thinks we are the sexiest women around. Also, people don't mess with you. When you go to eat, you don't get harassed and you always get your table right away. Like the restaurant wants you to get in and out as fast as possible. This is all the good side of the stereotype. Other people think we are sexy and have a lot of fun and wish that they could ride too. Just look at all those strangers taking pictures of us!"

Linda continues: "Harley culture is separate from the rest of motorcycling. And it *is* based on a lot of myths. It grew out of the movies and the Hells Angels stories. It's the myth of the very tough guy. You know, the guy who rides all day and never gets tired. The guy who can drink everything all day long and still function. The guy who can walk into a bar and every woman there wants him. The guy who fights all the time. The guy who's sexually insatiable. It's the myth that people believe about bikers. Most of it's not true, but there is just a little piece of it that is true and it's that little piece we all want.

"The stereotype can work well for you. If you ride, you can play the biker. Whatever part of the myth people want to have in their lives, they can play out. They can live it. We all have different parts of our personalities. This whole Harley thing is one way of letting out that part of our personality. For me it works well. At work, I'm a nurse. I dress in white, am superclean and sober and am always smiling and nurturing. I'm Miss Perfection. As a nurse I'm supposed to be. And that's all right. That's a part of who I am. But then I get on a bike and another part of me comes out. The exact opposite emerges. I wear black leather. I get dirty, full of grease and oil. When we camp out, sometimes I don't get a decent shower for days. When I'm part of the riding world, I also feel totally sexual. Riding lets out the wild, free, sexual part. Riding is something that gives me permission to do all those things that I want to do. For some of us, that's a big part of riding.

173

"But there is a bad side too. I could no longer go with a guy who wouldn't ride. I love all the parts of riding so much that he would just have to ride to share them. When I first started living with my ole man, one of the most wonderful things about our being together was that we could share our love of bikes. He rides all kinds of bikes. He can fix anything and he loves Harleys best. I prefer it when he rides Harleys but other bikes are fun too. Anything that gets you in the wind is good. That's when I relax. Besides, that's when I like to play, too."

"Hasn't the new helmet law cut down on your play?" I asked. "When Ken and I used to ride, I would nibble on his ear or play with his hair. Now that's really hard to do."

"That's true," Linda responded. "When you wear a helmet, you lose a little of that kind of intimacy, but there are other things you can do together. I love to pull up my shirt and bra from the front, and then pull up his shirt in the back and push my breasts hard against his back and then pull my vest around him and me so no one can see what we are doing. The first time I did that, pressed my naked breasts against his back while we were riding, I thought he would drop the bike. But he really likes it. Sometimes I'll put my hand against his leg or I'll massage his hand or arm or other part while he's riding. There are all kinds of ways you can be intimate on the bike."

"You've been around the biking scene for a while. Did you ever have trouble with other women? When you and your second husband split up, was it because of woman trouble?"

"When I first split up from my first husband—we married each other twice—he would go home with other women. There was one woman. She would go to the bike meetings even though she was not a member. She was not an associate member either. She just went to meetings to find a biker. She was looking for a guy who rode.

"Then after we were made up, one night I didn't feel like going to the meeting. Don went alone. But when he left the meeting, he did not leave alone. He left with this other woman on the back of his bike. He didn't come home until the next morning. He made up some kind of story because I was hysterical. At first I believed him but then this other woman called me (I will not name her) and she said that Don had been with her. She called my house to tell me that they had been together. I called her a liar. She described his tattoos.

"After a while I forgave him, but I never let him go to a meeting without me again. I knew that he had come back to me (it was a pride thing), because the motorcycle was parked downstairs in the garage. When a man's motorcycle is parked in your garage, you know the guy is there too. If he takes his bike away, you know that you're in trouble.

He is not going to leave his bike. He would be afraid that you might trash it."

"Linda, you have told me what you think about Harley culture, what about the word biker? Would you use it?"

"I hate that word. It's used in so many derogatory ways. I try to stay away from it. But then I also feel the opposite. To me, a guy I'm with must be a biker. In the good sense of the word. That's what really attracts me to him. It's not just a hobby or a game to him. It's part of his life. He's got to be completely involved in it. He *needs* to get out and ride. That need is part of his soul and spirit. It's part of me too. In spite of the fear and the doubt I experience about becoming a rider myself, I still want to do it. It gets really frustrating having to wait for someone else to get you in the wind. If I rode, I could be in the wind whenever I wanted.

"Riding is one of the very best things that ever happened to me. I hope that I'll be doing it to the very end of my days. If I knew that I was down to my last couple of days I would say, tie me to the back of a bike or put me in a sidecar, and let me have one last ride. One last sunrise and one last sunset on a bike. Then let me go."

Linda, her ole man, and Robin are a family who love to ride. But there isn't any such thing as a typical biker family. The following interview is with the youngest rider I met. If Robin is the youngest passenger, John Cannon is the youngest rider. He, like Robin, comes from a riding family. Unlike Robin, he was alone when I interviewed him. The rest of the family was away at the time. John started riding in 1994 at the age of fifteen. He had been passengering since he had turned twelve. He rode with his father.

"It looked like fun. I liked going out with my dad. I didn't know much about bikes then, but it looked really enjoyable."

"Were you ever scared when you passengered?"

"Not usually. Only when my dad decided that he was upset with someone and then chased after them. My dad can really travel fast when he wants to. But he's a really good rider. My mother wasn't ever worried 'cause she had ridden with him a lot. My dad is an experienced rider."

"When did you start riding?"

"Just this year. I got my own Sportster when I turned sixteen. I rode it the morning after I bought it. Then I crashed it."

"You what?"

"I crashed it. I went down the street and crashed into a driveway. I was only going five miles an hour and I wasn't hurt."

"Was the bike hurt?"

"The bike went down. But the only things broken were the passing lamps, the blinkers, and the mirror."

"How did you know how to ride?"

"I understood about the clutch and I knew how everything worked. My dad had taken me down the street and showed me how to ride. That's when I first crashed it. Then I got on and rode it around the parking lot before going home. The next day me and my dad went out riding on the back roads of Marin. I loved it. It's really relaxing."

When I asked about Harley culture, John responded, "I think there is a Harley culture. I wouldn't have bought any other bike. It wouldn't be the same. I don't know if it's a culture or a clan. It's really brothers and sisters getting together and doing something they enjoy."

"How did your mother feel about your riding?"

"I don't think that she liked it at first. She thought it was too dangerous. But then I took the riders' safety course in Novato and she felt much better. When I took the class I screwed up on only one thing. Mostly I did really well in the class. It was so easy riding those little bikes. In class they give you little bikes to ride. After riding my 883 those little bikes are fun. I was riding a little 125cc. After I completed the safety riding course, I automatically got my license. All you have to do is pass the course and you get your motorcycle license. Now my mother lets my younger brother Josh ride on the back with me. He's thirteen. I don't think he's going to ride when he gets older. He likes getting to a friend's house on the back of the bike, but he doesn't seem interested in riding. He doesn't like it like I do."

I thought with envy about the ease with which he got his license. The law has changed. When I took the safety class several years ago, no matter how well I did in class, I still had to go down to the DMV and ride around those damned little circles. Since 1994, a rider can pass the motorcycle license test by passing the motorcycle safety course. I was actually envious and thinking that in my day, all of two years earlier, we really had it tougher.

"The Sportster's my first bike. My dad's had a lot of bikes. He's had a Sportster, a Springer, and a Dresser with a sidecar (but that blew up so we got the Springer back). He's had a Heritage Softail and now a Dresser again. I just inherited his Heritage Softail when he bought the Dresser. So I am selling my Sportster."

His brother Josh rides on the back of his bike while his mother Regina rides on the back of his father's bike. A riding family. These four ride to movies, shopping, restaurants, and local events. His father, Joe Cannon, may have started the riding, but the whole family now participates.

"Mom won't get a bike. She won't passenger with me either. She

Regina and Joe Cannon (Courtesy of Regina and Joe Cannon)

loves her comfort. The back seat of my dad's Dresser is really comfortable."

All the time John was telling me about his mother's love of comfort, I was remembering. I have seen Regina ride thousands of uncomplaining miles on the back of a Softail. These bikes are notoriously rough rides with poor shocks and suspension. She never complained.

"Did you ever have problems in suburban Novato because of the bikes?"

"Well, last year when we had a reception at our house, we went over to all our neighbors and told them that there would be a lot of bikes here. We didn't want our neighbors to be worried. We wanted them to see that all the bike riders were regular people. All the guests belonged to HOG and all had jobs and businesses and families just like our neighbors. They were regular people, just like us."

John, like Robin, has gone to many motorcycle events. Last year he rode to Bridgeport on the back of his dad's bike. He not only rode to the event, he, his father, and my husband staffed the Bridgeport raffle booth. Hard work but a lot of compensation. No money but it made all three of them feel great. Their booth supported all the local community projects.

177

John considers himself part of the society of Harley riders. His parents showed an enormous amount of trust in him by permitting him to inherit his father's Softail. The kind of responsibility parents try to instill in their kids is a lesson easily taught when the object of that responsibility is a Big Twin.

10

Hanging with the Clubs

"Hey, look at this great bike over here," I yell to one of the guys during our stop at a local repair shop to get parts. The bike, a yellow Honda V 4, gleaming with elegance and power, sits on its pads.

"Shit! I thought you said you were going to show me a bike. I don't see a bike," remarks Detlef with disgust. "I thought you were going to show me a Harley."

The meeting room is in the basement of a garage. Bikes, tools, bike parts, and oddly mismatched chairs fill the cluttered space. As the garage doors open and close to admit new members, the air in the room shifts from the heavy odor of oil, gas, grease, and exhaust to the lighter smells of fog and city pollution.

Fifty to sixty bikers meet here every third week of the month to plan runs and take care of business. Almost all are men. Some have long hair and beards; some are short-haired and very clean-shaven. A few have shaved heads. Some have small and strong tattoos; some have tattoos covering almost every part of their bodies. A few have visible body piercings and studs; many sport an earring. Strong muscular arms hunch out from leather vests, legs are covered with leather chaps, and heavy leather jackets hang off the backs of chairs. Most of the vests sport patches. While black is the color of the day, here and there a brown vest, chaps, and jacket can be seen. The leathers are old and worn. This is a riding club.

Most of the men are big and wear a lot of hardware. Almost all have numerous tools hanging from their belts. They attach their knives to their belts and sport chains. The sounds of angry voices fill the space. Other voices rise to defuse the anger. There are factions.

Some men gather in small groups at the entrance to the garage. The air around them holds a confusing mixture of smells—grease, exhaust, grass, cigarettes, and cigars. No one smokes downstairs around the bikes. The No Smoking signs are visible, the gas and oil fumes are heavy, and the fine for breaking this rule is expulsion for the night.

179

Downstairs, the anger defused, the men form into small groups and talk bikes. They discuss their plans for bike chopping, for painting, for customizing. Tables are pushed against the wall for the display of club patches. These are available for sale. Raffle and 50/50 tickets are sold. At the end of the meeting, half the money collected from the 50/50 will be awarded to some lucky ticket holder. The rest will go into the club treasury. After the 50/50, raffle prizes are presented. The director is in charge of providing the raffle prizes. Usually these are no more elaborate than Harley T-shirts, but sometimes they include belt buckles or bike parts.

The men use Robert's Rules of Order when planning runs, parties, and official events. Sometimes the rules of order prevent chaos. Sometimes not. The men are all ages. Most fly their colors.

All the men are members. A few women in the room also wear club patches. They too are members. They are riders. All the other women come as passengers. They are ole ladies, wives, and girlfriends. Sometimes single women show up at the meetings. A few come alone, looking to meet bikers. From the viewpoint of the ole ladies, wives, and girlfriends, this is not a welcome sight. They pointedly ignore single women, refusing them seating and crowding them out of the bathrooms. Single women, potential threats, are always discouraged from returning.

There are many kinds of turf and many ways of guarding it. Ole ladies, wives, and girlfriends guard not just their men, but their rights in the club, this HOG chapter. Women who ride have rights of membership through their own riding abilities. All riders can join. Ole ladies, wives, and girlfriends, those who passenger, however, have only quasi-rights. They gain their membership privileges through their men. They are packed. They can never join as full and equal members. If they two-up, cram themselves between the sissy bar and the rider, or cling precariously to the tiny backless pillion pad and the rider's rump, they can gain a secondary, or associate, status. This gives them the right to hang around. That's all. In terms of the club, they are invisible. The rules, rituals, and rites of passage are male defined. While a man is packing her, his passenger is an appendage—sometimes a trophy but always a subordinate—and she is treated accordingly.

"So what do I call the passenger? If the guy is the biker, what do I call the passenger?" I ask one of the members.

"You don't call her shit! She's nothing; she's packed. She don't count."

Sometimes a woman is liked for her own attributes or out of respect for her man, but in a riding club only bikers have clout.

Enter a woman biker and all the men shift gears. The men, so distant and openly disdainful to women passengers, treat the woman rider with respect. She has passed the difficult test of membership. She rides.

"How did you start riding?" I asked one of the women.

"I loved riding on the back. I loved the bikes. I couldn't get enough of it. When my ole man and I split, I didn't ride for a while. Then my next boyfriend rode so I got on the back again. After we split, I missed it. My third guy didn't ride, so I figured, what the fuck, I can do this. I don't need anyone to get me in the wind. I can ride my own."

"Do you ever pack the guy you live with now?" I asked.

"Yeah! Right. You want me to lose him?"

As an anthropologist, I was lucky. Through my association with a biker (my ole man, my husband), I gained the right to hang around. Chafing under the double standard applied to riders and passengers, I still managed to participate. I had the right to attend meetings, passenger on rides, and be a part of Harley culture. As ole lady, wife, and girlfriend (these terms were frequently used interchangeably), I could hang with the other no-status women and take part in the activities open to us. Sometimes I got to hang with the men. This was permitted so long as I kept my mouth shut. This was hard to do.

In those early years, I was always in trouble. I talked women's rights. I backed a passenger's right to pack with another rider and had her ole man come after me with a hunting knife. An old-time member, a lifer with clout, came between me and the blade. He pulled the angry biker out for a ride. Cool-off time.

I tried to vote more women into positions of power. I objected to the slutty, seductress, naked-woman-on-bike calendar pictures that hung on the walls. More and more often my ole man, my husband, was regarded with sympathy and sorrowful looks from the other men. They felt sorry for him. Sometimes our male friends gave me lessons in biker behavior. They wanted to educate me before I acted in ways that would get us all killed.

At runs, right in the very heartland of America, I lost my cool and spoke up against racist remarks. I championed gay rights and women's rights. But I also learned to disappear very quickly into the nearest crowd. It took me a long time to learn to keep my mouth shut and listen. It took me a longer time to start acting like an anthropologist and not some pissed-off member of the community. It took me an even longer time before I began to understand, and finally appreciate, the dynamics of this complex culture.

Through my association with a rider, I could hang out. I could participate in the activities of the other women passengers and do my research on Harley groups. We went on runs. From the passenger's seat I learned to jam the wind.

Entrance into fieldwork is always a delicate matter. Questions come easy but the answers must be discovered with work and sometimes with difficulty. Will I be accepted? Will I be able to get my material? Will I be able to analyze my material in ways that make sense to me . . . and to others? Why am I doing this? Will anyone care about this work? Will I get killed?

Starting an unknown field assignment is always problematic. Fieldwork can be chosen for any number of reasons. Anthropologists may be hired by government agencies, research corporations, city institutions, or private foundations to research a particular group of people or some local problem. We may work for universities that require frequent publications. Or we may study groups because we want to, because they interest us and we want to learn more about them. Since my current work falls into the last category, I have the luxury of choosing my own time frame, my own methods, and my own motives. Still, regardless of the reasons for the work, entering the field is always scary. The unknown holds terrors. More so here, because to start this fieldwork I had to enter the field on the back of a bike. Approaching bikers in any other way would have been impossible.

At first, my decision to passenger was based on my belief that this was my only entrance into the community. How else could I get to the gatherings, go on the runs, or participate in Harley culture? Later I came to realize that this decision had large-scale field implications. Riding the wind is itself such a transformative experience that I would not have been able to appreciate or understand the culture without it. What started simply as a field method and entrance etiquette became part of my theoretical and analytic tool kit and part of my life.

But first I had to get onto the bike. My husband rode. He had ridden Hondas for years and was now into Harleys. My previous riding experiences were limited and far from pleasant. Plus, I am a natural-born coward—I do not fly, I dislike physical risks. I am uncomfortable in any area remotely resembling the great outdoors. Until I learned to ride sweep—to follow the bikes in an emergency vehicle over endless uncharted roads at obscene speeds—I had never driven farther than around town. The sweep vehicle bails out bikes in trouble. It's backup. For me, riding sweep was a pivotal experience. It was the first step on my journey toward learning how to ride the back of the bike.

The movies make it look so easy. You throw a leg over and away you go. Riding a bike is as American as apple pie, country living, and Norman Rockwell. The only problem is that I am a New York Jew, reared in the streets of Manhattan and the side streets of Brooklyn, and I had been born to read books not ride bikes. Being sedentary, sickly, utterly nonmechanically inclined, and a lover of the great in-

The author (Courtesy of Chip Vinai)

doors, I am more suited to appreciate museums than motorcycles. I am used to corridors and carpets, not canyons and woodlands.

Nothing in my urban, indoor, East Coast existence prepared me for jamming the wind. When you ride, you are right in the middle of nature. When it rains, you get very wet. When the sun is overhead, you can swelter. Protection from the elements is so minimal on a bike that you make friends with the elements or you don't ride.

My entire past city life of university teaching, child rearing, poetry writing, piano playing, and radical activism left me utterly unprepared for the glory and godawfulness of riding the wind. Only my innate fanaticism prepared me for riding. I had been, in mind-numbing order, a fifties beatnik; a sixties civil rights, radical politics, antiwar, women's liberationist, jail-going yippie; a seventies commune-living hippie (urban not rural); and an eighties down and dirty, fast-field professional anthropologist. It was revolution, sex, dope, and rock and roll all the way.

Part of that way included rearing two kids in counterculture communities and getting a Ph.D. in anthropology. I have had some experiences with risk taking. I have always rallied to a cause. I am adventurous. Authenticity alone requires that I live my values, not just teach about them. This frequently lands me on the wrong side of the law, the receiving side of welfare, and the libertarian side of any political discussion. My profile, at the start of this work, would have read urban intellectual and cultural cynic, as well as loudmouthed troublemaker. In the end, it was that fanaticism that got me on the back of the bike. That, and the exquisite patience of my husband.

Biking came easy to Ken. Raised in west Texas, a Vietnam vet, he is most at home out-of-doors. Rural, healthy, mechanically adept, soft spoken, and strong, he stayed in New York City just long enough to get me out of there. We met, married, and moved in the mid-seventies. I moved out of a commune and into marriage. He moved into parenting my kids. We all moved to California. I continued to research culture. There are a lot of urban subcultures in California. None of them required riding. But by the start of the nineties, I was looking around for another subculture to study. My husband mentioned his basement meeting with a group of bikers. He was thinking of joining. Did I want to come?

It took three months of practice to get even marginally comfortable on the back of a bike. It took buying a passenger seat as big as a house and as sturdy as an oak. We practiced until I could stop screaming in Ken's ears every thirty seconds. We rode for months until I could get up to highway speeds. Then we took our first run with the group.

Coming in last and discouraged, I despaired that I would ever be all right on a bike. Six years later, I still despair. Even though I can passenger now with a fair amount of ease and ride my own with growing ability, I have yet to achieve the skill or confidence level of any of my riding buddies. Whether I two-up or ride side by side, I am always the slowest on the road. I am always the last to arrive, the first to turn back. Every windswept bridge is my own personal demon, every tunnel a terror.

Sometimes I blame it on my age. If only I had started riding earlier, it would have been easier. Sometimes I blame it on my background. If only I'd been raised to be an active kid instead of one who thought physical activity and sports were dirty words. Through it all my husband kept encouraging me. Ken kept his cool. We kept on riding.

Riding is the entrance fee. It's the way in. I could not have done this field research without the bike. Yet, it is more than that. The bike is front and center. It is not only the means of entering the culture, it is the culture. It is both the symbol and the reality of the culture. Without the bike, there is nothing.

My research started the day I walked into that garage and observed the club meeting in progress. The research continues. It's been over six years since I started riding the wind. Since then I have been to many garages and seen many groups. I have passengered on too many runs to count and ridden to a few on my own bike. I entered this world on the back of a bike. I stayed in the world from the front seat of my own Harley and continue to confront it through the word processor on a computer. The scope of this work is small. It is limited to Harley riders. It is also limited to the groups I have traveled with and the clubs I have studied.

The clubs I am most familiar with are HOG, ABATE, AMA, and several small, local independents. I have met a great number of Harley riders in the past six years. Wherever possible, I hang with the women who ride and the women who passenger. Almost all my work has been with small-town, working-class bikers or with urban, blue-collar or professional bikers. I ride with both New and Old Bikers and have even had the privilege of riding with a few Old Timers. My experiences with One Percenters have been limited to going to occasional meetings at runs, notably Redwood Run, Bridgeport, and the Streets of San Francisco, shopping at the same after-market Harley shops, visiting at parties, and sometimes riding the streets and highways of Frisco.

I have even ridden three times with Dykes on Bikes in the San Francisco Gay Pride parade. The events, the meetings, the parties, the toy runs, the swap meets, the charity benefits, the campouts, the newsletters, the magazines, and the biker funerals all make up the stuff of Harley culture. When I started this book, I invited you to come along for the ride. I could not have written any of this if the community of Harley riders had not invited me to come along too. My methods are simple, my cultural group is complex, and the experience of writing this up is extraordinary. I suspect that I am writing, however, because it is California's rainy season and it's too wet to ride.

Finally, after many months of riding, I had the chance to go to one of those large inland meetings I kept hearing about. Finally I would see a group where women, I had heard, were equal in number to men and strong in membership. This one was off the urban track. No smelly garage for this group. They met in a pizza restaurant with ample seating, abundant food, and a playroom for the kids. Row after row of long tables filled the huge pizza hall. A crowd of around three hundred had gathered. I had come into the California heartland and Harley wasn't just a word—it was a word to live by.

"Man, you got a Harley! I got a Harley."

"I swear on my Harley that it's true. I swear on my Harley this happened."

Club officers took their jobs very seriously. Members attended the meetings and were penalized if they missed them. Meetings were family affairs. The pizza hall was packed with men and women of various ages. With them came kids, toys, dogs, and bike parts. The bikes stayed outside in a guarded parking lot. Amidst the children playing, babies crying, and waitresses yelling their orders, the officers conducted the meeting.

It looked like a reunion of a large, boisterous, unruly, and happy family. Mouths were crammed with pizza, garlic bread, and beer. Friends were hugging each other and shouting greetings across several table lengths. The somberness and menace of the urban garage crowd shifted to the family fun of middle America. Women, in equal numbers with the men, attended as both members and officers. The ladies' auxiliary was very strong; four women took on the task of running it, and all of them held titles.

I was amazed. In the first group I had observed, women were few in number. Women who rode were scarce and the women who passengered were silent. These women were robust, noisy, confident, and visible. They clearly believed they had the right to be present. It was their club too. This MC belonged to them all.

"So what do you ride?" I asked one of the women sitting next to me at the pizza table.

"I don't ride. My ole man rides. I'm a passenger."

"What about the rest of the women? How many of them ride?" I continued.

"We don't ride. Our husbands ride. I don't ride. My girlfriends don't ride. We all sit on the back."

"You mean," I persisted, "you don't ride and the guys still listen to you? You don't ride and you're still treated this good? Where I come from, if a woman doesn't ride, she's treated like shit."

"You should move out here. These guys wouldn't dare treat you that way."

I sat considering the differences among the groups. Different groups have different levels of bike appreciation, and this one raised Harley appreciation to spiritual status. They also raised the standards of eating, partying, and riding to epic proportions. Their motorcycle club was large and tightly formed. The group was primarily made up of couples. Couples of very long standing.

Both men and women were mainly in their late thirties and early forties. They had been around a lot together. Almost all had several kids. As families, they endured. In this small-town community, joining a Harley club was almost like joining the local Rotary or Lions Club. They were reasonably respected members of the community who also happened to ride.

The touch of the outlaw sat lightly upon them. Younger and more reckless men might look for riding excitement on the outskirts of respectability, but this group rode within the confines of bike, family, and God. Solidly middle America, stolidly small-town working class, they defined themselves as coming from the heartland and were very proud of it.

The women's groups were strong because the women partnered with their husbands. The women's associations formed the glue that helped keep the club together and the grease that kept it riding. The ladies' auxiliary had a strong hold upon the political reins of the club and in the life of the biker community. These women—farm women, small-town women, waitresses, tellers in local banks, nurses in the all-night ERs, partners in local businesses, and mothers—were a force to be reckoned with. They took no shit. They stood united and their men knew it.

"How come you ladies all have such a big role in the club? How come you are all so strong out here?" I asked my dinner partner. "How come, in such a small town, the club is huge?"

"Well, it's really very simple. You're from the city. You got lots of things to do. Out here, what's to do? We have our club. We have the only thing happening. We have long cold winters when we can't ride. So we party. We get through the winter by doing other things—by being friends, by having get-togethers. The guys tear down the bikes and get them ready for spring riding, while we hold our meetings and parties."

All the way back to the city, passengering at this point with a modest amount of aplomb, I realized with envy that I would never belong to a group that had that much female solidarity. These women rode in a universe far more ordered than mine. These women knew their place. It was a place of strength, courage, and power, but it was a gender-specific place. They shared the bike and club with their husbands and both accepted their complementary roles. But none, so long as they stayed in that group, would venture out of their defined roles and accepted behaviors.

Their behaviors were defined by club rules, by community standards, and by church affiliation. It worked. They had a good thing going and they all knew it. Unfortunately for me, it was their thing and, appealing as it was, I was not willing to join a small society with relatively rigid roles, no matter how emotionally gratifying the payoff.

If I had known what the consequences of another meeting I attended would be, I would have skipped it. But I was anxious to observe as many Harley groups as possible. Besides, this group wasn't so very different from the first group I'd observed in the garage, and I had survived those meetings.

The meeting hall, a big warehouse space, was daunting, but the familiar leathers and shades made me feel at home. This meeting space was so large that most of the bikes were parked inside. A long, narrow, and wicked-looking ramp lay right inside the doorway. The bikers maneuvered the ramp with the ease of long practice. I smiled and nodded at a few people but got back only blank stares. No one was friendly, but then this was an almost all-male group and I was a female outsider. Even my being there was somewhat suspect. I had come alone this time and on my own bike, and I was nervous.

The meeting started in the usual way—minutes were read, new members were acknowledged, guests were welcomed/observed, and upcoming runs were discussed. I settled back in my chair, relaxing, as I believed that nothing scary was apt to happen. I had been to hundreds of meetings and mostly they went just like this one. I even knew a few of the members from previous runs and local biker bars. The group was cool.

Unfortunately, just as I was getting comfortable, real-time politics intervened. The very real world of American diplomacy entered with a bang. News of Operation Desert Storm came over the radio and the room erupted in yells of patriotism and loud support for the troops. To a man, they welcomed the American invasion of Iraq.

The club chairman called for a Harley display of support. He asked for a show of hands. The motion on the table was to have all the riders ride in force downtown to meet the antiwar marchers. The bikers were going to ride through the crowd and scatter the dissenters. They were going to break up the antiwar rally.

Even though I was a guest at that club, I was a Harley rider. Having ridden in on my own Sportster, I felt qualified to talk. The chairman was polite enough to acknowledge me before he firmly called me out of order. I persisted. I argued that the marchers had a right to protest. They had the constitutional right to rally against a war they did not believe Americans should fight.

"I'm opposed to the war!" I shouted. "I'm sure that lots of us are," I persisted.

I had barely gotten these words out when everyone started for their bikes. As the engines revved, I did the only thing I could think of—I got on my bike and I tried to block the exit. I had to prevent the group from going downtown.

Luckily for me, one of the few members I knew grabbed me off my bike. "Are you crazy? Get on my bike and let's get the hell out of here!" he yelled. He sat me on the back of his bike and rode quickly away. No one harmed my bike, which stood in the path of the oncoming group. Everyone swerved around my Sportster. That was done out of respect for my bike, not for me. Had I been on the bike I might not have been so lucky. When I returned a few minutes later to get my bike, it was in perfect shape. I then rode downtown to warn the marchers. I arrived, of course, too late.

As I considered the similarities and the differences among the bike groups, one thing stood out first and foremost. Everyone saw their scoots, their Harleys, as central to their lives. All were serious riders. They differed in their riding ability, but all the riders defined themselves in relation to their motorcycles. The bikes formed a fundamental part of their identity.

Everyone also looked pretty much the same. It is hard to tell individual differences beneath all the leathers, shades, and brain buckets. Prior to the enactment of the California helmet law, there was greater individuality in style, and friends could be recognized from afar. Since the mandatory skid lid law took effect, everyone looks a lot more alike. But attitudinal differences are another matter. They vary widely. How the predominantly straight white male groups see women, minorities, and gays differs from club to club. How they view their own place in American society also differs from one group to another.

The backbone of Harley culture is white. It is also middle-aged and male. Whether a club appreciates women or puts them down, permits women to ride or keeps them as the bitch on the back, membership is still defined by males. Sometimes there are female clubs, female runs, and female gatherings, but this is still pretty rare.

Although there are some "minority"-specific groups, most Harley clubs remain pretty much white. White-only groups still exist in many areas of California. Black, Asian, and Latino riders are not accepted. Not all groups, however, are color specific. Some Harley clubs accept men of all races and consider their racial diversity a point of pride. While Harley culture includes all age ranges, most of the men in the riding groups, not counting the outlaws, tend to be middle-aged. Besides Congress and the hallowed halls of business, this is one of the last remaining places in America where it's still good to be a middle-aged white guy.

Class and sexual preference are different matters. Urban professionals and the rich are new players in the Harley community. There are whole groups of riders out there who have big bucks. Some also come complete with leftist leanings and liberal values, in contrast to the traditional mom and apple-pie Americanism of the majority of riders. These new riders are international travelers, largely single, amazingly mobile, and come in both sexes and all sexual preferences.

Newspapers write about growing Harley popularity among Hollywood celebrities, political figures, and well-known athletes. Jay Leno leads the Love Run. Elizabeth Taylor paints her Harley lavender. The newspapers also write about stockbrokers, lawyers, and doctors, but the new riders are far more numerous and more important than just those in a few professional groups.

These riders represent a serious and important part of emerging Harley culture. It is their presence that has so dramatically changed the face of the Harley community. That community is no longer the old homogeneous world it once was. It may still consist mainly of middle-aged white guys, but they are no longer narrowly bound by class or location. This new group parties around the country. On predominantly new bikes, they travel to many of the rallies and take part in the events; they spend a sizable portion of their income on their bikes, write for local Harley papers, and participate in the life of the culture. Indeed, they are helping to transform it.

A number of the new riders are also openly gay. While historically there have been a fair number of gay male clubs, they were usually open only to gay riders. Clubs that accept both gay and straight riders are relatively new. Many gay riders are not publicly out when they ride, but neither are they in the closet. Some fly the rainbow flag of gay liberation on their bikes. Others talk about the gay lifestyles they lead, though many may never mention it. But as the gay members (usually urban) of Harley groups travel across the country with the straight members of their own club, they all fly their club's colors. When they arrive at the run's end and party with other groups, they are seen as an integral part of their own club.

Middle America must now include gay riders as they ride to open events on their own Harleys. In the emerging Harley culture, women, gays, and riders of all classes, races, and colors are finding places within the older order of middle-aged white men.

Women now ride their own Harleys. While their numbers remain small, their impact on the culture is growing. Women riders represent over five percent of the overall Harley buying population in the country and eleven percent in California. Women are riding with friends, forming clubs, going on cross-country trips, and redefining the entire meaning of the term femininity. Women are responsible for their own survival on the road.

All biking women are extraordinary. Whether they ride or passenger, are hetero or lesbian, are members of a club or ride alone, they share a critical and compelling reality. They share their love of the road. These are ordinary lives made extraordinary.

In a society that leaches out most elements of primal excitement, biking is one of the few activities that retain a mix of adventure, immediacy, and bravery. Every biker knows this. Biking measures the biker with every ride. Biking women add a dimension of courage that is not experienced by males. Biking women endure the wrath of public outrage directed against women who dare to be radically different from almost all stereotypic versions of femininity. Whether they ride or passenger, women must forge their own definitions of femininity and their own definitions of self. Biking women risk much, but much is gained.

The price of admittance to the road is steep. The price is nothing less than your life. That is what is risked. There are safer rides and less safe rides, but ultimately every woman who rides knows that most risks are beyond her ability to control. The risks lie in the weather, the road, the motorists, the animals, and the unknowable. Unpredictability rides along on every trip. This growing community of women bikers exists as a primal tribute to their lust for freedom. Strong, gutsy, independent, fearsome, and wild, women are riding, and in doing so, they are changing the rules of the road.

11

Bike Lust

"The bike is like a living thing. It's real. It's an entity in its own right. It's family."

Six days ago I picked up my new bike, a Low Rider (FXD). She's black, of course, and incredibly beautiful. She's streamlined and sleek and powerful. All other thoughts pale in comparison to bike contemplation. I talk bikes to anyone who will listen. I call friends across the country who couldn't tell a bike from a bulldozer, and I babble about my Low Rider. I go and sit on her while she's parked in the garage. It's raining constantly in California and riding is at a standstill. But still I sit on my bike. I imagine the rides, the roads, and the wind.

Although I have had my Low Rider only six days, she has already been ridden eight times. I confess, a totally female thing, that I did not ride her home. I bought this bike without ever having ridden a Big Twin. I bought her because I wanted more stability in the wind than my Sporty was able to offer. I wanted a stronger, sturdier, and heavier bike. I was not looking for speed or power, but apparently I got both. I got the complete package.

Since both my husband and my riding buddy Debby were at work and I refused to ride the bike home alone, I asked one of the guys at Dudley Perkins if he would ride for me. Mark Kammueller said he would. He thought it was a strange request, but hey, nothing is too odd when it comes to bikes. Besides, Mark was always giving me a hard time at the shop so this was right up his alley. I appreciated his help and recognized that giving someone a hard time was Mark's way of being nice. So there we were—me in the car, Mark on my Low Rider, and the wet pavement sprinkling my new bike with water.

As soon as Ken came home that night, we went riding. Within seven seconds, I knew that this was the right bike, the right time, the right everything. My sleek, stripped, gorgeous Low Rider is absolutely the most incredible ride on the road. Ken calls my fascination and love of this bike "obsession" and says he's been there more than once. I call it "bike lust."

She had to be modified, of course. No Harley stays the way it rides out of the shop. My bike got a Bandlander seat, new muffler, pipes, and air cleaner. The carb was rejetted and the easy-pull clutch grip installed. I now had a bike that was two inches lower, easier on the clutch, and sounded like a Harley. She rumbled, she roared, she purred. This was bike lust. She also had a name. Most men do not name their bikes. Most women do. Not all women and definitely not all men follow this rule, but it covers many. The men who do name their bikes rarely talk about it. It's seen as much too sentimental.

Some Harleys are referred to as female. Some Harleys are seen as male. Ken's bike, the Beast, is neither male nor female. But out of respect, he will never call his bike "it." He always refers to the bike as "the Bike" or "the Beast." His new Road King has yet to be named.

My Low Rider is Lady. There is never any doubt that the name fits. She is all things a lady should be. She is strong, beautiful, lusty, powerful, and fast. She purrs or roars depending upon mood. When passing a car that might consider turning into our lane, she growls and screams. She has a mind and heart of her own. My other bikes also had names. The wonderful Honda 250 that I learned to ride only four years ago was called Baby. Selling her was hard to do but with a brand-new Sportster in the garage, I had no choice. If I had kept the Honda Rebel, I would never have ridden the Sportster. It was a hard transition. The Sportster, appropriately named Beauty, has lived up to her name. Both of my bikes now sit in the garage. It is time to sell Beauty. I feel disloyal even as I write this, but I know that if I keep Beauty it will be hard to ride Lady. Lady is over 650 pounds, has a 1350cc engine, is real fast, quick, big, and scary. Besides, we need the money. Harleys are not cheap.

I knew that I had gone over the edge when Ken jokingly suggested that we park Lady in the living room and I took him seriously. Although I considered the logistical difficulties of riding her through the narrow hallways, I never doubted the rightness of his suggestion. Something happens when you bond with a bike. It is not a cliché to say that you two become one in all kinds of critical ways. Your life depends on it. Your life, your lifestyle, the things you wish to do, the company you wish to keep, the money you wish to spend, all depend upon that relationship. Harley ownership is not for the casual or the cavalier. Am I a true believer? It's either that or bike lust.

All women riders are familiar with this territory. Riding always puts us over the edge. I remember the last good talk I had with a group of riding women. We were recounting some of the great and not so great things that had happened to us since we had started riding.

"One of the first things I noticed when riding a Harley is that people scurry across the street. It's because I'm on a Harley. People just really move fast when they see me coming. The bike is so big and so loud that people get out of the way."

"Wait a minute, Debby," I asked with my anthropological seriousness. (Some things never get turned off.) "How do you know it's because you were on a Harley? Maybe it's just the fact that you were on a bike?"

"Nope! I know it's my Harley 'cause when I ride the Honda they just walk in front of me. People only scurry when I'm on my Harley."

I remembered all the times when I rode my Honda Rebel and I had to wait for places in traffic to open so I could creep into them. I remembered all the times that people had deliberately opened car doors directly in my path, causing all kinds of havoc. I remembered the names I was called (everything from "dyke" to "bitch"), none of them meant as a compliment. I remembered the rotten fruit thrown and the debris hurled as I rode down the city streets. I asked other women and many of them shared similar experiences.

Then I got my Harley. And all the harassment stopped. The street problems stopped cold. It was so sudden and so complete that I felt like I had sprouted muscles and menace. And I think that may be part of the answer. Harleys do appear formidable. But I think that something else is going on as well. People who would think nothing of harassing me because I am a woman rider might refrain from doing so because I ride a Harley. It isn't out of respect or fear of me. Street behavior became polite out of respect for my bike. It's now a common occurrence that when I'm riding in a city and stopped at a stop sign or waiting for a red light to turn green, from out of nowhere a man in a car, truck, or van will sidle over to me and compliment my bike. It has happened so often that I now take it for granted. When I rode my Rebel, this *never* happened. Appreciation of Harleys appears to extend way beyond those who ride them. A large proportion of the San Francisco public apparently shares my respect for Harleys. As a woman on a Harley, I get the kind of street respect that I never received before. Far more typical, for most women, are street hassles. Debby told a story that started out pretty average. Her ending, however, had a nice twist.

"I used to get hassled on the street all the time. We are all familiar with that one. You can't be a woman and live in the city and not have that experience. Well, I was walking down Haight Street and this guy said something really gross—no, I'm not going to repeat it, but it was really gross. I just kept walking but feeling really bad inside. You know, like I wanted to tell him to shove it but was afraid to. I was alone and didn't want reprisals from him. So I just kept on walking. Kept on feeling bad though and played in my mind all the things I would have liked to say. Then I got on my bike to ride home. I always ride in the city and only take the car in emergencies. Well, several blocks away, I'm crossing Oak and Masonic and this same guy is crossing the street right in front of me *and he doesn't recognize me.* We all look alike with our helmets and greatcoats on. Actually, we all look like men with all that gear and those helmets. I was wearing all black that day and had on my full face helmet.

"Here was my moment and it was great. Slowly I inched my bike toward the crosswalk. I waited until I got close enough to see his face and have only him directly in my line of riding and then I popped the clutch. The bike, only a few feet away from this creep, violently jumped forward. The guy jumped too and looked scared shitless. Six hundred and fifty pounds of Milwaukee's finest bore down on him. I stopped in plenty of time, of course, but it was sure fun."

"Did you then remove your helmet and let him see it was you?" I asked.

"No, I was so pleased with myself for being able to do that, that I just concentrated on the bike and what the bike could do."

We all listened to Debby's story with great interest. We agreed it was a great payback to street creeps and I thought that we should all learn how to pop the clutch. But as an added flourish, we should remove our helmets so the guy who did the harassing would know that it was a woman who had scared him silly.

Then our talk turned to helmets and we noted interesting changes in public attitude since the dreaded California law passed. Prior to the law requiring helmet use, a large contingent of Harley riders disdained skid lids. Even with the law in place, many of us wear the smallest helmet money can buy. They are not street legal but will usually pass. When stopped we get ticketed, but most of us are willing to take our chances. To wear no helmet is to invite ticketing and general hassling from cops. A beanie helmet, though illegal and light, usually goes by undetected.

Being forced to wear a helmet has pissed off many riders. Riding bareheaded is not just part of the experience of riding, it is such a fundamental part that the helmet often produces profound disorientation. We ride for many reasons. The helmet interferes with most of them. It makes us less safe on the road. It blocks out sound, sight, depth perception, and judgment. If a rider is caught in an accident, it can be helpful. It can, however, cause accidents in its own right.

Wearing a brain bucket does have two notable and otherwise unavailable side effects. It holds head gear in place. It anchors scarves, hoods, glasses, and goggles. It also gives anonymity while on the bike. This last part is a surprise. We lose our everyday identity while wearing a helmet. If we cannot even recognize friends at a distance, the general public has no clue as to who is riding. It is simply assumed that we are all men.

Since the enactment of the California helmet law, many riding women have reported a significant drop-off in bad remarks, road hassling, and rude behaviors. Yet some women wish to be recognized as women on the road. Women who want to be so identified have gone to great lengths to feminize their outfits. Some pin long braids to their helmets to give the appearance of very long hair. Others paint their helmets light colors or paste flowery designs on them. Other women wear outfits with bright colors and prints. Some women have gone so far as to paint their bikes pink.

Real women on real bikes most frequently wear the same kinds of protective gear as men, however. They would have a hard time riding if they were wearing biker magazines' fantasy outfits. Only on rare occasions, when the weather is really hot, do women passengers take off as much clothing as possible. The unshaded sun scorches. On rarer occasions, women riders do the same. But mostly they wear the same clothes as men. The clothing preference is easy to explain. We all face the same road conditions. Only once did I ride with women who broke all the rules of bike wear—a group of new Amazons called Dykes on Bikes. And it was a hoot.

With a fierce sense of achievement I participated in several of San Francisco's Gay Pride parade rides. I rode with Dykes on Bikes. I was doing research on women riders. I was learning to ride. But mainly I wanted the wonderful experience of riding with hundreds of women in an important public parade for lesbian rights.

While Dykes on Bikes, now called the Women's Motorcycle Contingent, is not a club, it is famous. The group changed its name a few years ago when it came to their attention that someone had trademarked the Dykes on Bikes label, but many still use the old name. Since this is not a club, there are no rules for membership. Any woman who rides is encouraged to participate. The first few times I went to meetings for the parade, I brought it to the attention of the person running the meeting that I rode "only" a Rebel, was an anthropologist interested in researching biking women, and had a male spouse. All three disclaimers were important because I did not wish to be accepted with a false identity. I had to make sure that no one felt uneasy or betrayed by my presence. To my relief and surprise, the women I spoke to accepted me. This was a turning point in my own biking career since all women were encouraged to come and ride in the parade. No one cared what I rode or whom I slept with. My Rebel became famous. Eleven women took their motorcycle riding tests on my Rebel. They all passed. Riding those endless circles at the DMV is difficult and can drive you crazy on a big bike. The Rebel was just the right size for the circles. During the second parade I rode my Sporty and I carried a passenger. The third time, I rode my wonderful FXD Low Rider.

Like my riding buddies from other groups, Dykes on Bikes shared stories, swapped ideas about road-worthy clothes, and talked bikes. Then came my first parade. The women, most of them, to my great astonishment, dramatically changed their clothes. They looked like something out of a biker magazine. What a switch! I was expecting functional road gear. I was an innocent. I had not gone to many Gay Pride parades. The parade is awesome.

It starts with a sound—the slow, low, thump-thump-thump of a helmet truck almost silently stalking Market Street. Helmets are legally left on the truck for the duration of the parade. The thump is full of promise, pride, and menace. A portent of things to come. A million eyes are watching. The crowd, waiting stock-still, draws in a great collective breath. Half a million people strain to hear the coming sound. This is what they have come to feel and see. They wait. They wait for the roar. They wait for the thunderclap of bikes to slash through silence. The bikes do not disappoint.

At exactly 10:30 A.M. on June 27, 1993, a large contingent of bike riders started their engines. Five hundred loud, strong, determined bikes rumble down the road. They are all ridden by women. Eight hundred women, riding and passengering, glide into glory on the wheels of steel, riding every make of bike imaginable. According to the next day's *San Francisco Chronicle,* "They were a motorcycle army in dreamlike mythic costumes of feathers, tattoos, lace and black leather, . . . part theater, part home grown Mardi Gras and part political statement."

The newspaper got that right. This army of bikers belongs to the Women's Motorcycle Contingent, and their roar signals the start of the Gay Pride parade. Every year, on the last Sunday of June, the Gay Pride parade strides, dances, marches, roller blades, sashays, and rumbles and roars down Market Street. Everything goes. Some women dress in riding gear: leathers, chaps, vests, and goggles. They look no different from any rider, anywhere. Some, however, are dressed in fantasy out-fits. One rider is wearing fishnet stockings, spike heels, a G-string, and a short vest. That is all. Another has dyed her pubic hair, which is carefully curled, to match her rainbow-colored head. Tattoos and piercings, hair colors and designs of grand variety and great imagination make their appearance. There's a woman with a giant tiger tattooed over her belly, a tiger paw cupping each breast. She sports a nose tusk. Here's a woman wearing only a lacy bra, fringed brown leather vest, thong, and pointy heeled boots that ride to her thigh. A number of women have shaved heads. Multiple earrings, large and dangling, are making a comeback. The styles are outrageously outré. It is way over the top. During my second parade, my passenger wore purple panties, chaps, a vest, and little else.

Half-naked and high-heel-shod women balance, in slow motion, large bikes down trolley-car-tracked Market Street. Women from many clubs, most flying their colors, join the throng. Women wearing Harley-Davidson patches and ABATE patches, dressed for a typical Sunday putt in jeans and jackets, add their color and consciousness to the crowd. Anything goes. At this moment of license, all is permitted. Dykes on Bikes do it all while riding difficult and dangerous motor-cycles. And they do it all with style and grace and glory. They do it for the parade.

The parade is political. It marks the anniversary of the 1969 Stone-wall Bar police riots in New York's Greenwich Village, where gay men who were harassed and hassled by the police openly fought back. Their battle spilled out onto the streets where an entire sixties count-erculture community, schooled in activism, street theater, and human rights causes, entered into the fray and sparked an instant parade. "Remember the Stonewall" became the rallying cry and historic touch-stone for gay pride.

The parade is theater. It is a spectacle of giant proportions. It's the best free show in town. After centuries of being closeted, a walk in the sun is triumphant. A public walk, where half a million spectators line the streets and millions more view the participants on TV, is sublime. Gay pride is famous as the news reaches the far corners of the country. The open thrill of lifestyle affirmation is joyously, exuberantly, and out-rageously acted out.

"Look at me!" the costumes, floats, flags, and colors shout. "Look at me!" the clowns, dancers, musicians, drag queens (all in full costume), members of athletic clubs, mothers, fathers, children (on bicycles and in strollers) roar. "Look at me!" the army of church groups sings. "Look at me!" the rows and rows of older, gray- and white-haired lesbians, thrilled to finally be there, chant. "We're here, we're queer, get used to it," scream the younger participants of the parade. "We're gay and proud!" proclaim the oldest, most sedate marchers. The parade is a hoot and everyone hollers.

The parade is opportunistic. The mayor walks along (or rides in an open car, depending upon age and physical fitness). This is, after all, San Francisco, and the gay vote is a big deal. Every politico looking to be elected participates in the parade. It gives the "right" public message. It says, "I'm a politician who cares about your vote and your problems. I sympathize. I will support your issues." It is also a time for gay politicians to strut their stuff.

The parade can be scary to straight folk. To those of us, gay and hetero, who live in the Bay Area, the parade is our annual street fair, our time of license and free fun. To lesbians and gay men nationwide, it is a testament and victory. It is not unusual for gay folk to travel from New York, Florida, Colorado, Vancouver, Paris, or Dakar just to walk that mile of march. They are, as are we Friscans, used to the excesses and profound factions within the gay community. The rest of the straight world is not. Fifty marching mothers, following two hundred marching schoolteachers, following twenty-seven marching athletic clubs all get edged out of the news. Shown on TV and newspapers are the excesses that sell. Look! There's a man, dressed as a woman, marching in glitter, heels, and boa. Look! There's a whole truck full of drag queens, sequined to the teeth but exposing pierced nipples, penises, and tongues. Look! There's a whole group of men wearing nothing but women's thongs, leaving all the unmentionables, mentioned, hanging out and swinging loose. Look! There's the controversial man/boy love contingent, boycotted by many and adored by a few. Look, look, look. Some of the women bikers are dressed in glam gear, but most are not. How plain and ordinary most of the parade women look in comparison to the men. Here and there a woman in full S/M leather gear whips her slave along the route, or a butch/fem team, one in Barbie satin, the other in a Ken tux, smooch it up along the way. But for most of the marchers, it is a time of rejoicing and acceptance of the community's diversity.

The parade still remains scary to straight folks. It's not just the dramatic weirdness of some of the costume presentations, it's the gender bending. American society has gotten a lot looser when it comes to acceptable gender behaviors. There is now a range of roles that women and men may take. The roles have widened. But there are still many behaviors seen as outside the range. Pierced nippled men in thongs and women on big bikes stretch beyond most people's comfort zone. Women bikers make such a strong visual statement that they are the show stoppers as well as the show starters.

Dykes on Bikes kick starts the parade with a roar and sets the stage for all to come. The group's been going strong for twenty years. It's the highlight of the parade.

The pre-parade planning group meets at the Eagle Tavern. This sets a tone. Picture every dark, forbidding, foreboding, outlaw, under the bridge, behind the tracks, sleazy/alluring meeting place every imagined. Enter through a main door and come face to body with black leather draperies so dense and thick that all sun and street light is blotted out. Pass through. Along the dark wood walls are barely visible posters for male mud wrestling, tattoo and piercing establishments, music and dance events, and political rallies. Light comes from soundless TVs and randomly placed brilliant neon strobe lights. Bike parts, sculptures, and pictures rear out of the darkness. There is a pool table along the back wall, near the lockless toilets, but no one is ever playing. Above the front entrance just after the passage through the leather drapes is a color security camera trained on the parked bikes outside. You have just arrived at a gay men's motorcycle leather bar.

Outside, behind the main bar, in the courtyard stocked with dartboards, folding chairs, barbecue grills, more posters, and throbbing music, is an outbuilding complete with an idle bar, pictures, a TV, and a table and chairs. This bar room has good lighting and a feeling of closeness. Dykes on Bikes meets here. The Eagle Tavern has been the group's meeting home for eight years. It is an easy camaraderie. Women walk through the main bar, sometimes stopping to pick up a drink on their way to the outbuilding. This is where the parade agendas are discussed. Who are these bikers? How do they differ from women riders all over the country? A quick survey around the room shows a mixed group. Dykes on Bikes come in a variety of colors, mostly but not all white; a variety of ages, young to old but clustering in the thirties and forties; and a range of styles. Some of the women are plain by conventional standards. Some are conventionally pretty, and some are gorgeous. Some have shaved their heads. Some choose a short cropped style. Some have wavy hair, long and flowing. Some sport multiple rings, makeup, and hair coloring. There is no consistency. There is no particular style of Dyke. All the riders have but three traits in common. With few exceptions, all ride motorcycles (an activity closely identified with males). With few exceptions, all are lesbians (a group oppressed for refusing to be straight in a hetero world). And all are female (a gender struggling for rights and recognition). According to Lynn May Rivas, a Berkeley graduate student in sociology, "Dykes on Bikes are an incredible mix of strength, sexuality and rule breaking. They break all the stereotypes. They are supposed to be these tough dykes and yet some show up in heels and lace. They are the parade.

Some years that's all I go to see. They are the highlight for everyone. They project toughness and dominance. They are top dog. The fact that they are first, says it all. Everyone else in the parade follows them.

"There is something incredible about watching women riding big bikes. It's definitely about power and it's absolutely sexual. Some of them show a lot of skin. And they can. They get to do it all, to break all the rules. Watching them brings out our animal urges and gives us a great sense of wildness and freedom. Sometimes I can't decide if I want to be them or just take one of them home. The rest of us are like putty in their hands. We watch, while once a year, the Amazons come to town. They are like Goddesses."

At the end of the parade, after traveling down the length of Market Street in slow motion, aware that if any of us dropped our bikes, half the TV world would see it, we arrive at the special parking section set aside for the bikes. We leave our bikes and go to watch the rest of the parade. One year, when I returned there were a number of business cards stuck to the seat of my bike. They all offered invitations to join the card owners in after-parade festivities. All were from women. My favorite added just one line to her name and occupation. It asked, "Are you as hot as your wheels?" That year I was riding my Harley Low Rider. Years before, when I had first ridden my Honda Rebel, no one had left a single card on the seat.

12

NFGs

The New and the Old

"An outlaw biker has turned riding in the wind into something to live for. He has made the motorcycle the cornerstone of his identity, the master symbol of his lifestyle, and a metaphor for his personal freedom.... He has found ordeals and tests that confirm his manhood. He has found ultimate experiences that transcend the earth-bound traps of the ordinary. He has found core values around which to focus a lifestyle." (Wolf 1991, 59)

Bikers need feedback and reinforcement. Some get it from friends. Some get it from reading biker rags. Some get it from joining clubs. However the lifestyle is attained, it's cherished. Time, work, money, energy, danger, broken bones, broken families, and confrontations with the law have gone into forming this lifestyle.

In the past, Harley riders bought entrance into the life with blood, sweat, and swears. Whether a rider was a One Percenter, a Ten Percenter, an Old Timer, or an Old Biker, the wages of membership were steep. Membership demanded commitment. The bike defined the biker not only in terms of the outside world, but in terms of himself.

From the mid-forties until the mid-eighties, the Harley world knew its own. It was male. It was tough. It was dangerous. A man could ride in, but he couldn't buy in. Whether a man joined an outlaw club, rode solo, or rode with friends, he made recognizable commitments to the culture. A novice had many mentors. In this world—a world that persisted for over forty years with few changes—a culture flourished. It was John Wayne, Clint Eastwood, and Jesse James. Outlaws shared the rules and road with other Harley riders. They understood the terms. They understood the turf.

The terms and turf demanded certain things from a man. They demanded self-reliance, independence, a willingness to fight, a defense of ideals, an ability to go it alone, and an ability to back up your brothers in a fight. Jamming the wind, riding for its own sake, riding to live, living to ride: all of these were real. Before these words became contemporary clichés, they were words to live by. Every biker could tear down and build up his bike. Every biker could wrench. It was the elementary entrance into the culture. The language of wrenching was biker language. It provided the boundary between bikers and outsiders. It permitted bikers to identify each other on foreign turf. It provided the communication oil necessary to score tranny oil. A man had to know bikes. He had to be able to build one from a basket case, fix it in any and all circumstances, and ride out on any road.

The rules were simple and venerable. They provided each biker with a set of survival skills for dealing with the cops, ole ladies, bosses, family, or the government. When all else failed, there was the bike. Throw a leg over and be gone. Life gets unmanageable? Goodbye! It was a culture of quick exits.

Then things began to change.

"Yeah, there used to be a Harley culture," announced Old Biker Pablo Lopez, reflecting upon his years of riding. "It arose out of the people who lived it. We were able to live our dreams. Riding was part of our American dream.

"Now you have baby boomers out there, guys who are bored and restless, and they are looking around for something to do. They got their kids grown. They got their jobs and their house all paid off, so now what are they going to do? Now they get a Harley-Davidson. They put on leathers, chaps, boots, and gloves and they think they are bikers.

"Six, eight, ten guys walk into a bar and everybody goes ooh or aah. These guys automatically think they own the place. Then they go home and put on their white shirts and ties. These guys don't understand any of the mystery or mystique or history of Harley-Davidson. They just took out their checkbooks and thought they were buying an identity. They become guys with dual personalities. They act like big, bad bikers on the road and Mister Respectable at home."

"Pablo, somehow I get the feeling that you don't appreciate these guys."

"I call them NFGs. It stands for New Fuckin' Guys when you are in a good mood and No Fuckin' Good when you are not. They think they can buy into a culture. They think they can buy respect. You can't. The road has to be earned. These guys haven't earned it."

Woody, a Ten Percenter, drawled out his comments. "There are those bikers who have gone down, and those bikers who have yet to go down. Sooner or later, everyone loses it. When these new riders lose it, it's all over for them. The bike goes. Now you walk into most dealerships and they look more like boutiques than motorcycle shops. With all the clothing and gift sales and kids' toys, you don't know you are in a bike shop."

Things continue to change.

Bradley "Rooster" Brown, a New Biker, has a shorter time perspective than Pablo or Woody. Bradley can do some wrenching, uses his bike as his primary means of transportation, and is thoroughly committed to riding.

"My bike is major in my life. It's got my marks on it. I've customized the bike the way I want it. Like Native Americans on the plains put their handprints or marks on horses, I've put my mark on my bike.

"For a while, I thought I'd join some other groups. Thought I'd join the Vietnam Vets or the Iron Souls. But I'm not really a group person. I'm not much of a joiner. I ride with the FogHogs because I have friends there.

"But I can't identify with the FogHogs anymore. I got really pissed at the last meeting. All these new rich riders. They spend money like it's easy to get. They talk like everyone's rich. They talk like they don't want people like me around. These rich new guys act like they are above everyone else. At one of the last meetings I went to, one of the officers said that the next run should cost $25 a person. That would be the sign-up. I figured, that's rich people's prices, so I said so. I was told that anyone who can afford a Harley can afford twenty-five bucks a person to go to the run. Shit."

Harley riders aren't the only ones taking pot shots at NFGs. Open up *CityBike*, the San Francisco biking newspaper, and turn to almost any column. Sooner or later every columnist blasts the Harley community. In an article entitled "Safer than Sinning," Joseph Glydon has fun with the newer Harley riders:

> A while back I went on a ride originating at R&J in Vallejo, and ending at the locus of the annual Capay Valley Almond Festival, Esparto, California. Also availing themselves of this stimulating destination were a couple thousand new age Harley riders. You know, the ones who network to create packs of rumbling it's-my-day-off-and-I'm-in-a-scowling-mood homeowners. Packs rich in noise, color and taxable income that invariably string their bellowing multitudes out between the Mustangs and Miatas that haunt scenic California byways on sunny weekends.
>
> Downtown Esparto was graciously hosting these daydream felons, and they were reciprocating by spending their way up one side of the craft-infested Main Street and down the other. I noticed something, perhaps new for this outlaw riding season; no effort was being made by this group to give any pretense of weathered authenticity. Maybe it

was just this crowd, maybe it's a trend, but there wasn't one unsightly scuffed jacket seam, one trace of dental truancy, one leaking primary, or one Crazyman Iron Sportster.

With no social scar tissue looking on, hygienic suburban values had reasserted themselves to deodorize this otherwise typical biker scene. Clearly these folks had managed to overcome any pathetic dependence on unsanitary, small-bore criminals for validation of their Genuine American Motorcycling Experience. Perhaps credentialized bikers are just getting too old or selective to casually endure the tortures of a rigid Pan just to keep the company of party instinct deficient taxpayers.

The Harley-Davidson motorcycle may have evolved into a sort of bulky ROM game module to be surreptitiously slipped into the suburbo-corporate mainframe. Something for the sedentary but over-worked cyberslave to petulantly indulge in to spite the wife and the boss; a sparkling Sunday afternoon's delusion of vitality and independence that's much safer than sinning. (*CityBike*, June 1995, 9)

Rich Urban Bikers and Occasional Bikers are both butts of traditional Harley scorn and the joke of the non-Harley motorcycle world. New Bikers, however, hold a pivotal position. If they learn to wrench, that combined with their years of riding experience will allow the traditionalists to accept them as serious bikers. If they never learn to wrench, they will continue to get grouped with the dreaded RUBs and OBs.

Not everyone, however, views RUBs and OBs with disdain. Dealers, of course, love them. All the aftermarket shops look upon them with delight. These are people who have money and know how to spend it. They are a merchant's dream.

There are other voices of approval as well. Mike Molinari, Old Biker, had a few kind words to say: "You hear a lot of grumbling about the new rich riders. All the hard cases make jokes and refuse to ride with them. This is silly. I've met any number of newer riders who I would rather ride with than many old timers. There are lots of riders, RUBs, who get serious about their bikes, fall in love with riding, and end up as great riding buddies. Just because someone didn't come to biking at fifteen doesn't mean they can't be good at it. Just because they didn't learn to ride in the dirt doesn't mean they can't become intense. This myth about biker purity is bullshit."

Most surprisingly, even Easy Ed Gilbertson expressed approval of the NFGs. An impassioned rider, a Ten Percenter, he found them promising. He found their presence important.

"I get irritated when I hear people knocking the newer riders or different kinds of bikes," he told me. "We don't all like the same things. Nor should we. I don't put down touring bikes. I don't ride them, but

I don't put them down. Same thing for sports bikes. That new Buell might just be right for some young guy into real speed. It corners well, is fast like a pistol, and has the sports-bike look. Not my taste, but so what! I've never been down for the Blessing of the Bikes in San Jose, but I hear that every type of bike shows up there. It takes place on Easter Sunday and the priest blesses the bikes. It's done to keep everyone safe for another year. There's always a good turnout. Lots of new riders show up.

"I think HOG is a great idea. It's a great opportunity for new riders or new-to-the-area riders, or first-time Harley riders to meet people to ride with. It's open membership so the group gets very large. People come from all different backgrounds and have all different views. Everyone gets a chance to join.

"Today, there is something for everyone. That's an improvement. For those who want to ride full tilt, the H.A.'s are still there. For those who want serious friendships and serious riding, there are a number of independent clubs. For those who want to get casually involved, there is HOG. HOG serves a definite purpose within the Harley community. It helps the new rider get his first entrance into Harley touring groups. And we are lucky. Here in California, all biker groups get along pretty well. This is not true of the East Coast or most of the rest of the country. Things are quiet here, the roads are safe here, because the territory is uncontested. One group rules the roads in California and everyone knows it.

"You can measure how things have changed by looking at the dealerships. Look around at Dudley Perkins. It's run professionally. Back in the fifties and sixties and even into the seventies and early eighties, motorcycle dealerships were greasy, dirty holes in the wall. They were housed in cheap, rickety old buildings in run-down, dangerous parts of town. You walk into a dealership now and you see a dramatic change. It's like walking into a little Nordstrom's. It's all been standardized and sanitized. This is a real shock to most hard-core bikers, but I think that it's an improvement. The dealers now hold runs, take their customers more seriously, and give much better service.

"But most important of all is the economic impact of the newer riders. If they weren't around buying bikes, there wouldn't be any Harleys for the rest of us. These newer riders really saved Milwaukee's ass. They are responsible for Harley still being a viable, growing, prospering American business. Let's not knock them. They are part of the Harley revival. All these newer riders with their money-to-spend finances and their buy-American attitudes have helped turn Harley around. I, for one, am glad they're here."

The tensions between the old and new riders reflect differences in class, economics, commitment, and community. The new riders do not fully understand the criticisms leveled against them. They ride the wind. They take their chances. They think that they are paying their dues every time they survive a bad storm or live through ten miles of bad road. Some of the old bikers look at the new riders with both surprise and disdain. They are surprised that the new riders consider themselves bikers. They are disdainful because the new riders are unwittingly destroying the very culture they wish to join. By their entrance into the biker world, they are changing the rules. They have not given their souls to riding. It is not their life. They are weekend warriors.

I am a weekend rider. I spend my weekday life teaching, researching, writing, and working within the confines of a college and a museum. I am very far away from being a biker. But I remember the subcultures I once lived within and the contempt I held for weekend warriors. Except then we called them day-trippers. To be authentic within alternative societies, a person had to live that subculture twenty-four hours a day. It had to make up the stuff of your life. Anything less was inauthentic. Anything less was held in contempt.

I remember how much I disliked the sixties weekend hippies who played at psychedelia, preached radical politics (while partying), and pretended to understand poverty. They behaved like activists all weekend and then went home to middle-class suburbs. When problems arose, they were always bailed out.

I remember my own disgust at their fellow traveler status. I considered them to be ripping off my culture. I was a full-time radical living on the fringes. During my days in the civil rights, antiwar, feminist movement, all the time I spent in jails, hospitals, and free clinics was part of paying my dues.

I never did make my peace with the part-time activists. They had never burned their bridges to respectability. We, living within the sixties and seventies counterculture, bought into that culture with our own blood, sweat, and swears. We were outlaws.

Weekend radicals and day-trippers played a part in making social change. Yet as a fully committed activist, I had a hard time seeing it and I resented their getting the cultural benefits of outlaw status without paying their dues. Our dues were paid in poverty, fear, hunger, broken bones, lost jobs, cultural marginality, and societal disapproval. Authentic activists burned their bridges to the straight world.

Now I am day-tripper. Within the biker world, if I were male, I would be considered a weekend warrior. It's a hard position for an old radical to be in. My heart lies with those who authenticate the culture but my life has brought me to riding from a faraway place. Over immense distances of age, gender, class, background, and political positions, I have made contact with bikers. I have reached the biker world in my late years. This does not diminish the wonderment of the contact. It adds to it. Even though I will never be more than marginalized within this world, just the edges of it bring me the glory of jamming the wind. There are times I even forgive myself the day-tripper status. I know, however, that those who have spent their lives within this world will not.

The rest of the weekend warriors have no apologies to make. They too are legitimate within biker society. They are something new and not loved by the hard cases, but so what. They do not need to be. They know who they are, why they ride, and make no excuses for it.

PART 3

Jamming the Wind

13

An Intimate Account of the Redwood Run

Our First Year

"There's nothing like the real thing."

I awake with serious nausea and a sharp sense of things gone wrong. Check out Ken, no problem there. He snorts in oblivion. Roll out of bed with the stiffness of having lived too many inactive years and curse my laziness. Check the cats, the house, and the phone. No cat shit, no break-ins, and no callers. Something's wrong, I'm just not sure what it is.

The sun is up and out. The day is dry. It is a day made for riding. Memory hits. Damn, I had prayed for rain. I wanted Frisco hit. I wanted to revel in the biggest baddest rainstorm in creation. I wanted the rain to obliterate all traces of outdoor life. I wanted unrelenting fury. I wanted rain rage. Anything to keep me off the bike. Anything to keep us from riding.

This day of my first Redwood Run starts out hot and healthy. I start out sick and scared. Even before Ken can focus his eyes, I have mentally gone over every plausible excuse for not going. Why am I about to jump on the back of a bike and stuff my rear into an open seat going seventy-five miles an hour down a sun-blinded highway, when I could be comfortably reading a book at home?

Redwood Run is a long two hundred mile trip. The body starts to ache, sag, pound, blister, and stink. Everything hurts. And that's before you factor in fear. It's the fear that wakes me up early. It's the fear that keeps me praying for rain. It's the fear that makes me sick. But it's my fury at that fear that keeps me on the bike. Fuck the fear—I will ride.

Despite the odds, despite sanity and reason, I will ride behind Ken today. We will ride to Garberville and participate in Redwood Run. I'll be OK just so long as we stay away from the pit.

It's hard to rouse Ken, and the morning bagels taste like straw. The juice is bitter and watery with tiny clumps of pulp. Ken puts up toast instead, and I dump the bagels and juice. Considering all the gear I have to wear, a light breakfast sits better. Jeans, chaps, jacket, vest, boots, goggles, and cap get jammed, tucked, and pulled over my body. Everything is brown leather, including even the pointy brown hat that resembles nothing so much as a German World War I army helmet. The hat is soft and supple. No skid lid is yet required.

This is to be our first Redwood Run. It will be the last one we will attend without brain buckets. The following winter, Dick Floyd will pass his helmet law through the California legislature and Pete Wilson will sign it. Helmet hatred goes deep. Resentment of authority goes even deeper. This is going to be the last chance to ride bareheaded through redwood mountain country. Freedom's last gasp!

On this day, our heads are covered with leather. As the day warms, headgear will change to neckerchiefs, worn bandito style around our foreheads. As the wind whips up, another handkerchief will be pulled across the face—bank-robber fashion—and knotted in back. This will keep out the bugs, the road grit, and the sun. By day's end, only our eyes will be showing.

I've crammed my gear into the saddlebags. I've got water, food, shampoo, and toilet paper. But am I psyched enough for this trip? We barely know the guys we're riding with. Can I trust them on the road? Are the bikes in good enough shape? Will there be enough bathroom stops? All the past fears and uncertainties crowd back into my mind. And for a second, terror returns.

To calm myself, I think about all the runs in our lives. I have loved them all and lived to tell about them. But Redwood Run, at this point, is still a mystery for me. I expect to party and visit. I expect adventure. The pit, Redwood Run's infamous attraction, is the only place I expect to avoid.

Whenever a run lasts more than a day, clothes, tents, food, and bike tools must be figured into the trip. What to wear simplifies down to, What do I need and will it fit on the bike? There are Lady Bikers who ride with nothing but hairdryers and condoms in their saddlebags. I am not one of them. I know I will need rain gear even though the sun is shining and the forecast says "clear." Too old to be reckless, I prepare. Later, as I ride the back seat, I remember all the things I forgot to pack. I brought the toothbrush but forgot the toothpaste. I remembered the soap but forgot the Band-Aids.

Some of the newer bikes, the full Dressers, have complex communications systems. Dubbed "Harleybagos" by the hard-core, they come outfitted with radios, walkie-talkies, mobile phones, and other communications equipment. There are even gadgets that allow the passenger to talk to the rider when both are covered in full face helmets. I, however, use the old-fashioned method: I shout in Ken's ear. I also nibble and bite that ear for attention. Riding two-up keeps us very close.

The time to mount has come. Carefully, Ken lowers the passenger pegs and slides to the very front of his seat, giving me maximum room to board. I place my right foot on the peg, swing my body high up behind him, and settle myself into the passenger seat. After a number of wiggling movements, clothes adjustments, and groaning complaints about my lack of space, we are ready to roll.

"Go slower, go slower," I scream, more out of habit than alarm. Ken loves me. He listens. "Go slower," I continue relentlessly. "Watch that car! Why are we slowing down? What's the matter with the engine, it's making funny noises."

Ken has the patience of a saint. His riding buddies feel sorry for him. Once when he left me at the side of the road (by accident, he claims), his friends applauded. Passengering, I am a pain in the ass.

Once we're underway, a wonderful transition occurs. There is the roaring sound of the engine, the complex and changing sounds of the road, the rush of the wind, and the internal sounds of my own thoughts. As I finally relax into the ride, an internal quiet descends. I can feel Ken's body loosen and settle into his own rhythm. We are both at peace.

The awesome and scary stories about Redwood Run make me afraid to travel alone. We need friends on the road. We need traveling buddies. Ken and I don't yet know a lot of other riders, but we have made a few quick friends at the bike shop and we're riding with a group today. There are nine bikes and ten people. I am the only passenger. I am also the only woman. This is not good news.

For the first few miles, all goes well. The men slow their speed to accommodate me and the weather holds sunny, the road hot and clear. Forty minutes out of town we stop at the first open-air biker bar. There are hundreds of bikes here already, crammed into small spaces, parked at impossible angles, all sitting at the sides of the road. Cigarette, beer, and bike fumes compete for available air space. The day is young and we have not yet begun to sweat in our leathers. The bar is filled with men. What with bear hugs, beer swigs, and lively bike talk, it takes us an hour and a half to get back on the road.

Less than fifty minutes later, another bar beckons. This one is indoors and filled with food as well as bikers, beer, and smoke. Still, only the occasional woman appears. I hurry over to a lone women sitting on a stool at the far end of the long wooden bar, but by the time I get there, she is already sliding off her stool. I am shocked at the difference in our appearances. Dressed in full riding gear and wearing road grime like a second skin, I am less than fastidious, with wild, dirty, tangled Harley hair and no makeup. She looks cool and pulled together. Her makeup is perfect and her hair shiny. Most telling, however, is the coordinated outfit. The tube top and the cutoff jeans show off her very long, bare, tanned legs. At the end of those long legs are feet sporting high spike heels. She turns to me with a look that slides away. She is here looking for a biker. I am beyond noticing.

By the time we leave our third roadhouse, we've been traveling over five hours, are less than halfway there, and are filled to the gills. Without saying a word to us, the group we've been riding with abruptly decides it is time to move. We are left in their dust.

Many years later, I will find out what shits our first riding buddies were. At the time, though, it doesn't occur to me that they should not have left us without warning. Bikers frequently separate during trips but not usually without advance planning. Alone, on our own, and more confident than we have a right to be, we start for Garberville. This first Redwood Run will be our entrance into the wider Harley culture. Before this, we have traveled only the local streets and highways of the Bay Area. Now we are riding for real.

The day grows hotter and we soak our clothes with water as we ride. We spray our bodies from a plant sprayer and slowly strip away heavy layers of leather. The wind will take whatever it can. The wind is always greedy. I have learned to change almost all my clothes on the back of a bike. I am careful, for whatever I cannot hold on to, the wind will steal.

As we ride down the highway, off comes the outside vest, the one with the HOG patches, then the jacket, then the sweater and gloves and hat and long-sleeved shirt. All clothes are deposited underneath me on the seat. As my seat grows, I am riding higher and higher in the saddle. As I tug and pull at one of the sleeves, I clamp the shirt ends into my teeth. Using both my hands to maneuver, I need another body part to clamp onto the shirt now loosely whipping in the wind. I press the shirt between my arm and side while holding that arm tight against my body. It works.

Gloves, before they can be deposited in pockets, must first be swung under shirts and into halter tops, so they will not become the wind victims of this back-seat striptease. Wallets, taken from inside jacket flaps, get crammed into crotches before being safely transported to zippered pockets. I am now sitting on all the cast-off clothes.

"For God's sake sit still," Ken growls as I wriggle around too much, but the burning heat gives justifiable and furious momentum to my stripping.

When I get down to the T-shirt and the halter beneath, I stop, then carefully pull the shirt over my head. Ken gives a very sudden "What the hell!" and I realize that from Ken's view, from the rear-view mirror, I look naked. From the front seat, the small halter top is not visible at all.

We are off that highway in two and a half seconds.

Leaving the road for Ken's visual inspection of my halter gives us a few precious minutes in some shade. It's too hot to cuddle. It's too hot for sex. But there is time for Ken to wet down my whole body. The tepid water dries almost on contact but he's having a good time. We giggle, lurch, clutch, and fall over on the grass. Slick and slippery, I climb back on the bike. I am wearing only a loose, short skirt and the halter top. My thighs stick to the saddle and my legs are going to burn in the sun, but I don't care. Before Ken fires the bike into life I take a minute to tie a handkerchief around my face. Now only my eyes are visible.

With those eyes I watch the road. I see women, alone and in groups of twos and threes, standing in the sweltering heat along the highway. Their tank tops are rolled up to pencil-thin lines and their cutoffs are crotch high. They are wearing a lot less than I am. They wait, moist-lipped and dripping sweat, by the side of the road. They wait, pursed-lipped and doused with water, along the entrances to biker bars.

"Ah, the camp followers," mutter the bikers. "Show us your tits!" yell the men riding by.

The women comply, and I realize suddenly that they too want to go to Redwood Run. They are hitching rides with the bikers.

"Holy shit!" I look on in shock. I can't believe my eyes. These women are eager to get on a stranger's bike. But they wouldn't know shit about his riding ability! They wouldn't know shit about his attitude toward women!

We pull over at a roadside store to pick up food. I notice one woman standing apart.

"Are you alone?" I ask.

"I'm waiting for a ride to Redwood Run."

"Are you waiting for your boyfriend?"

"No, I'm waiting for the right rider."

"How can you tell?" I ask in awe of her confidence.

"I can tell," she says and walks away from me toward the highway.

This is an act of uncommon courage and faith. It is also nuts. Her blond, almost white, hair is braided into a neat French knot. Her tank top and shorts are baggy and she sports no makeup. Since most of the hitchhikers have tight shorts and bulging breasts and are wearing their hair long, hot, and loose, this woman stands out. She is an island of cool in the burning sun. She is also beautiful. Her rounded face, pointy chin, and enormous eyes shout of youth. Her flat-footed and erect stand says she's prepared to wait. Her eyes continue to search to road. She does not show her tits.

Suddenly a large group of riders, three-piece patch holders all, rides by. Almost all of them are packing women. An outlaw club on its way to Garberville. How I envy these women who ride the rear with such casual confidence. I watch them speed by, bodies positioned high, legs bent halfway to their butts, as they perch on tiny, tiny, unpadded princess seats. I wouldn't last five seconds on such a seat, but these women, on Panheads and Shovels without benefit of rubber-mounted suspension, ride with grace and style. They carry themselves with an arrogance equaled only by the style of their mounts. The women know how to ride the back with class. They are all young. I figure it is the bravery of youth.

Several miles farther down the road, Ken and I take a pit stop at an air-conditioned Chevron station when five of the outlaw women burst into the bathroom.

"Did you see what Mickey did? What an asshole!"

"Didn't you tell him to slow down and knock it off?"

"No, I didn't say nothing. When I complain, he just goes faster."

"So were you scared?" I broke in, unable to prevent myself.

"No shit!" She looks at me as if I were some recently released incompetent. "Of course I was scared. When he goes really fast and does something really dumb, I close my eyes and pray."

"Me too!" says her friend. "I can't look. I close my eyes like I don't want to see what's going on. I sit real still so I won't rattle him or throw off his concentration."

"Boy this trip's a bitch. I've had to pee for over an hour and Mickey wouldn't stop. And now I'm getting all sunburned."

After listening to the women, I feel a little better. Like me, they too get scared. Unlike me, they have learned not to show it. Their men do not put up with any bullshit. Their men don't take their feelings seriously. Mickey stops when he wants to, not because his ole lady has to pee. I am suddenly filled with appreciation for Ken.

These women are used to riding in a group. They put up with speed and rough rides and bursting bladders and sunburned bodies because they have to. It's their entrance fee. It's their ticket to ride. In some parts of the biker world, women have learned to keep their legs open and their mouths shut.

Riding to Garberville, I think about the other runs I have loved. Bridgeport and the stunning steeps of Sonora Pass, the sheer drops that go for thousands of feet. And me with height fright! Instant therapy. Baking in the burning sun of Redwood Run, I still taste the incredible cold of the Bridgeport High Sierra mountain air. I still see the hills of flowers, the sweet-smelling lakes. Riding the wide roads of Redwood Run, I remember the narrow roads to Bridgeport and how they wound between mountains and meadows where cows grazed on one side and deer on the other. My loose hold on Ken's waist as we cruise the gentle Redwood Run hills contrasts with my gut-lurching grip on him as we slid sideways down a wet, gravel-filled Bridgeport fire road. Bridgeport was a four-day run that lasts a lifetime. Redwood Run has just begun.

There's a lot of time for thinking on the back of a bike. I have known women who are able to drift off, fall asleep, zone out in the passenger seat. Lucky ladies! I have never ridden with anything less than full alert. On a quiet stretch of road I might let my mind wander, but most of the time I am fully awake and very attentive. While watching the road, I am, however, alone with my thoughts. Sometimes I reflect on my ambling progress through life. Sometimes I think about runs.

I think about Sturgis, the most famous run of all. Hundreds of thousands of bikers converge on that small South Dakota town every summer. At the fiftieth anniversary run, over half a million tattooed, wired, pierced, sweaty, drunken, fringe-haired, half-naked bikers got themselves there. Maybe next year we'll make it. One day we may even make it to Washington and the Ride to the Wall.

The word "run" is not a Harley term. It's a road term. Travelers—from truckers to Teamsters—toss this word about. Deliverymen and shipping companies refer to their regular routes as runs. Bikers, however, have added some special meanings.

It's a term I love. It's a term of movement, excitement, and activity. It's a shivery term filled with implicit danger. The road is a twisty, windy thrill that bikers live for. The road is unpredictable, rough, and difficult. The road is predictable, smooth, and easy. You never know. Tied up in the term is my knowledge that I will be sharing the road with real bikers. A run can last three hours or three days. It can last a month or a lifetime.

Runs can be planned or impromptu. An inspiring patch of clear weather can produce an instant run.

"It's a clear day," I whisper in Ken's ear. "Let's go on a run."

Five minutes later, boots, jacket, helmet, and hat securely in place, we are off riding the crisp-aired mountain roads of Marin.

Other runs, like the Redwood Run, can take months of planning. I think a lot about these runs before they happen. I worry, plan, puke, get the runs, and call my friends to say good-bye. Even spontaneous runs require time for both reflection and planning. Nothing on a run is simple, and the longer the journey, the more complex the planning.

Runs are always complex. They raise questions. How well are Ken and I getting along? When you passenger, it's real important not to fight with the rider. You do not want him mad at you. You want him happy and confident. You do not want him taking his anger out on the road. You want him calm.

Runs mix a number of contradictory elements. When you partner, you are very close, but also very alone. When you ride, you are right in the middle of nature, yet you are completely apart from it. When you jam the wind, you pay for it with hours at the side of the road.

The first contradiction. When you two-up, you are physically very close to your partner. You could not be closer. Each depends upon the other for survival. If something goes wrong, you both go down. Yet as you travel together down the road, you stay within your own world, within your own thoughts.

The second contradiction. While you ride, you are in the middle of the natural world. There are trails you can reach only on a bike. They are not approachable any other way. The natural world shimmers and shines out in front of you and there are no windows, walls, floors, or ceilings to distort your senses. Yet you enter that world on a roaring, powerful, smoking, mechanical beast that scares and scatters every critter within miles. You pass like a thunderbolt slicing through tranquility. You're there with a rush and then—in a lightning flash—you're gone.

The third contradiction. While riding, you experience an extraordinary sense of freedom. Nothing is comparable to riding the wind. Even the rough moments, if you live through them, become the classic ones of memory. All of the bad times amazingly become good times the instant they are over. Yet everyone who has ever loved a Harley knows the experience of bike failure. One minute you are gloriously riding down the road and the next you are sitting at the edge of that road tinkering and waiting for help. After many, many breakdowns, all in out-of-the-way places, I threatened to make a sign that would read, "If we owned a Honda we'd be riding now." When you ride, you experience a powerful sense of movement and activity. This contrasts profoundly with the long hours you spend wrenching by the side of the highway. Keeping the bike up and running has always been a problem for owners of Harleys.

In Harley culture, runs make up the stuff of life. In some clubs, run attendance is mandatory. In others, it's considered the best way to spend a day or weekend or a vacation. The run, with its double function of being both transportation to the event and the event itself, once again puts the bike front and center.

Finally we make it to Garberville and check out the lure of this one-street town—a town that sits in the very lap of the redwoods. How foolish were my worries about surviving the six-hour bike trip. This trip never takes six hours. A car might make it in that time but bikes are different. No one rides directly to Garberville. Between the pit stops, the bar stops, and the visiting, it takes the entire day. Redwood Run is party time and the party begins the moment you mount the bike.

We arrive only to discover, however, that there is no arrival place. It's just a quaint, tree-lined village clotted with bikes, bikers, and booze. This realization leaves us a bit startled. We had expected . . . What! We had expected . . . More! We wanted action. The only action is our first walk in a bike-choked street. Bikes are parked everywhere. They are parked in the street, in the corners, in front of every store, on half the sidewalks and, in some places, in the middle of the road. It's a bike-mad world. It's beautiful.

Redwood Run has been a Harley tradition for a long, long time. Starting as a dealer's run, it was taken over by the Kiwanis Club in 1992. It's an event where outlaw MCs ride side by side with mom and pop clubs and novices get a taste of Harley life. To the outsider, not much appears to be happening. Bikers swarm all over the little towns, making Garberville the center of the run and Piercy its party place. Garberville has the town, the walkable streets, the restaurants, the motels, and the bars. Piercy has the pit.

Along the mountain roads to Piercy, thick among the redwoods, are rows of vendors selling bike parts.

"Ken, I want a new bandanna. I want new gloves."

I want one of the colorful stickers that proclaims, "It's True, I've Fallen In With The Wrong Crowd." I want, I want. There's no end to the things I want. Ken's wants are more practical; he eyes the windshields, the fairings, the solo seats. He especially eyes the solo seats. We cluster with hundreds of bikers sampling the beer. Whole bike clubs meet at vendor sites. Bikes are parked along the roadside as riders stop and visit and drink beer. Hundreds of bikes sit proudly on their kickstands, and we walk among them admiring the saddlebags of one, the paint job of another.

"Hand me my shades," Ken says to me as we bike hop.

The glare from all that chrome is painful as it dazzles and blinds in the noon sun. Finished with riding, buying, and beautiful roads, we head for the action. We head for the pit. At last we ride to Piercy, fifteen miles south of Garberville and, after much hesitation, descend into the pit.

14

The Pit

Layered and Loud

"Sometimes the real thing is too real."

"That's what the Redwood Run is all about, a bunch of goofy guys and a few biker chicks running off to the woods for a three-day party. Lots of others go on the run, and while some of them come down to the pit for a short time, most stay and play elsewhere. Different strokes for different folks, but if ya didn't get down and dirty in the pit, ya missed the party. I was tired and dirty with a head floating somewhere in the treetops and there was a mean little animal growling in my stomach. But then that's what the Redwood Run is all about, isn't it?" (Easy Ed, *FogHog News*, August 1991)

I have always dreaded the pit. Heard stories about it for years. Every woman I knew said "Stay away." Every man I knew said "Go for it." The pit is the stuff of legends. It's where the main action of the run takes place. The pit is where you earn your right to boogie. Getting into the pit is the first rite of passage. Descending into the pit, I leave all expectations about behaviors behind. The pit makes its own rules.

The pit is an enormous canyon with a river running across one end and terraced hills rimming three sides. On the fourth side, the granite goes straight up. Arriving at the lip of the pit, we are smacked in the face by the music. Music vibrates off the canyon walls. Loud, live bands vie with each other for raunchier, bluesier sounds. Music rebounds off the canyons, creeps into the tents, spirals along the carburetors, and ejaculates among the shitters. The pit is music-happy and it doesn't matter if the music is blues, rockin' blues, rhythm and blues, rhythm and country, or rock and roll. By the end of the weekend, no one can hear a bloody thing. Drawn by the music, Ken and I go deeper into the pit.

To get into the pit, you must descend, on bike, down a very steep, winding, mountain road overlain with gravel, dirt, straw, and rocks.

With the mountain on one side and the cliff edge on the other and a road full of gravel and ruts, there is not much room for error. The road is pitted with deep grooves and potholes of enormous dimension. The road down, narrow and broken, has only one lane for bikes both entering and leaving. Great security. Other vehicles remain outside. Vendors, bands, and food concessions are already in the pit by the time the bikers arrive.

Entering the pit is never done casually. Even in the best of weather, the steep dirt paths must be navigated with care. The road that winds down the mountain has no shoulder and provides little traction. It is slow going to get either in or out, and once in you're pretty isolated from the rest of the world. A perfect biker hangout.

The entrance is guarded by security people checking wrist bands.

"We are comped," I comment to Ken. "We don't have to pay."

We are covering this event for *Thunder Press*, the Harley newspaper, and Reg Kittrelle, the editor and publisher, has gotten us in for free. Everyone else has to show their tickets at the entrance to receive their brightly colored wristbands. Tickets costing as much as $50 a person are purchased beforehand at the local bike shops or at the run's entrance. We give our names at the entrance booth and get our bands. They will be worn all weekend. Since the wristbands are fitted to individual wrists, some riders make them as loose as possible. This permits them to later slip the bands off and pass them to friends. Since no one enters the pit with a naked wrist, friends share bands only when they are through with them.

From the back of Ken's bike on the way down, I watch the unescorted, nonriding, single women crashing the gate. Without the neon-colored wristbands, they can't get past the guards. But it's just a temporary setback. After only a short wait, the women get picked up by bikers, are bought the expensive at-the-gate tickets, and are given wristbands. Many married bikers choose to ride solo to Redwood Run. They leave their ole ladies, wives, and girlfriends at home. It's party time! It's common for a man to ride single to the pit, pick up a hitch-hiker at the gate, and party with her the whole weekend. It's rare for single women to ride solo into the pit. Not unheard of, just rare. Most of the women ride in with their men or get picked up at the gate.

Halfway down the mountain, we pass Miss White Hair, the young woman with the French braid. She's clinging tightly to the back of a biker as their bike loses traction and slides halfway off the road. Several hands reach out to help them as Ken and I pass close to their fender. Her hair's still in its neat braid but she has dark smudges around her eyes and a swollen mouth.

"You OK?" I yell, as we pass. She looks up in recognition but starts to turn away. "I'll see you at the bandstand," I continue to shout, but she has completely turned from me and faces the men with the helping hands.

They steady the falling bike.

"Shouldn't we stop and help them?" I ask Ken as we pass. "Didn't you recognize her? She's the one from the roadside looking for a ride."

"I guess she found one," replies Ken as we keep going down into the pit.

"Why didn't we stop?"

"We don't need to," he answers. "They had a lot of help. We would have just been in the way."

"But I wanted to talk to her," I add.

"You'll see her later," he answers. "She's pretty hard to miss."

The pit has some impressive if informal rules. In the early part of the day, the men take on an air of exaggerated politeness. Theoretically, no one packs a weapon. Theoretically, all drugs and hard booze are left outside. In reality, anything goes. This is an open, all-Harley event where many clubs participate. Not all of them like each other. Not all of them are friendly. I suspect that the exaggerated politeness is a peacekeeping device. It is a way of making the area safe. The pit becomes neutral territory.

The pit is terraced in such a way that each level has bikes, tents, and shitters. Ken pulls into a level about halfway between the bandstand at the bottom and the entrance at the top. He finds an open spot overlooking the bandstand. He steadies the bike as I climb off and immediately sets about parking it away from the gravel road. We pull off our remaining gear and bungee it to the seat of the bike. As we start walking down toward the bandstand, I accidentally step on a zoned-out biker's jacket and apologize profusely.

"Not to worry," he nods, as he extends an enormous hand to help me over the rest of his gear. "Don't fall," he cautions, as I thread my way around the slippery side of the mountain.

It's a safe space. All groups can party on this common ground. For this time-space, all groups are welcome. And for the most part this works. Even though many bikers are packing weapons, drinking continually, and mixing assorted drugs with abandon and flair, the area remains hospitable. Despite the potential for mass lawlessness, the pit actually provides an atmosphere of camaraderie.

As we walk I stare down into the pit and I realize I could be looking into the ninth circle. People are camped out in every scrap of space. Tents of every size and color cling to the sides of the mountain, stacked along the flat plains of the terraces and perched high above the arena overlooking the bandstand. Rows of colorful green shitters perfume every level.

The pit during the day is a time for swimming, setting up camp, and kicking back. It's a time for listening to music, drinking beer, smoking dope, and visiting friends. The pace picks up at dusk, when the music gets louder, the crowd noisier, and the mood rowdier. By full nightfall, the crowd is aggressive, drunk, and into hell-raising. The lights from the shitters and vendor stands cast a murky, eerie glow around the terraces. Where the lights cannot reach, shadows and darkness chase each other with only thin moonlight filtering through. A laugh, a scream, a deep-throated whoop punctuate the night between the sets of music.

On a narrow straw-strewn hill, I watch a biker, fully unclothed, ride his scoot over a ridge with an equally naked woman clinging to his back. He downshifts and leans his bike hard to the left as another nocturnal, naked, and drunk rider careers over the same ridge. He rides with his feet over the handlebars even while hard-twisting the throttle. It's not the riding style taught at motorcycle training school. Bikes are big, tough machines and human bodies are inconveniently vulnerable. Bare legs burn easily on hell-hot bike pipes.

"My Gawd, Ken, the guy's nuts are sitting right there on the gas tank!" I yell.

Any error, the slightest miscalculation in judgment, and all three riders are history. They roar off laughing into the night. The wild ride ends in triumph. Tonight they ride for free. No flesh is demanded in payment for pleasures. Tonight no piper will be paid.

At night the pit, greatly enhanced by nitrous oxide nips from colorful balloons, takes on a color and shape of its own. It's a time of license. It's a time for fucking in the tents, on the hills, and under the trees, pissing in the bushes, and drinking beer nonstop. From one tent comes a woman's scream, from another, a purr. Distant cries and curses can be heard between the breaks in the music. A woman runs drunkenly along the mountain's edge while two men chase her. I am beginning to worry about her, when all three of them collapse in gales of laughter. People lie in tangles of twos and threes and fours around campfires. With so many men and so few women my worries are not unfounded. The men are drunk; the women had better be willing. But then, I remind myself, no one forced anyone to attend. The danger, the sexuality, and the adventure are all part of the pit. The rules are informal but acknowledged. The warring clubs stay cool and the women stay hot.

I catch a glimpse of Miss White Hair dancing in the moonlight, her long hair loose, the white strands having escaped from the confines of the French braid, her baggy clothes shed. She moves in mystery. As the moon, the music, and the mood rise, Ken and I leave our first experience of the pit for the safer, quieter comforts of our teepee.

Preparing for our first Redwood Run meant reserving a place to stay ahead of time. Every room in Garberville was already filled. They had been booked for years. Once a biker finds a room, he keeps it forever.

Using all of my anthropological smarts, calling in academic favors from around the country, I landed us a teepee in a campsite some fifteen miles from Garberville. The anthropological community is large and I was owed a favor or two by friends who had friends who knew someone near Piercy. We are lucky. The campsite offers not only the teepee (which includes cots) but a restaurant and bathrooms. The teepee has flaps at two ends and poles for supports, but it is far too open for my taste. The protective covering stops an important two feet from the ground. This means that critters have access to our sleeping area.

Despite my worry about insects, reptiles, birds, and other beasts, late that night I fall right to sleep. The sheer exhaustion of riding all day and visiting the pit all evening, combined with the sun and generous amounts of beer, make sleep easy. The constant rumbling and growling of the big bikes vibrates the ground like cataclysmic orgasms. Sleep follows the release. While much of the world considers the triumphant roar of an unmuffled Harley noise pollution, for us it's slumber music. Our sleep is comforted by the screaming and coughing of the bikes as they ride all night past our teepee.

Then in the very early, very quiet predawn hours, I awake to another sound. This one is not pleasant. Right next to our teepee, closer than I ever want to consider, a wildcat screams loud and long. It is as eerie and awful a sound as a city woman is ever likely to hear. The next thing I know, I am screaming loud and long at the wildcat. I screech and scream and wake the entire woods. I out-shout the wildcat. I out-shout the late returning bikes. I wake the camp but I vanquish the cat. The next day we ride back to Frisco. The trip takes five hours. It's the end of our first Redwood Run.

15

The "Wetwood" Run

Frigid and Freezing

"You're not going to believe this!"

Two years later, Ken and I are off to our next Redwood Run. We are more experienced riders. We are more savvy in the ways of the road. We make plans to ride with friends we trust. A whole horde of them expect to share the road with us, and two special friends, Jonathan and Kitty, become our mainstays. Ken and Jonathan ride. Kitty and I are packed. The men say they don't mind packing us but I have my doubts.

"If you were riding your own bike," says Ken, "I would have more room in my saddlebags. If you were riding I could use your seat to store more of the gear."

I consider briefly the thought of riding my own scoot the full 200 miles. I think about the possibility of rain, heat, exhaustion, and saddle sores. As a beginning rider, both my feet and hands are occupied at all times. Once settled into the ride, I remain in that very position until I stop. All that time in the saddle without room to extend, flex, or move. "It's all yours, dear," I respond to Ken, "I love to be packed. That way I can still nibble on your ear."

In back of Jonathan's bike is a small trailer, infamously and beautifully named the Jade Box. The weight of the trailer makes us all go slow. All right with me. This year I have snagged a room in Garberville. Once a year, the Garberville Motel permits reservation calls. These start at 8:00 A.M. on New Year's day. Whatever rooms are unfilled by last year's bikers go out for rent. By 8:02, all the rooms are rented. I started calling at 7:45 and kept calling until 8:01 when Nina, the manager, answered the phone and assigned us the one room still available. It is a miracle. We have a room. Kitty and Jonathan have their camping

Kitty and Jonathan Gould (Courtesy of Kitty and Jonathan Gould)

equipment. They plan to stay in the pit. We all have supplies. Redwood Run, here we come!

We meet at Dudley Perkins's shop at 10:00 A.M. on the windiest, wettest day imaginable. The sky, gray and thick with storm clouds, crackles with energy. When the rain comes, it will come hard. The horde of expected friends never shows. Everyone but Kitty and Jonathan cancels at the last minute. The folks at DP's take bets on how far we will get. No one expects us to last till Santa Rosa, fifty miles north. It's only drizzling now, but we know it's going to get worse.

"What do you think you're wearing?" asks a friendly voice. I turn, point, and show off my new leathers. He shakes his head and points to the rain gear.

"I'm really comfortable in my new chaps," I explain.

"Doesn't matter," he softly adds, "you're gonna need more than leather when the rain hits."

The service people at DP's insist that I buy a real rainsuit, and for once I listen. They stuff me into a bright, yellow, one-piece plastic sack. I cannot move my body in any direction but forward. The suit does not bend. It does not turn. It reminds me of a straitjacket. It will, I hope, keep me dry.

Brimming with self-determination, the four of us take off. Two more riders join us for a short distance but are forced back by the rain. We too do not want to ride in a steady downpour. But somehow, disregarding all sanity, we persevere. We keep hoping the forecasts are correct. They predict only scattered showers.

"Ken, ride slower! I can't see in all this rain."

"Hey, Barbara," yells Kitty, turning to shout across two lanes of traffic, "are you still up for this? Do you think we should go on?"

I nod and give her a thumbs-up. For the first fifty miles we keep telling ourselves—and believing—that we can always turn back. But after leaving Santa Rosa, we know we are committed and pride keeps us going. These decisions aren't rational. We are too numb to think. Vanity, stubbornness, and the genuine desire to participate in the soon to be historic "Wetwood" Run keep us moving.

"Ken, pull off, over there! Let's stop, I'm freezing."

"Kitty," I yell straight through the rain, "are you and Jonathan ready to stop?"

As we pull into one of the traditional Harley-occupied roadhouses, we are greeted by a shivering, dripping group of bikers. The contingent is much reduced in numbers. No one is talking. No one is visiting. No one is joking. The few on the road this day are miserable and morose. I suggest to Jonathan, who always wears a patch that reads "If it's got tits or wheels it will give you trouble," that he change his patch to read "If it's got tits or wheels or weather it will give you trouble."

For my husband, all three give him trouble. He has problems with the weather, with me, and finally with the bike. The rain is becoming torrential, and I am wet, cold, and cranky. "I'm too old for this bullshit!" I groan in his ear.

The rainsuit tears and icy cold water pours down my crotch. I am forced to patch up during pit stops. Kitty winds duct tape around my yellow rainsuit and patches plastic garbage bags over the rips. Ken takes pictures. He thinks I look wonderfully funny. Funny enough to win some hokey contest about glamorous women on Harleys. Later, he has to cut me out of the whole damn mess.

The wheels also give him trouble. Just outside of Ukiah we break down. Quick calls to Harley hot lines, biker road services, and the local dealership. Fortunately, the local Harley shop says it will fix the bike next day at dawn. Ken, in protective mode, drags all our wet clothes over to the Laundromat. We spend the night warm and dry in a Ukiah

228

motel. Kitty and Jonathan continue. Piercy is just over the next mountain. Over their objections, we give them our key to the Garberville room and tell them to use it. They want to camp in the pit but none of us knows how wet it will be.

The next day is worse than the first. Now it's cold, wet, and windy, and we still have a mountain to pass. The frigid air takes huge bites out of our lungs as we ride the last seventy-five miles to Garberville.

"My nose is frozen and I can't feel my hands. I can't take any more of this!" I keep saying, over and over.

"Stop complaining and save your energy. We're going to make it," says Ken as I cling to his sides.

I hold on to Ken, close my eyes, and curse most of the way there. To keep from going crazy, I play a game with myself. I think of all the things I have to be thankful for. For the next seventy-five miserable miles, I concentrate on my "grateful" list. Aren't I fortunate I don't have a cold? How would I be able to blow my nose? My wet gloves couldn't hold a tissue. Isn't it great that I love my job? How good to be an anthropologist and get to choose the groups I study. If I had chosen another group, I wouldn't be clinging to the wet back of a dripping biker riding right into the wrath of a storm. Isn't it lucky I don't have to go to the bathroom? It would take a derrick to remove me from the bike. I am wearing twenty-two items of clothing plus three plastic bags. When we finally arrive, I need two helpers to get me off the bike. Their laughter still rings in my ears. The sight of me makes their morning. In the middle of a dreary, depressing Garberville, my ridiculous outfit becomes the one light spot in a heavy day.

Upon arrival we find a very grateful Kitty and Jonathan. Frozen from the ride over the mountain, Jonathan had to drag Kitty into a steamy shower to unfreeze her bones. That first night they slept in the motel room. The pit is one great mud hole. We share the room for the entire weekend. Kitty sets up camp in the middle of the room. They blow up their air mattresses, pitch the tent, and lay out their sleeping bags.

"Smell the mud?" I ask each morning. "We all smell like wet rubber, old socks, and wet fur." No matter how high we set the thermostat, the room feels damp and moldy. "Don't you feel like we've been damp forever?"

But Kitty never gives up hope. She's sure the damp will clear and the pit will be livable. I'm less optimistic. Each time we leave the room our riding trips are short and difficult. The heavy rains force Ken to pull over every few miles to wipe his glasses. Much of our travel time we travel blind. Motorcycle helmets do not come equipped with windshield wipers.

229

This year we return to find the pit completely awash in mud. It is now one gigantic sinkhole filled with wet straw; crushed, soaked gravel; and soggy, drunken, miserable bikers. It has been raining for three days. Those who have pitched tents have done so against all the odds and all reason. Tents slide down ravines, bikes sink into the mud, their kickstands all but disappearing into the ooze. Fires won't start. Nothing stays dry. Even the food is filled with mud. This trip we find that the mud hole is occupied almost exclusively by men. With so many men, so few women, and such difficult weather, I am very grateful to have a room in Garberville.

This time there are no single women waiting at the entrance to the pit and it is far too wet for any of the men to stand around with signs saying "Show us your tits." There are very few single women in the pit and those who are, are disinclined to undress. It doesn't take me long to discover that the single women have far more sense than the male bikers. Most of them are warmly ensconced in motel rooms.

Two women, young and far too pretty, move into the room right next to ours. They keep their shades up and their pants down. Kitty and I can't figure out at first why our men keep going outside to smoke. All weekend long, bikers visit next door. And just this weekend Ken and Jonathan develop an urgent need for nicotine. We try to act pissed about it, but Kitty and I think it is just too funny. Because we are there, our men can only look. We can deal with that. We also notice that there is a sudden increase in the number of windowless vans parked in the motel lots. Some of them never stop rocking.

In spite of the rain, the cold, and the wind, I am glad we've come. This is one run pin we earned.

16

Redwood Run Rerun
Heat, Harleys, and Havoc

"Say good-bye."

For our third Redwood Run, I have pulled strings to upgrade from one small room into nine wonderful double rooms with porches and air-conditioners. All our friends are going to be there. It will be a nonstop, three-day party. The weather is clear and dry, the pit passable, and the music promises to be superb. Once we arrive, it'll be party time. It takes us, however, twenty-eight hours to get there.

Ken and I, along with Jonathan and Kitty, now our permanent Redwood Run buddies, leave a day early. This year, with the dry weather, Kitty wants to get a good spot for camping in the pit. I want to relax before the hordes arrive. Nevertheless, we still manage to limp in a day late. This, on a Harley, is not hard to do.

"Ken, I really am dying of the heat!" I moan. "I've got to stop in some shade."

It was hot when we left DP's but by the time we hit Santa Rosa, the temperature's well over a hundred. The enforced wearing of the skid lid, now law in California, has raised the heat level beyond that. Hot, dazed, dizzy with the heat, we head for the coast.

Highway 1 is wonderful any time of year, but in the middle of a heat wave, it is sublime. The trip's a bit longer but is worth every cool, comfortable, glorious extra second. Unless, of course, you break down.

Somewhere, just south of Sea Ranch and way out of the reach of any cellular system, Jonathan's bike stops dead. An electrical coil has gone bad and the bike has given out. Once again we are experiencing a Harley moment. We are stranded by the side of the road. But this time the wait will take eight hours. We are on the coast road somewhere between two very distant bike tow sites. Neither wants to claim

231

us. Ken and I, with the only working bike, ferry food and information back and forth. After four trips we are able to relax and settle in for the long wait. Jonathan and Kitty, however, are feeling no pain. They've had the pleasure of waiting by the ocean with a cooler full of beer.

We join them on a grassy knoll overlooking the fog-strewn sea, drink beer, and stare at the water. It's a beautiful spot to break down. We sit and drink for hours. No one stops to offer help.

"Are we invisible?" Jonathan asks.

"No, we are bikers and this is a snotty region. We are lounging in the land of the rich," I slur. "We should be hauling their trash, cleaning their grounds, and shopping for their groceries. The homeowners here don't expect to share their scenery with us."

"It's different when you come in a car," announces Kitty. "We stayed in a lodge near here last year. Hot tub in the room, room service, and lots of privacy."

"I'll bet it cost a bundle."

"Worth every penny. It was the most romantic weekend Jonathan and I ever spent."

Around ten in the evening, the tow truck arrives and we have the unique experience of loading two bikes in the middle of a moonless highway.

"Swing that light higher," yells Kitty, as I flash the flashlight at the oncoming traffic.

"I'm swinging as high as I can," I giggle into the night. The beer has had its way with me.

Only the bright signals from our flashlights keep the oncoming cars from crashing into us. Only the constant waving of arms wards off the cars and other night demons. For two hours we make like fireflies in a land that doesn't remember them, in a land that doesn't even see us. Finally, just short of 2:00 A.M., we arrive for the third year in a row in Ukiah.

Kitty is full of news. As we start up the mountain the next morning, she tells us of her new business. It's called TITS—Tip Income Tracking Services. Jonathan who now sports a DILLIGAF (Do I Look Like I Give A Fuck) patch says it's about time they were finally making some money off Kitty's TITS.

Our third return to the pit brings sunshine, sex, and surprises. The place is filled with more women than I have ever seen. Solo women riders brave the trip and the entrance. They arrive triumphant. They strut, they swagger. Their confident, cocky walk announces their accomplishments and their pride. They ride their own Harleys. These are women to be reckoned with.

The pit too has a different feel to it. It is still filled with activities but it feels friendlier. Even when all the men jump down from the ridges to watch the wet T-shirt contest there seems to be less of the lawlessness of previous years. There is also a little less wildness. There is still balloon nipping and there are prodigious bouts of drinking, but the atmosphere is subtly modified. It's still loud and lewd and loose and most rules still get left at the entrance. It's still a time of license and leer. Men still forge casual and temporary truces with one another and women still ride the line between wariness and anticipation. Sexual tensions still fill the spaces between the truces. It is still a place where too much ain't enough. It's still the pit but some things have changed.

The new pit has more events crowded in. There are now wet shorts as well as wet T-shirt contests. Men still pay hundreds of dollars for the privilege of wetting down the female contestants. But women also pay for this equal opportunity ceremony. "Who'll pay $50? Who'll pay $75? Look at these fine hung men. Which of you ladies will pay to wet him down?"

The wet T contest always draws a noisy, cheering, rowdy crowd. The area around the bandstand and stage packs tight. Men shout, dancers strip, and the name "wet T" becomes only a label. Before too many seconds pass, the first woman has peeled to a thong.

"Off! Off! Off!" The men's chant is heard above the music. They clap in rhythm.

"Uh-Uh-Uh," pants the dancer as she wiggles, jiggles, and giggles herself across the stage.

Heavy applause from the men as she lovingly runs her hands up and down her wet breasts. Heavier applause as she plays peek-a-boo with her nipples. Thunderous applause as she removes the thong and, holding it at both ends, slowly starts to rub it back and forth between her legs. And this is just the first act. There are four more wet T-shirt dancers to follow. The second dancer, not to be outdone, rhythmically runs her fingers in and out of her cunt. For her finale she languidly licks those fingers.

"Put your eyes back in your head," I shout over the music as Ken busily snaps away with the camera.

"It's professional interest," he claims.

He's been editing the *FogHog News*. "Professional interest? Right!" I laugh as the third woman starts her dance. (Later, we find out that the local camera shop will not print his pictures.)

Dancer three performs for herself and not for the men. Dancer three is fat. Suddenly women start crowding into the spaces between the men at the bandstand. We all watch the third contestant, who dances with abandon. She is applauded by the women. She is appreciated by

233

every woman who has ever viewed her own body and gone "Yuk!" This dancer is grooving on the music. Head thrown back, hair flying in all directions, she looks like she is really enjoying herself in spite of not having a traditionally "perfect" body.

The winner, decided by applause, is not number three. Men outnumber women in this audience five to one and they vote for the first dancer.

The wet shorts contest is new. Women ogle, stare, clap, and stomp their approval of naked men. The wet shorts dancing started only a few years ago and reflects some of the changes in the pit. As the women hurry to the bandstand, most of the men hurry to leave. The male audience is not missed. We women hoot, holler, wave, and applaud our favorites. Women bid for the privilege of wetting down the dancers. Loud cheers go up as the bidding intensifies. The winner gets up on stage and after intimate hugs, throws the water over the men. Then she douses herself.

"It's cold!" shouts the first dancer as the pail of water hits him. Nevertheless, he takes a long time wiggling out of his shorts.

Few of the men dance with the grace, style, or abandon of the women. They are less at ease on stage. Some just stand at the edge of the stage and flex their muscles.

"Show us what you've got! Show us your butt," yell the women around me.

"Shut up," I yell back. "Let them dance."

One man dances with the fluid movements of a Chippendale. The rest hobble through their numbers. Most of the men strip down to their jock straps, a few pull out their cocks and play with them. Some wiggle around stage dancing their balls to the music. One man, however, refuses to remove even his shirt. He poses arrogantly, struts to center stage, smiles, turns his back to the audience, and flexes his muscles. He is wearing a tight tank top.

"Show us! Show us!" the women yell again and again but he teases and taunts and once more presents only his back.

Unlike the women dancers, he never gives the group what it wants. At contest's end, he is the winner.

"So what did you think of that?" I ask Ken.

"I think it's great! If they have dancers for men, they should have them for women."

"Would you ever do it?"

"No, no way," he first answers. Then he thinks about it. "I don't know. I'd have to be pretty drunk. I mean, it kind of goes against the way I was brought up, privacy and all. You'd have to be pretty uninhibited to get up there and do that. And do it good. You also have to be really pleased with yourself. It takes a lot of guts and probably took a lot of drugs."

"Did you feel sorry for the guys?" I ask.

"No. No one dragged them up there."

"They all had small cocks! Did you see that? Every damned one of them was little," I complained.

"Well, sure. They would look small to us," responded Ken. "We're far back. Unless it was hanging down to their knees, it would look small from here."

"I only saw three of them dancing with their balls," I added. "I think the women did better."

The new pit has bike shows, bike games, and a popular Slow Race. Lots of women talk about the games.

"Bite the weenie is disgusting," announces one of the participants. "Last year I got mustard all over me and almost choked on the hot dog."

"No, it's not disgusting! I think it's fun," answered her friend.

"You think I'm going to stand up in the passenger seat and try to bite that damned hanging hot dog while my ole man rides?"

"What's your problem! I did it last year."

"Well, I think these bike games are ridiculous."

Both women have passengered in the pit for years, but the games are relatively new. Only a few of the women join in.

There is far greater participation in the Slow Race. From start to finish, the race course covers, at most, only seventy feet of track. Bikes race against each other and the clock. The slowest one to cover the distance wins. Moving a 700-pound motorcycle through space is a challenge. Moving it slowly with precision is a rare skill. The riders twist, turn, clutch, shift, and rock. There are moments when the bikes stand still and shimmy back and forth. There are times when the riders cannot hold them steady and the bikes go down. The crowd remains alert. Out-of-control bikes can instantly veer toward the watching crowd, jump over chalk lines, and crash into spectators. Women have just begun to enter the Slow Races. For now they offer no competition to the men.

Beer and food concessions dot the terraced landscape. This is Bud and Miller country and beer is served around the clock. No other beer is ever considered. Stick food is the meal of choice. There are hot dogs on a stick, chicken on a stick, beef on a stick, and corn on the cob. Dessert is a nip of nitrous oxide. Plates are optional. Napkins mandatory.

A walk down vendor row reveals the most colorful people in the pit. There are body-piercing artists, nipple-piercing specialists, and tattoo designers of every style. Bikers used to choose a predictable set of tattoos. Vivid skulls, brightly colored dragons, girlfriends' names, big-busted women, and wild animals were the common designs. Contemporary bikers now often go for abstract design, monochrome colors, and total body tats. While both men and women get tats, the designs and sizes are different. Women's tattoos tend to be smaller, located in hidden places, and more picturesque. There are exceptions. One of the solo women riders shows off her winning tat. She has an eagle tattooed on her chest, its claws grasping her pubic bone.

The pit still runs hot and burns with excitement. The energy is still raw but not quite so dangerous. The pit has become less predatory. We stay late into the night before returning to our motel.

Redwood Run is worth every stranded, overheated highway mile. The motel, packed with our friends, is a welcoming sight. When we arrive, Wild Turkey gets shoved into our hands and our butts get shoved into lawn chairs. With feet resting on the railing of the motel porch, we watch the endless parade of bikes pass by. The weather holds for the rest of the weekend, and the music in the pit rocks. Somehow, the ride home is always short, safe, and without adventure.

The changes in Harley culture are evident at the run. The riders are getting older. They are more settled. More riders are coming from middle- and upper-middle-class clubs. They party differently. They want more comfort. They don't want to tangle with the law. They have too much to lose from a confrontation with the police. Working-class men, while still the mainstay of the culture, are now bringing their wives, girlfriends, and ole ladies with them on the run and into the pit. The willingness of these women to follow their men into the pit has played a major part in its transformation.

The wives, girlfriends, and ole ladies have different expectations from the women pick-ups at the entrance gate. They will not be left when the weekend ends. It is also becoming more difficult for a biker to leave his woman at home. If he does go alone, the emerging women's network will insure that his wife, girlfriend, or ole lady finds out how he behaved in her absence. Her girlfriends will be there with their men, and they will report back.

The pit used to consist mainly of men, some couples, and some single women. The large-scale admission of wives, girlfriends, and ole ladies has changed this picture. Their presence has been transformative. So too has the presence of women riders. Women riders now ride their own bikes into the pit. They are riders. They demand respect. The ratio of men to women has grown more equal. Over the past ten years, the number of women riders has grown greatly and they are demanding partying privileges. Much has been gained. The pit has become an equal-opportunity party. Much has been lost. The pit was one of the last holdouts of raw, sexist, male-dominated partying. It came complete with the competing behaviors of gallantry alongside aggression, camaraderie coexisting with brutality, and rape in the midst of shared sexuality. The Redwood Run with its long history of lawlessness and male license is changing. We are witnessing the taming of the pit. Many will mourn the change. Many will applaud it. Me, I'm glad I got the chance to see it.

PART 4

Polemics and Philosophy

17

Bikers' Dirty Little *Open* Secret

The Racism Rap

"So my friend said, 'How can you ride with those people? Aren't they all racists?'"

Standing in front of Dudley Perkins's shop were two of the biggest, brightest, most lacquered to perfection, brand-new Buells ever seen. This newest addition to the Harley family of bikes is a masterpiece of mechanical engineering and market strategy. The Buell looks like a sports bike. With its wrap-around fairings, humped gas tank, and sleek-for-speed lines, it requires a rider to lean over the hump while riding. It produces a smooth aerodynamic effect when the rider is aligned lengthwise with the bike. Gone is the cruising, upright position of the typical Harley rider. Enter, the superb cornering and speed of a sports bike. The sports-bike rider is the one Milwaukee had in mind when it developed the Buell. There's a big sports-bike market out there and Harley wants it. That market tends to be young, multiracial, multi-cultural, and hooked on speed. Not your typical asshole on a Harley. With a bored-out 1,200cc super Sportster engine, the Buell is a contender.

DP was offering demo rides when Easy Ed rode up, saw the two Buells idling at the curb, and offered to "drag me for beers." The demo man in charge of the Buells blanched until he realized that I would not take up the challenge. Unlike the nervous demo man, I had a rare, genuinely mind-expanding experience during that brief incident.

I realized that I could, in fact, drag Ed for beers. I would lose, of course, but I could get on that Buell and ride away. I have my motor-cycle license. I ride a big bike. The thought, while it would have been ordinary to most bikers, left me thunderstruck. Another riding threshold had been crossed. The impossible could be easily accomplished. I could probably ride, albeit with great care, just about any of those bikes around. What a thought.

More important, in my musings about the Buell, was the recognition that Milwaukee was genuinely reaching for another riding population. The desired new population would be far more racially diverse and culturally mixed than that of the usual Harley riders. Sports-bike riders come in more colors, ages, ethnicities, statuses, lifestyles, class backgrounds, and religions than do most Harley folk. If Buell succeeds in opening the Harley community to a variety of other subcultures, some basic, hard-core, unresolved issues within the Harley world will have to be addressed.

Bikers' dirty little open secret would be out of the closet. Harley riders, as a group, are racist, anti-Semitic, homophobic, and misogynistic.

The big truth would also fly. Most of America is racist, anti-Semitic, homophobic, and misogynistic.

There are, of course, exceptions. Not everyone, every time, succumbs. There are also differing definitions of racism, anti-Semitism, homophobia, and misogyny.

"Race," said Bradley, "tells you where you can or cannot go in this country. When I ride, there are a lot of places as a black man I do not want to go. There are a lot of groups I cannot ride with. A lot of the time, I feel damned uncomfortable around most of the outlaw clubs. I'm not welcome there. My friends and I used to travel a lot. We made up a good team, the three of us. Woody, Blood, and me. But even when we travel together, we are treated differently."

Bradley spent some time considering his travels with Blood. Johnny Blood, or JB, is, like Bradley, a black man in America. Woody is white. Woody, with his total body tattoos, wild hair, beard, and wilder expressions, JB, with his cowboy hat and spiffed up bike, and Bradley, with his three-foot-long ponytail, make up a fearsome, extraordinary biking trio.

"Woody and JB would be lane-sharing and riding up ahead of me. Neither could hear for shit. Woody would yell out something. Blood would veer his bike toward Woody's yelling, '*What! What!*' Woody's got his hearing aid off and Blood's got his ear plugs in and both would be yelling, '*What! What!*' I'd be riding in back laughing, and then when they got too close to each other, I'd think, 'Oh shit!'

"So the three of us are riding like this, and a cop comes along and pulls me and Blood over. I was mad. 'How come,' I ask him, 'you only

Johnny "JB" Blood (Courtesy of Johnny Blood)

pulling over the two black guys?' I'm saying this while Woody is sailing right on by.

"The cop looks down at my taillight and says, 'You got a Blue Dot in the middle of your taillight. That's illegal.'

"Blood and I knew that he stopped us because we were black guys on expensive bikes and he wanted to check to see if the bikes were ours. He thought we might have stolen them. Why us, and not Woody? You know the answer."

"Do a lot of bike situations feel like that to you?"

"Enough. I remember when I first joined HOG a guy called in and asked if there would be any trouble if he brought his wife. I thought that was real strange, so I asked him why he called. 'She's Asian,' he said, 'so I thought that I had better ask!'"

"Bradley, what was he thinking?"

"He was thinking that someone might be rude to her. He was worried about us being racist toward her because she's Asian. I let him know that the FogHogs are a very mixed group and he had nothing to worry about."

"But doesn't that mean he shared the common belief that all bikers are prejudiced?"

"You bet."

Johnny Blood, who rode with Woody long before he hooked up with Bradley, discounts tales of racism among bikers.

"I never experienced racism when I rode. Other places, of course, but not when I rode. I've hung out with them all. No one ever gave me a hard time. I rode with the Angels, with the Jokers, and with others. I never did join 'cause if you join one, you can't hang out with the others. I liked to ride with everyone. Most of all, I rode with my buddies. Me, Woody, D. C. Dick, José. We were all young then. We were a rowdy group of guys. We used to ride drunk a lot, we used to ride drugged a lot. Then I got sober. Over thirteen years now. With three kids and a wife, I don't have time to join a club."

Bradley listened thoughtfully and responded.

"He may not have felt the racism, but it was there. He was never invited to prospect for any of those clubs."

Every rider has his or her own perspective on racism, as was clear from a conversation with Bradley, his wife Susan, Lillian, and Debby. Debby rides her Low Rider while Lillian borrows Debby's Sportster. They joined Susan, Bradley, and me for coffee. Susan, Bradley's wife, is a passenger.

Debby is a white woman married to a black Fijian man. Lillian is a black woman married to a white man. Susan is a white woman married to a black Native American man. Ken and I are both white, but we come from different backgrounds. His roots are Southern Baptist, rural, and Texan. Mine are Jewish, urban, and New York. We are all mixed. We vary in race, class, ethnicity, religion, and gender. All of us have strong feelings about bikers and issues of prejudice.

"Hey, I was so nervous when I first went to meet Bradley's biker friends," announced Susan. "I had bought into the stereotypes. I was afraid that they would all show up drinking Jack Daniels and looking to crash on my couch. I was afraid that they'd be missing their front teeth. My first comment to Bradley was, 'Do they have their teeth?'"

When I asked Debby whether she had ever experienced racism, she said, "No! I've never experienced any racism, but I know that most motorcycle groups are all white. I've always noticed that. Being white all my life I may not have noticed racism even when it was there. I am sensitive about race, but since my husband doesn't ride, this hasn't yet been an issue for us. But recently, I've been thinking about going with my family on long trips. Now I'm beginning to edit towns in my mind. There are towns I'd better not stop in. Since I got married, it has come to my attention that there may be places I don't want to go. As a white person, you ride wherever the road leads and you never think twice. But being an interracial couple, you have to think twice. Some places we will just ride through."

"There are lots of places I won't go, or if I go, I do so with great caution," I commented. "As an anthropologist, I know that when anyone steps or rides out of their local area, they have to watch their step. It's easier to see when there's white racism against blacks 'cause it's so common, but the reverse happens as well. There are lots of places I can't go 'cause I'm white. There are lots of black neighborhoods where I would not be welcome."

"I've never experienced racism in the slightest with my close riding buddies. No, no way," declared Lillian. "But I am very aware of it existing in some of the all-white groups."

"But Lillian, if you haven't personally experienced it, how can you say it's there?"

"Well, I base that on the fact that it's everywhere. Everywhere in America. It would be very strange it you didn't find it among bikers. My close riding friends are wonderful, but I haven't been around too many outside groups or been to many large gatherings."

"Well, I experienced it," I announced, "directly and in a terrible form. Ken and I were at our first Redwood Run, and there among all the beautiful trees and mountains was this disgusting sticker and statement on an old and chopped Shovel. There was this round circle painted on the bike. In the circle there was a caricature of a black guy, and there was a line through the circle. The logo stood for 'No blacks

245

Lillian Jackson (Courtesy of Lillian Jackson)

allowed.' Next to the logo, there was an arrow pointing to the rear seat. This was a narrow, princess-type seat about six inches wide, and next to the arrow were the words 'whore's place.' I saw this and wanted to kill the rider. I stood there waiting for the biker to come along. I didn't have to wait long. He could tell right away I was pissed. I didn't like the seat or the words or the logo. I made that clear with my comments. We started to get into a real argument, when I saw Ken coming toward us. I signaled him to stay away. The guy I broadsided with my

246

anger would have loved to get into a fight. But there would have been no honor for him to have fought with me and I didn't want to give him the opportunity to take his anger out on Ken."

"What good did it do you?" asked Bradley.

"What do you mean what good did it do me? I was so mad I wanted to kill him!"

"Barbara, what good did your anger do? You didn't change his mind. In fact, you just reinforced his feelings. Look, you can't force people to like you. People have a right to like who they want. You can't go around telling people how to feel."

"Bradley, are you saying I should have just walked away?"

"Yes. I would have. Why was it your business what he felt or believed? Of course I would have walked away. It's part of the bikers' code. You mind your own damned business.

"People have a right to think what they want, hang out with who they want, and believe what they want. Just 'cause I don't like it, so what! That's my business, just like his racism is his. Now if he had gotten into my face, that would have been different. But he wasn't giving me any trouble. We were both attending a run. You should have left it alone. Racism exists in the community, but unless it's directed toward you, leave it alone. It's not your business. It's not your place to educate others. We were there to ride and to party. We were not there for lectures."

"I can't believe you, Bradley! You would have walked away from racism?"

"You've got to know when to make your stand. America is riddled with racism. You fight every comer, you do nothing but fight all the time. Just last week, I was at the market and this guy was talking out loud. 'Those fuckin' niggers,' he kept saying. 'Those fuckin' niggers.'"

"So I walked over to him and said, 'Hey man, you got a problem with black folk?' He kept on saying, 'Those fuckin' niggers.' Now, I had a situation. If the guy had been muttering to himself, that would have been his business. But he was talking loud enough for me to hear him. He wanted me to hear him. Now that was a situation that had to be answered."

"So what did you do?"

"I walked right up to him and repeated, 'You got a problem?' But the guy kept backing up on me. He wouldn't stand up and defend his own racism. He had the backbone of a jellyfish, so I told him so. I kept walking closer and closer to him. I was getting in his face. He kept backing up until he was out the market door. Then he split."

"What made your situation any different from mine? Weren't the stickers on that guy's bike the same as 'being in my face'?"

"No, no way. This guy at the market, he saw me coming. He chose to insult me. So I took care of it. If he hadn't turned tail and run, I would have busted him up. It was personal. What you saw on that guy's bike was his general views. He was not directing them at you. He was sending them out to everyone, not to you personally. You should have left it alone.

"Knowing when to fight and when to let it alone is real important. If you don't learn it, you wind up fighting all the time. You wind up never having time to do anything else. Someone attacks you, you fight. Someone insults you, you fight. Someone is racist or sexist and doesn't fuck with you, who cares? That's their business. If you don't learn this, you're going to have a hard time in the biker community. Bikers want to be left alone. They don't take kindly to being told how to live."

Stickers and statements make obvious shows of racism. Then there are all those tattoos of iron crosses and swastikas, pointed helmets, and other symbols of Nazi Germany. While apologists of the symbols claim that they became integrated within the biker community as icons of liberation with the returning World War II veterans, they remain symbols of anti-Semitism for most of the Jewish population. Most bikers are white Christians. Anti-Semitism is as all-American as racism.

Misogyny in the form of sexism is a mixed bag. Women as well as men participate in it. Women pose for the nudie shots, dance for the wet T-shirt contests, and climb onto the backs of strangers' bikes. Women participate as groupies in a biker culture that is male defined and male dominated. There is no question of the masculine bent to the culture. Every woman present is aware of this reality. While the offensiveness of the omnipresent "Show us your tits" signs is questionable, that of the "Shut up bitch" ones is not. Women, while a necessary part of this aggressively hetero culture, are shown at gatherings and depicted in pictures as cycle sluts and biker babes. Wives, women riders, and girlfriends of long standing stage an uphill fight for quality acceptance within the culture. This is especially true at large, exuberant gatherings.

Homophobia is the Johnny-come-lately of big-time open prejudices. It's only in the past twenty-five years that lesbian and gay lifestyles have been sufficiently out of the closet to be openly and routinely condemned by American society. Even the FogHogs, as a multiracial, multicultural, mixed-gender group, have problems when it comes to homophobia. Every few years someone flies the rainbow flag of gay liberation on their bike. And all hell breaks loose. The first year this happened, one of the old-time members caused an enormous fracas by trying to physically remove the flag. Membership opinion was divided on what was the right thing to do.

Group one, the smallest of the groups, thought that the guy should be able to fly anything he wanted on his bike. It was his concern and his business. An important part of biker code is to mind your own business.

Group two, a larger group, thought that the guy should fly whatever flag he wanted *but not* when he rode with the FogHogs. Doing so at FogHog events was seen as stepping over boundaries and onto other peoples' toes. Most of the chapter was afraid that it would look like he was representing the entire group with his gay liberation flag, and they did not want to be associated with gay liberation.

Group three, the next largest, felt that the flag should not ever be flown on a Harley, but that the guy who had torn it off was, himself, out of line. A more important feeling than homophobia was the belief in the sacredness of the bike and the bond between a man and his motorcycle. No one should mess with that.

Even in this small, urban, multiracial community, most of the bikers felt seriously uncomfortable riding behind a gay liberation flag. The most common flag flown is the American flag. The issue that some bikers might feel uncomfortable riding behind an American flag is *never* raised. A love-it-or-leave-it philosophy is firmly in place. Patriotism is assumed.

Patriotism can mask a number of fairly significant prejudices. As a predominantly white, Christian, family-oriented, working-class, male community, the biker world is not exempt from most white, Christian, working-class, male prejudices. America has always been a nation divided. We separate first into the haves and the have-nots. Using various minorities as scapegoats to explain why many hard-working, tax-paying, working-class people have become part of the have-nots is common. Scapegoating explains and excuses various forms of prejudice.

Problems with money? Blame it on the Jews. Everyone knows that they have it all.

Problems with finding jobs? Blame it on the blacks. Everyone knows that they have all the jobs as a result of affirmative action.

Problems with the kids? Blame it on feminism. If women remembered their place and took better care of the children (and their men too), the kids would be better off.

Problems with the state of the world? Blame it on the homosexuals. If they hadn't started screwing up the family and the relationships between men and women, the world would be a better place.

Scapegoating is old. It is also effective. The hard-working, tax-paying, working-class man does indeed have reasons to be mad. More often than not, he does end up getting a shorter end of the stick, a

249

smaller piece of the pie, and the bad end of rotten clichés. But this continuing state of inequality within America is not caused by Jews, blacks, women, or gays. Inequality has been woven into the fabric of the country and the multiple causes for it are vast and complex. They vary by region and class and include inheritance laws, class and status structures, access to upward mobility, and chance. With all this complexity, it is so much easier to blame a group. There is so much more satisfaction in scapegoating. You cannot quarrel with historical circumstances. You cannot quarrel with the historical inequalities of money and position. But you can pick a fight with a minority. Blame your troubles on a minority, and you have a concrete face to punch and a flesh-and-blood ass to kick.

Bikers, mainly white working-class men, are no different from the rest of America. Bikers are themselves a minority. It is prejudice against bikers that expects them to be better than the rest of society. They are not.

Neither are they worse. This comes across clearly in Daniel Wolf's work with the outlaw club:

> The outlaw-biker community is an enclave of right-wing patriotism. Major biker events, such as those held at Sturgis and Daytona, feature a plethora of stars-and-stripes flag waving. For their part, the Hell's Angels went out of their way to defend returning Vietnam veterans against militant peace marchers at the Los Angeles airport. Outlaw bikers are staunch defenders of *laissez-faire* democracy wherein the individual becomes solely responsible for his own destiny.
>
> Outlaw bikers envision themselves as social rebels who defend their personal freedom and who exercise their right to choose and their freedom to associate. The outlaw biker feels that he is different because he has not been completely subdued by social routines, rules and regulations over which he has no real control. For him a large part of the appeal of being an outlaw is living according to his own law. (1991, 54)

Sometimes right-wing patriotism is expressed through the contempt most Harley riders feel for Japanese motorcycles. The "buy American" creed translates into both concern for American workers and personal fear of unemployment. "Jap crap," the term used most frequently, after "rice rocket" and "rice burner," to describe Japanese bikes, has both personal and political overtones. At large rallies, Honda-bashing can be pretty common. Everything from bad-mouthing to literal bashing takes place. There have been Honda drops, burials, and smashings. Hauling the bikes by crane high into the sky and letting them drop is one kind of entertainment. At one rally, everyone paid a buck to whack a Honda with a sledgehammer. It was a popular event. Anger over the Japanese-made Harley lookalikes is also intense. Honda, Kawasaki, Suzuki, and Yamaha all make Harley knockoffs. These bikes have started encroaching upon Milwaukee's market. The imitations are all big bikes with the characteristic Harley V-Twin engine look.

To Harley riders, nothing sounds, feels, rides, or performs like a real Harley, and the Japanese knockoffs just add fuel to the already burning fire of Harley chauvinism. The fact that the Japanese bikes have been known to outperform, outlast, and outride Harleys, while costing only a fraction of the price, is irrelevant. Harley loyalty transcends these boundaries. In this area, Harley loyalty reinforces ideals of patriotism. The biker is buying American.

Racism expressed in Japanese bike bashing has made popular the bumper sticker that reads "Honda, Suzuki, Yamaha, Kawasaki, from the People Who Brought You Pearl Harbor." It is clear that racism is in operation, because British, Italian, and German bikes are never trashed.

Outlaws aren't the only ones who show contempt for "ricers." Nor are they the only bikers who have made Sturgis and Daytona their major events. It's an all-Harley run. It's important. It's history. Most of the Harley clubs, HOG chapters, and independent groups try to make one or both of these runs.

Freedom runs deep as a theme for all bikers, along with the idea that you have a right to associate with whomever you please.

"I want to stick with my own kind" is an emblematic statement. To some, this is a statement of natural preference. No racist, anti-Semitic, homophobic, or misogynist implications are intended. One's own kind usually refers to someone of the same race, religion, gender, and sexual preference. It's both an inclusionary and an exclusionary statement. It simply means "I bond best with people who share my background" and "I can be uncomfortable around people with a different one."

To others, "I want to stick with my own kind" is a statement of acknowledged prejudice. It is a statement of rejection and dislike. It means anyone who is not of *my* race, *my* religion, *my* sexual preference, or *my* gender should go away.

There is a profound difference between these two meanings of the statement. Since the same statement can be used to describe the thinking of two groups of people whose viewpoints are actually quite different, a problem of interpretation emerges. In a society only too willing to put down bikers, the second interpretation will almost always be put forth as the one that describes their views.

Bikers are assumed by general American society to be prejudiced. Nonbikers will say, "Those damned assholes, everyone knows those bastards are racists!"

Bikers do tend to be separatists. Almost all private clubs, outlaw clubs, Christian clubs, mom and pop clubs, and local clubs are separatist. Separatists are those who prefer to "stick with their own kind." They may or may not be prejudiced against others. While they openly display their preference to "stick with their own kind," that does not mean that they dislike those who are not "their own kind." But they vigorously defend their right to choose their companions.

There are a few groups, however, that take on all comers. The nonseparatist groups accept membership across lines of race, gender, ethnicity, religion, and sexual preference. They are openly and proudly mixed. Nonseparatist groups are rare. Those that do permit a crossing of lines are mainly big-city groups. They are often filled with bikers who, in their personal lives, are bicultural or interracially married and are good friends with both hetero- and homosexual riders. Most often, these groups are not formal clubs, but consist of riding friends who travel together often enough to have the appearance of a club. They usually lack the name, patch, or specific items of identity that come with club membership.

A second kind of nonseparatist group is not a club at all in the traditional sense, but a group with institutionalized membership. While it permits entrance to all comers, it usually has an economic or political agenda. HOG (Harley Owners' Group) is one of the inclusive groups. HOG membership is based on Harley ownership. You buy a bike, you become a member. ABATE (American Brotherhood [or Biker] Aimed Towards Education) is another. This is a political action group dedicated to protecting bikers' rights. Its major agenda is to abolish all discriminatory motorcycle laws. AMA (American Motorcycle Association), born out of the racing industry, purports to speak for and champion all motorcycle causes. It too has open membership.

When it comes to the private clubs, however, most are separatist. They "stick to their own kind." To insure that the clubs get "their own kind," they have established a tradition of recruitment. This consists of a period during which the club prospect is assessed as a potential member. The prospect enters into a hazing, or proving, period. It can last from one to five years. During that time, the club members get a good sense of the prospect and determine whether or not he "fits." Private clubs can have formal or informal, easy or difficult, short or long prospecting periods. But they all serve the same purpose. They let the club's members and the prospect know that they are on the same wavelength. They let the members know that the prospect is someone like themselves *and* someone they can depend on. He is "one of their own kind."

Daniel Wolf documented the formal process of prospecting for an outlaw club (in Canada, the term for prospect is "striker"):

> The striking period is a socializing process. It is made up of a series of learning and testing situations that ultimately serve to integrate the prospective member into the club. . . . There are a number of club activities whose performance both demands and symbolizes certain personal qualities in the members, qualities that become part of the outlaw biker identity. Being a member of an outlaw club includes "partying," "drinking heavy," and "riding hard," while avoiding "dying fast. " A biker "lives to ride" and "rides to live." (1991, 88–90)

Sticking to your own kind doesn't necessarily mean that you are prejudiced against others. But it does ensure the perpetuation of group distance. If you ride only with your buddies, you are less likely to party or hang out with people different from yourself. Eventually the distance grows until separations appear inevitable. Differences and separations are the stuff that foster prejudices. It's easy to dislike someone you don't know, or don't see very often. It is also easy to stereotype people who are different from you.

It's easy to distrust them. It's especially easy if their color, religion, or sexual preference is different from your own. Since clubs promote identity and each club reinforces a different identity, breaking down the barriers is difficult. Most don't want to, anyway. Bikers pride themselves on choosing a lifestyle that puts individualism first. Why try to understand, sympathize, or appreciate someone different? Their form of individualism will not be your form. Separatism, as natural as birds flocking to their own, may eventually lead to distrust or avoidance of others.

Bikers are labeled racist, anti-Semitic, homophobic, and misogynist for a number of reasons. It's true that some of them are. It's also true that some of them are not. And as long as they band together in separate clubs, they will be seen as prejudiced. But times are changing. Harley riders are coming under new influences.

Women riders are forging changes. Inclusion of women passengers, girlfriends, wives, and ole ladies into that long-cherished bastion of male control—the weekend run—has begun. It is starting to change the feel of those runs. Redwood Run has lost some of its wildness, and the pit now holds less of a reputation for mayhem than for music. As more HOG chapters, defined at the outset by Milwaukee as family-oriented organizations, start attending mixed regional runs in large

253

numbers, the complexion, gender, and sensibilities of these runs will change. HOG chapters are frequently mixed by race, religion, gender, and sexual preference. The accepted sensibilities of an all-male, white, Christian group will no longer be the only sensibilities at the party. They will no longer be the only game in town.

Bikers, unhappy with the inclusion of the newer riders, will probably create new and exclusionary runs for themselves. But even while they move to more private pastures, there will still be parties, rallies, and runs that *all* groups will share. Sturgis and Daytona are just too filled with Harley tradition to be left unattended. HOG chapters already add significant numbers of mixed groups to the rallies. If the Buell motorcycle is successful in capturing the youthful, sports-bike-riding population, another new crowd will come into the Harley orbit. Diversity will increase.

Harley riders are not out to end prejudice. Neither are they out to spread it. They are not out to save the world. They are not political activists. They are out to ride.

Friends (usually academic friends) ask, "How can you stand being in a community that is so openly sexist?" They see the pictures and articles in the biker rags where women are portrayed as subordinate and submissive sex objects. Biker women are expected to accept this image. Some do, some don't.

Friends, when they ask about biker sexism, are really making two comments. The first is, "Look what a terrible community it is." The second is, "How can you justify your participation in such a community?"

The biker community is *not* a terrible community. Actually, it is quite wonderful. While it lacks none of the problems found in the rest of America (including all forms of prejudice), it has found unique ways of dealing with them. Unlike most Americans, bikers are honest about their feelings. Bikers don't hide their sexism, racism, or homophobia. They do not hide behind gentlemen's agreements, myths of color-blindness, equality, nor politically correct language. When a biker is prejudiced, it's right there in the open for all to see and for all to make comments upon. It's in your face.

While bikers stand behind their views, they also are capable of changing them. There is less bullshit and less investment in looking good for the general public. Bikers are strong-willed individualists participating in unconventional lifestyles.

Prejudice exists. Yet it is easier to deal with the honesty of a biker who looks you straight in the eye before putting you down than it is to cope with the civilian world which does not. In a society in which women earn less than men (for the same job), it is harder to relate to the smiling official who pretends to believe in equality than it is to relate to the biker who believes women are inferior. The biker has the potential to change. The other does not. The official espouses equality in an unequal situation. He may even believe it.

Bikers are willing to bear the responsibility for their beliefs because they are totally up-front about them. Being up-front about their views is what has gotten them into so much trouble. It's what adds to their bad rep. In a society that routinely double-talks, bikers are willing to talk straight.

Bikers themselves are a minority group subject to both societal censure and moral condemnation from the rest of society. The harsh and often punitive laws directed against bikers reflect general public attitudes. Bikers maintain a lifestyle that requires strong commitment in the face of frequent adversity.

In answer to the second comment, how I can justify my participation in such a community, I respond, "I do not justify my participation, I take pride in it."

In a multidimensional society filled with groups pulling this way and that, Harleys are a source of American identification and pride. They are big, beautiful, powerful, expensive, and functional.

There is much in America to be proud of. There is much that is extraordinary, dramatic, unique, and special: our landscape, our size, our endurance, and our ability to govern vast amounts of land and diverse peoples.

Our history is one of both great justice and great injustice. The battles for human rights and personal freedoms are noble. Our history is charged with the legacies of democracy, independence, and success. Yet our history is also charged with the legacies of racism, inequality, and poverty.

We are a country both blessed and flawed. To our credit, we continue to struggle with these flaws. Our problems hit the papers daily. Our successes get less press coverage. We are a country that has, for a half century, focused on its flaws.

Harleys have highlighted our successes. Harleys wear the "made in America" label with pride. The flawed past will always be there, but the flaws need not follow us into the future. Harleys promise a future filled with positive actions, community spirit, and a chance to make things better. Harleys open doors. They offer an identity.

Thousands of clubs participate in charities. It is direct giving and not filtered through large, indifferent, impersonal bureaucracies. Pride in giving back to the community functions in life-affirming ways.

Americans are a people in search of an identity. Harleys provide a peer group, a support club, and a general way of life that emphasizes shared values. Bikers may differ on religion, politics, and meaningful employment, but Harley riders share a great many common bonds, beliefs, and ideologies. Part of the Harley explosion comes from reaffirming pride in being an American, pride in finding a community to participate in. That's a tall order for one bike to fill. Apparently, Harleys have no trouble filling it.

Glossary
References
Index

Glossary

ABATE. American Bikers (or Brotherhood) Aimed Towards Education (in California; different state chapters interpret the acronym differently). A motorcycle rights organization whose main aim is to fight discriminatory laws against bikers.

AMA. American Motorcycle Association. The original motorcycle organization that scheduled the bike races. Now a motorcycle rights organization, it is still involved with racing schedules.

Ape hanger. A type of handlebar which requires the riders arms to be above their shoulders.

Badlander Seat. A product brand of a stylish and comfortable saddle.

Bagger. A disrespectful name for a fully dressed, large Harley-Davidson in the FL series.

Big Twin. A Harley model containing a powerful V-twin engine; includes the Dresser and the Low Rider but not the Sportster. *See also* Softail.

Bitch Seat. A passenger seat on the bike that is traditionally reserved for a woman, who is then sometimes referred to as the bitch on the back. Also known as riding bitch.

Brain bucket. An impolite name for a motorcycle helmet. *See also* skid lid.

Buell. A new American sports bike sold by Harley dealers and manufactured by a company that has shared ownership with Harley-Davidson. Contains a high-performance Sportster engine.

Cages. The name bikers use for cars.

Chopper. A chopped bike. To chop a motorcycle is to reduce its bulk and pare it down to bare essentials. The bike is redesigned. Typically the front forks will be raked (extended and its angle increased) and the whole bike will be lowered.

Crotch rocket. A Japanese sports bike with enclosed engine and humped tank. A fast bike, known for its turning ability. Usually a disrespectful term. Also called rice rocket.

Dresser. A Harley Big Twin in the FL series. Usually comes with floorboards, fairing, saddle bags, and large passenger seat. A polite term for Bagger.

Evolution. A Harley-Davidson engine design developed in 1984. Fuel-efficient and oil tight. *Evo* for short, also called the Blockhead.

259

Fairing. A wraparound windshield usually installed on Dressers and Buells.

Flying colors. *See* Patch holder.

FogHogs. The nickname for the Golden Gate Chapter of HOG.

Harleybago. A fully-equipped Bagger. Usually comes with a sound system, heated seats, and walkie-talkies for rider-passenger communication. *See also* Bagger.

HOG. Harley Owners' Group. An association sponsored by Harley-Davidson. Each dealership sponsors its own association within its region, but members must first sign up for the national HOG, which is run out of Milwaukee. Anyone with a Harley can join by paying dues. Some HOG groups permit members to ride other makes of bike. Passengers can join as associate members.

Jamming the wind. The experience of riding. Also known as to jam the wind.

Knucklehead. A Harley-Davidson engine design developed in 1936 and produced through 1947. Knuckle for short.

LOH. Ladies of Harley. A subsidiary group within HOG. All women may join whether they are riders or passengers.

MC. Motorcycle club.

MMA. Modified Motorcycle Association. A bikers' rights organization that sponsors events. More hard-core than the AMA.

Ole lady. Biker female companion; wife or girlfriend. A good term.

Pack. To carry something special on the bike. Guns and women are both packed.

Panhead. A Harley-Davidson engine design developed in 1948 and produced through 1965. Pan for short.

Patch holder. Member of a motorcycle club who wears the distinctive club patch on his jacket or vest. A distinction is made between a three-piece patch (usually an outlaw club) and a one-piece patch (a local club). Wearing the patch is flying (or wearing) the colors.

Poker run. A popular run event. Individual cards are drawn at designated stops. The rider with the highest, and sometimes lowest, hand wins.

Rice rocket. *See* crotch rocket.

Ride to the Wall. The Vietnam Veterans Memorial run every year to Washington, D.C. The ride is to honor the service men and women whose names are inscribed on the wall.

Rubber mount. A type of mounting of the engine to the frame that makes for a smoother ride. All Dressers and Low Riders are rubber mounted. Sportsters and Softails are not.

Run pin. Groups who sponsor runs may sell run pins at the start of the advertised run.

Scoot. The bike.

Scooter trash. A derogatory term for someone whose motorcycle, and motorcycle behavior, are not acceptable. Can be used as a compliment when friends are calling each other by affectionate names.

Shovelhead. A Harley-Davidson engine design developed in 1966 and produced through 1984. Shovel for short.

Sissy bar. The high bar behind the passenger's seat. Keeps the passenger from sliding off the back of the bike.

Skid lid. An impolite name for a motorcycle helmet. *See also* brain bucket.

Softail. A Big Twin. Rear shocks are mounted horizontally underneath the frame. They are not visible. The Softail does not have rubber mounting.

Sportster. A Harley-Davidson that is narrower, leaner, more lightweight, and comparatively smaller than a Big Twin. It has a characteristic small, peanut-sized gas tank.

Sweep. Usually a four-wheeled vehicle, a truck or van that follows the bikes on a run. It is brought along as backup in case any of the bikes or bikers get in trouble. Sometimes motorcycles can also ride sweep.

Tat. Tattoo.

Toy run. A charity event to bring toys to children in hospitals. A frequent occurrence among all motorcycle groups.

Trike. Typically an open three-wheeled vehicle. Most trikes look like bikes with double wheels in the rear.

Two-up. To ride with a passenger.

V-Twin. The distinctive Harley-Davidson engine, with two cylinders arranged in a *V*-shape. All modern Harleys are V-Twins.

Wrench. To fix your own bike. To be able to mechanically care for your Harley.

References

Baker, Amy Brooke. 1988. "Bugs in Her Teeth." *Christian Science Monitor*, 6 July.

Birkitt, Malcolm. 1992. *Cruisin 'n' Posin: All Part of the Harley-Davidson Experience.* Milwaukee, Wis.: HD Osprey Automotive Press.

Bolin, Anne. 1988. *In Search of Eve.* New York: Bergin & Garvey.

Condert, Jo. 1989. "'Go for It Lady!' Elderly Woman Buys Motor Scooter." *Reader's Digest*, January.

Dizard, Jan E., Robert Merrill Muth, and Stephen P. Andrews Jr. 1999. *Guns in America: A Reader.* New York: New York University Press.

Doyle, James A. 1983. *The Male Experience.* Dubuque, Iowa: W. C. Brown.

Ferrar, Ann. 1996. *Hear Me Roar: Women, Motorcycles, and the Rapture of the Road.* New York: Crown Publishers.

Forkner, William. 1986. "'Wino' Willie Forkner: All the old Romance Retold. " *Easyriders* 16, no. 159.

Fox, Kathryn Joan. 1987. "Real Punks and Pretender: The Social Organization of a Counterculture." *Journal of Contemporary Ethnography* 16 (3): 344–70.

Hamblin, Ken. 1996 *Pick a Better Country: An Unassuming Colored Guy Speaks His Mind about America.* New York: Simon & Schuster.

Harris, Max. 1985. *Bikers: Birth of a Modern-Day Outlaw.* London: Faber and Faber.

Hazleton, Lesley. 1990. "Working on the Mechanics: Author as Motorbike Mechanic." *New York Times*, 14 January.

Hochswender, Woody. 1991. "Born to Be Wild but Feminine." *New York Times*, 16 July.

Hopper, Columbus B., and Johnny Moore. 1983. "'Hell on Wheels': The Outlaw Motorcycle Gangs." *Journal of American Culture* 6 (summer): 58–64.

Hopper, Columbus B., and Johnny Moore. 1990. "Women in Outlaw Motorcycle Gangs." *Journal of Contemporary Ethnography* 18 (Jan.): 363–87.

Imes, Joyce. 1996. *Harley-Davidson 101.* Tacoma, Wash,: Semi-Serious Ink Publishing.

Joans, Barbara. 1992. "Problems in Pocatello: A Study of Linguistic Misunderstanding," In *Applying Anthropology*, ed. Aaron Podolefsky and Peter J. Brown, 160–63. Mountain View, Calif.: Mayfield Publishing Co.

Joans, Barbara. 1995. "Dykes on Bikes Meets Ladies of Harley." In *Lavender Lexicon*, ed. William Leap, 87–106. New York: Gordon and Breach.

Joans, Barbara. 2001. "Women Who Ride: The Bitch on the Back Is Dead." In *Athletic Intruders: Women, Culture, and Exercise Sport*, ed. Anne Bolin and Jane Granskog, 73–95. Albany: State University of New York Press.

Languist, Norman. 1987. "Totems, Flight and Fetishes: Shamanic Elements in Biker Culture." Doctoral dissertation, Eastern Arizona College.

Lavigne, Yves. 1987. *Hells Angels: Taking Care of Business.* Toronto: Ballantine.

Lavigne, Yves. 1996. *Hells Angels: Into the Abyss.* New York: Harper Paperbacks.

Lawrence, Elizabeth Atwood. 1982. *Rodeo: An Anthropologist Looks at the Wild and the Tame.* Chicago: University of Chicago Press.

McDonald-Walker, Suzanne. 2000. *Bikers: Culture, Politics, and Power.* New York: Berg Publications.

McGuire, Phillip. 1986. "Outlaw Motorcycle Gangs, Part 1." *The National Sheriff,* April–May, 68–75.

Quinn, James Francis. 1983. "Outlaw Motorcycle Clubs: A Sociological Analysis." Master's thesis, University of Miami.

Reid, Peter. 1990. *Well Made in America.* New York: McGraw Hill.

Schouten, John W., and James H. McAlexander. 1992. "Hog Heaven: The Structure, Ethos, and Market Impact of a Consumption Subculture." Paper presented at the Annual Conference of the Association for Consumer Research, Chicago.

Spradley, James P. and Brenda Mann. 1975. *The Cocktail Waitress: Women's Work in a Man's World.* New York: Wiley.

Spradley, James P. and David W. McCurdy. 2000. *Conformity and Conflict: Readings in Cultural Anthropology.* Needham Heights, Mass.: Allyn & Bacon.

Sucher, Harry. 1990. *Harley-Davidson: The Milwaukee Marvel.* Milwaukee, Wis.: Haynes Publication.

Thompson, Hunter S. 1967. *Hell's Angels: A Strange and Terrible Saga.* New York: Random House.

Urseth, Mike. 1990. *Sturgis 50th Anniversary Book.* Minneapolis: Midwest Rider Publications.

Watson, J. Mark. 1980. "Outlaw Motorcyclists: An Outgrowth of Lower-Class Cultural Concerns." *Deviant Behavior* 2:31–48.

Wethern, George and Vincent Colnett. 1978. *A Wayward Angel.* New York: Richard Marek.

Williams, Lena. 1988. "Yes, Real Women Do Ride Motorcycles." *New York Times,* 11 May.

Wintner, Robert. 2000. *The Modern Outlaws: A Road Saga.* Lincoln, Neb.: iUniverse.com, Inc., toExcel.

Wolf, Daniel R. 1991. *The Rebels: A Brotherhood of Outlaw Bikers.* Toronto: University of Toronto Press.

Wright, David. 1993. *The Harley-Davidson Motor Company: An Official Ninety-Year History.* Foreword by Willie G. Davidson. Osceola, Wis.: Motorbooks International.

Index

Index

Ladies of Harley (LOH), 86; criticized as separatist, 119; as empowering to women, 127–28
Lady Bikers, 104, 105–15, 131; gender-specific behaviors, 104, 109, 115, 131–32; public reactions to, 106, 194
Lady Passengers, 90, 94–97
Laidlaw, Bob (Harley dealer), 20–21
Legal and legislative issues: helmet laws, 42, 46, 130, 174, 195–96, 212; insurance, 50; licensing and training, 176
Lesbian bikers, 120–21, 143, 196–201
Libertarianism, 71; responses to racism and sexism, 247–48
Lindblom, Debby, 124–30; birth of son Joe, 154–55; on gender/femininity, 146–47
Lopez, Jayne Kelly de, *73*, 105–8; on gender, 146
Lopez, Pablo, 72–74, *73*; on Harley culture, 203; mechanical skills, 85
Low Riders, 26

Male disenfranchisement, 17, 28, 250
Marketing, 121; dealership errors, 25; of Harley culture, 121; Harley-Davidson Motor Company strategies, 43, 45, 86, 241–42; of Japanese motorcycles, 24; women depicted in advertising, 65
Masculinity, 77, 84; and bike ownership, 85; erosion of gender roles after World War II, 85; in Harley culture, 38; Harley identity and, 56; male promiscuity and, 114–15, 118, 236; Old Timers and, 63; Outlaws and exaggeration of, 144; riding clothes and image of, 140–41; traditional definitions of, 144–45
Masuwale, Usaia, 128–29, 146
McKay, Bernie, *67*, 99–101; on gender/femininity, 149
McKay, Dick, 62, 66–68, *67*, 83; definition of femininity, 149
Mechanical skills (wrenching), 14; as aspect of biker culture, 202–3; biker identity and, 65–66, *66*; dealerships and, 32, 36; of first-generation riders (Old Timers), 63; of Lady Bikers, 104, 109–10; motorheads, 38; of Old Bikers, 75; "one-kick Harley" as exemplary, 71; of Women Bikers, 104, 116, 117
Media: biker stereotypes perpetrated in,

101, 113, 141; biker women as portrayed in, 97
Military: uses of motorcycles, 22; Women's Army Corps (WAC), 65
Minorities: bikers as, 250. *See also* Anti-Semitism; Racism; Sexism
Misogyny. *See* Sexism
Models, 26–27; Buells, 55, 241; Huggers (838 Sportster), 86; Knuckleheads, 62
Molinari, Mike (CEO Performance Productions, Inc.), 46–50, *48*, 171; on Rich Urban Bikers, 205
Morty's (biker bar), 110–11
Mosley, Ken, 166
Motorcycle clubs, 179–92; antagonism between, 223; Bay City Motorcycle Club, 67; cultural variations in, 186–87; diversity in, 206, 251–52; Hells Angels, 68, 110, 169, 250; identity and, 189, 253; inland meeting described, 185–87; males only, 38; outlaw clubs, 8, 14–16; politics and, 188–89; prospecting and recruiting, 252–53; racism and sexism, 75, 181, 189; San Francisco Motorcycle Club, 67; as separatist or exclusionary, 251–52; sexual orientation and, 189; socioeconomic classes and, 189–90; wars between, 169; women and status in, 85, 123, 180–82, 186–87, 190
Motorcycles: protection of, 137–38, 160
Motorheads, 38
Movies, 8, 56; *Easy Rider*, 24; motorcycles as symbols in, 23; outlaws in, 8
Ms. Harley-Davidson contest, 168
Mythos, 52, 141, 173

Names and naming of bikes, 69, 193
Nature, 125–26, 129–30, 130, 183, 218, 225; animal encounters, 125–26; bears, 153–54; on campouts, 164; riding and intimacy with, 97, 98–99, 152–53, 172; weather, 226–30; women and, 172
Nazi symbols, 248
New Bikers, 63, 74–78
New Fuckin' Guys (NFGs), 203–8. *See also* Rich Urban Bikers (RUBs)
Nostalgia: Softails and, 26–28

Occasional Bikers (OBs), 63, 81–83, 205
Odysseys, 136–37, 155–58
Old Bikers, 63, 72–75